Encounters at the Counter

Bringing together a diverse collection of studies from a team of international scholars, this pioneering volume focuses on interactions in shops, exploring the dynamics of conversation between sellers and customers. Beginning with the emergence of a 'need' for a product before the request to a seller is actually made, all the way through to the payment phase, it explores the rich and deeply methodical practices employed by customers and sellers as they go about the apparently mundane work of buying and selling small items. It looks at how seller and customer interact, both verbally and by means of manipulating the material objects involved, across a range of different kinds of purchase. Providing new insights into multimodal human interaction and the organisation of the commercial activity, it aims to bring about a new understanding of the fundamental ways in which economic value, possession, and ownership are achieved.

BARBARA FOX is Emerita Professor of Linguistics at the University of Colorado Boulder. She works at the intersection of grammar, the body, and social interaction. Her book *Grammar in Everyday Talk* (with Thompson and Couper-Kuhlen, Cambridge University Press, 2015), won the Best Book Award from the International Society for Conversation Analysis in 2018.

LORENZA MONDADA is Professor of Linguistics at the University of Basel. Her research focuses on social interaction in ordinary, professional, and institutional settings, within an ethnomethodological and conversation analytic perspective. She has co-edited several collective books, and published *Sensing in Social Interaction* (Cambridge University Press, 2021).

MARJA-LEENA SORJONEN is Professor of Finnish language at the University of Helsinki. Her studies cover interactional practices in mundane interactions and in a range of institutional settings, conducted from conversation analytic and interactional linguistic perspectives. She has co-edited several volumes, and published *Responding in Conversation* (John Benjamins, 2001).

Studies in Interactional Sociolinguistics

FOUNDING EDITOR
John J. Gumperz (1922–2013)
EDITORS
Paul Drew, Rebecca Clift, Lorenza Mondada, Marja-Leena Sorjonen

1. *Discourse Strategies* John J. Gumperz
2. *Language and Social Identity* edited by John J. Gumperz
3. *The Social Construction of Literacy* Jenny Cook-Gumperz
4. *Politeness: Some Universals in Language Usage* Penelope Brown and Stephen C. Levinson
5. *Discourse Markers* Deborah Schiffrin
6. *Talking Voices: Repetition, Dialogue, and Imagery in Conversational Discourse* Deborah Tannen
7. *Conducting Interaction: Patterns of Behaviour in Focused Encounters* Adam Kendon
8. *Talk at Work: Interaction in Institutional Settings* edited by Paul Drew and John Heritage
9. *Grammar in Interaction: Adverbial Clauses in American English Conversations* Cecilia E. Ford
10. *Crosstalk and Culture in Sino-American Communication* Linda W. L. Young (with foreword by John J. Gumperz)
11. *AIDS Counselling: Institutional Interaction and Clinical Practice* Anssi Peräkylä
12. *Prosody in Conversation: Interactional Studies* edited by Elizabeth Couper-Kuhlen and Margret Selting
13. *Interaction and Grammar* edited by Elinor Ochs, Emanuel A. Schegloff and Sandra A. Thompson
14. *Credibility in Court: Communicative Practices in the Camorra Trials* Marco Jacquemet
15. *Interaction and the Development of Mind* A. J. Wootton
16. *The News Interview: Journalists and Public Figures on the Air* Steven Clayman and John Heritage
17. *Gender and Politeness* Sara Mills
18. *Laughter in Interaction* Philip Glenn
19. *Matters of Opinion: Talking about Public Issues* Greg Myers
20. *Communication in Medical Care: Interaction between Primary Care Physicians and Patients* edited by John Heritage and Douglas Maynard
21. *In Other Words: Variation in Reference and Narrative* Deborah Schiffrin
22. *Language in Late Modernity: Interaction in an Urban School* Ben Rampton
23. *Discourse and Identity* edited by Anna De Fina, Deborah Schiffrin and Michael Bamberg

24 *Reporting Talk: Reported Speech in Interaction* edited by Elizabeth Holt and Rebecca Clift
25 *The Social Construction of Literacy, 2nd Edition* edited by Jenny Cook-Gumperz
26 *Talking Voices, 2nd Edition* Deborah Tannen
27 *Conversation Analysis* edited by Jack Sidnell
28 *Impoliteness: Using Language to Cause Offence* Jonathan Culpeper
29 *The Morality of Knowledge in Conversation* edited by Tanya Stivers, Lorenza Mondada and Jakob Steensig
30 *Conversational Repair and Human Understanding* edited by Makoto Hayashi, Geoffrey Raymond and Jack Sidnell
31 *Grammar in Everyday Talk: Building Responsive Actions* Sandra A. Thompson, Barbara A. Fox, and Elizabeth Couper-Kuhlen
32 *Multimodal Conduct in the Law: Language, Gesture and Materiality in Legal Interaction* Gregory Matoesian and Kristin Enola Gilbert
33 *The Suspect's Statement: Talk and Text in the Criminal Process* Martha Komter
34 *How Meditation Works: Resolving Conflict Through Talk* Angela Cora Garcia
35 *Action Ascription in Interaction* edited by Arnulf Deppermann and Michael Haugh

Encounters at the Counter
The Organization of Shop Interactions

Edited by

Barbara Fox
University of Colorado Boulder

Lorenza Mondada
University of Basel

Marja-Leena Sorjonen
University of Helsinki

Shaftesbury Road, Cambridge CB2 8EA, United Kingdom

One Liberty Plaza, 20th Floor, New York, NY 10006, USA

477 Williamstown Road, Port Melbourne, VIC 3207, Australia

314–321, 3rd Floor, Plot 3, Splendor Forum, Jasola District Centre, New Delhi – 110025, India

103 Penang Road, #05–06/07, Visioncrest Commercial, Singapore 238467

Cambridge University Press is part of Cambridge University Press & Assessment, a department of the University of Cambridge.

We share the University's mission to contribute to society through the pursuit of education, learning and research at the highest international levels of excellence.

www.cambridge.org
Information on this title: www.cambridge.org/9781009216029

DOI: 10.1017/9781009216012

© Cambridge University Press & Assessment 2023

This publication is in copyright. Subject to statutory exception and to the provisions of relevant collective licensing agreements, no reproduction of any part may take place without the written permission of Cambridge University Press & Assessment.

First published 2023
First paperback edition 2025

A catalogue record for this publication is available from the British Library

Library of Congress Cataloging-in-Publication data
Names: Fox, Barbara A., editor. | Mondada, Lorenza, editor. | Sorjonen, Marja-Leena, editor.
Title: Encounters at the counter : the organization of shop interactions / edited by Barbara Fox, University of Colorado Boulder, Lorenza Mondada, University of Basel, Marja-Leena Sorjonen, University of Helsinki.
Description: Cambridge, United Kingdom ; New York, NY : Cambridge University Press, 2023. | Series: Studies in interactional sociolinguistics | Includes bibliographical references and index.
Identifiers: LCCN 2022023679 (print) | LCCN 2022023680 (ebook) | ISBN 9781009215992 (hardback) | ISBN 9781009216029 (paperback) | ISBN 9781009216012 (epub)
Subjects: LCSH: Consumer behavior. | Business communication. | Interpersonal communication. | Customer relations–Social aspects. | Retail trade–Social aspects. | BISAC: LANGUAGE ARTS & DISCIPLINES / Linguistics / Sociolinguistics
Classification: LCC HF5415.32 .E5278 2023 (print) | LCC HF5415.32 (ebook) | DDC 658.8/342–dc23/eng/20220617
LC record available at https://lccn.loc.gov/2022023679
LC ebook record available at https://lccn.loc.gov/2022023680

ISBN   978-1-009-21599-2   Hardback
ISBN   978-1-009-21602-9   Paperback

Cambridge University Press & Assessment has no responsibility for the persistence or accuracy of URLs for external or third-party internet websites referred to in this publication and does not guarantee that any content on such websites is, or will remain, accurate or appropriate.

Contents

List of Contributors		*page* ix
1	Encounters at the Counter: An Introduction LORENZA MONDADA, MARJA-LEENA SORJONEN, AND BARBARA FOX	1
2	Approaching the Counter at the Supermarket: Decision-Making and the Accomplishment of Couplehood ELWYS DE STEFANI	37
3	Customers' Inquiries about Products: Establishing Grounds for the Decision to Buy KATARIINA HARJUNPÄÄ, LORENZA MONDADA, AND KIMMO SVINHUFVUD	73
4	Offering a Taste in Gourmet Food Shops: Small Gifts in an Economy of Sale LORENZA MONDADA	109
5	Embodied Trajectories of Actions in Shop Encounters: Giving or Placing Products on or over the Counter LORENZA MONDADA AND MARJA-LEENA SORJONEN	144
6	Unpacking Packing ANNA LINDSTRÖM AND BARBARA FOX	184
7	The Request-Return Sequence: What Can Happen at the Interface between Picking up a Repaired Item and Paying for It BARBARA FOX AND TRINE HEINEMANN	214

8 Moving Money: Money as an Interactional Resource in
  Kiosk Encounters in Finland   255
  MIA HALONEN AND AINO KOIVISTO

Appendix: Transcription Conventions   279
Index   283

Contributors

ELWYS DE STEFANI (University of Heidelberg and KU Leuven)
BARBARA FOX (University of Colorado Boulder)
MIA HALONEN (University of Jyväskylä)
KATARIINA HARJUNPÄÄ (University of Tampere)
TRINE HEINEMANN (Independent scholar)
AINO KOIVISTO (University of Helsinki)
ANNA LINDSTRÖM (Uppsala University)
LORENZA MONDADA (University of Basel)
MARJA-LEENA SORJONEN (University of Helsinki)
KIMMO SVINHUFVUD (University of Helsinki)

1 Encounters at the Counter
An Introduction

Lorenza Mondada, Marja-Leena Sorjonen, and Barbara Fox

1.1 Introduction

1.1.1 Why Study Shop Encounters? Some Analytical and Conceptual Issues

This book is about shop encounters in which material products are bought and sold, face to face, at the counter, within situated interactions between sellers and buyers. Entering a shop, selecting products or services to be bought, and purchasing them is a mundane and recurrent practice in the lives of citizens of modern commercial societies. While shop interactions are often brief and simple, and seem therefore at first glance to be hardly worthy of scholarly examination, analysis of their moment-by-moment unfolding reveals a closely organized orderliness. This orderliness enables both an investigation of general features of institutional encounters and a study of the specific details that constitute the commercial transaction around products. Both rely on the systematicity of talk, body, and materiality in interactions in institutional settings, as in situ achievement of sociality, culture, and economy.

Shop encounters are a perspicuous setting in various respects. First, they are a routine type of encounter, exhibiting regular interactional patterns: they enable the study of methodic practices, their systematicity across contexts, and their specific adaptations to local ecologies and contingencies. Second, encounters at the counter are interactions in which the participants use talk and the body to request, refer to, and manipulate products as co-present objects, thus being a setting in which talk, body, and materiality are exemplarily intertwined. Third, shop encounters are an example of institutional asymmetric interaction, in which the categories of seller and buyer are quickly established, albeit at the same time being constantly re-elaborated by the participants. Fourth, beyond multimodal actions with objects, shop encounters make observable the constitution of sociability, economic value, and culture: shops and market stalls are a place where shoppers and sellers engage in sociable actions beyond the mere transaction, where shoppers are socialized in a world of cultural objects that are not just products to sell, and where the value of the products is not only given by their price, but also by and within the interactional event that leads to their purchase.

1.1.2 Situating Shop Encounters in a Broader Context

Shop encounters are at the crossroads of various academic interests that arise from different disciplines and foci.

On the one hand, they have attracted the interest of linguistic, pragmatic, sociolinguistic, interactional, and anthropological studies as a canonical activity in which sociality, formality, and institutionality are manifested through language and corporeal conduct. They are also seen as important to study because they offer a setting in which routine actions are recurrently observable and comparable, affording systematic analyses of regularities of contact. Finally, they are a context in which embodied actions not only accompany talk but are a key resource in the engagement of participants with materiality – since in these encounters people manipulate, inspect, describe, and assess products as objects.

On the other hand, shopping practices have been more recently revisited within research in economy, sociology of economy and consumption, and marketing – after having been neglected for a long time, in favor of more global perspectives on economic processes – not only as a type of social activity that is embedded in larger cultural, social, and economic contexts, but as a relevant locus for the study of the negotiation and establishment of the value of goods (Simmel 1900), practices of selection, reasoning, and decision-making (Cochoy et al. 2016), practices of consumption (Campbell 2021; Douglas & Isherwood 1979; Miller 1998; Warde 2017), and material culture and the definition of things as commodities (Appadurai 1986). Even though these advances in the cultural, social, and economic study of the market exchange, seen from the perspective of shopping practices, are still rarely associated with detailed analyses of the shop encounter, they show that shopping, the circulation of goods, and consumption are fundamentally related to in situ actions of buying and selling.

However, there is a kind of paradox in the distribution of analytical and theoretical interests across this multidisciplinary landscape. On the one hand, often studies centered on the language and talk in shop encounters have *not* been interested in the specifics of the commercial transaction and in its economic consequences (and have sometimes used the transaction as a *pretext* for studying social relations, politeness, or social stratification, as, for example, in the sociolinguistic study of department stores as a place to observe the correlation between phonological variables and social stratification, Labov 1972). On the other hand, and conversely, socioeconomic approaches have not been interested in the situated details of the sociointeractional organization of shop encounters and have rather insisted on the importance of more global orders defining the economy of the exchange.

Rather than attempting to overcome this divide, our ambition in this book is to understand better the constitutive actions that build a shop *encounter*, such as requesting, asking questions, choosing, tasting, and paying for products. These will cast some light on the specificity of *shop* encounters, concerning the way participants deal with commercial issues, orient to service, and bodily engage with products as material objects.

The next sections will sketch the panorama of research that has characterized shop encounters in order to situate the contributions of this book. For doing that, it adopts a broader multidisciplinary perspective on the studies of language and talk in shop encounters, before taking a more focused approach centered in ethnomethodological and conversation analytic (EMCA) studies of shop interactions, which enable us to locate the chapters of this volume.

1.1.3 Situating the Study of Shop Encounters in a Genealogy of Studies

The observation that shop encounters are frequent, recurrent, and routinized kinds of interactions, which facilitate the constitution of rich audio/video-recorded data sets, affording their systematic analysis, has prompted various projects to base their studies on such data. One of the very first studies based on naturally occurring shop encounters is Merritt (1976a), based on a corpus of more than 700 encounters audio-recorded in the USA. Aston and colleagues in Bologna exploited the recurrent features of shop encounters to initiate a comparative project (PIXI: Pragmatics of Italian/English Cross-Cultural Interaction), looking at bookshop encounters in Italy and the United Kingdom (Aston 1988). The idea of invariants and variation also characterized a similar project developed in Lyon (Kerbrat-Orecchioni & Traverso 2008), focusing on shop encounters in France, and comparing them with similar encounters in the Maghreb and the Middle East (Traverso 2001, 2006, 2007).

This book has emerged from several projects that have been developed in recent decades, based on audio- and video-recorded shop encounters in a variety of cultural and social contexts.

A project on service encounters was initiated at the Research Institute for the Languages of Finland in Helsinki during the late nineties and developed into a larger project (2002–2007) by Sorjonen, Raevaara, and Lappalainen. Social interactions in kiosks (convenience stores), other types of shops and other service encounters, like insurance offices and hairdressers, were video-recorded in a diversity of locations in Finland. This regional diversity enabled the researchers to examine regional linguistic variation (Haakana & Sorjonen 2011; Lappalainen & Raevaara 2009; Raevaara 2011; Sorjonen & Raevaara

2006, 2014). The subproject on convenience stores has inspired several other initiatives, such as the following.

The project *Multimodality: Reconsidering language and action through embodiment*, developed by Mondada in Helsinki in 2015–2017, took inspiration from the previous project, focusing on video-recording a large corpus of shop encounters, not only in kiosks, but in diverse food shops like bakeries, and especially cheese shops, documented in a dozen languages across Europe (Harjunpää et al. 2018; Mondada 2018a, 2019b, 2020, 2021; Svinhufvud 2018). The focus was on the multimodal organization of actions constitutive of these encounters, such as requests, on comparative analyses (Mondada & Sorjonen 2016), as well as on the study of the embodied formatting of actions dealing with the materiality of products, approached in terms of multimodal and multisensorial engagements (Mondada 2021).

The project *Requests at local businesses*, developed by Fox and Heinemann in 2013–2015, was similarly inspired by the project in Finland. In order to create a somewhat comparable corpus of shop data, encounters at convenience stores, a bike shop, a university bookstore, and a shoe repair shop were video-recorded in a small town in the USA. The focus was originally on the linguistic and embodied formatting of customer requests, but eventually expanded to include investigations of other moments in the interactions (Fox & Heinemann 2015, 2016, 2017, 2020, 2021; Heinemann & Fox 2019).

These projects were not only able to gather a substantial amount of data but also paved the way for systematic and comparative analyses taking into consideration talk, embodiment, and materiality.

1.2 Delimiting the Field: What Kind of Shop Encounters?

Abundant research exists on shop and service encounters, based on different theoretical and analytical approaches, and adopting different methodologies, ranging from fieldnote-taking to audio-recordings and to video-based studies. The variety of the encounters studied has prompted early classificatory attempts, which we refer to here less to propose a typology of encounters than to discuss and position the face-to-face shop encounters exchanging material goods that are the target of this book.

Shop interactions are *encounters* in the sense of Goffman (1961), that is, focused interactions or "situated activity systems" that are characterized by a face-to-face engagement in a "mutual eye-to-eye activity" (1963: 92). They contrast with other practices of sociality, such as *gatherings*, which are rather a form of co-presence, where individuals might momentarily glance at others within forms of civil inattention (1963: 24).

Studies of shop interactions as 'encounters' in Goffman's sense can be traced back to Merritt (1976a). Merritt not only conducted one of the very first interactional studies based on a substantial audio-recorded corpus of shop encounters; she also precisely defined the activity of "service encounter" for the first time, as

an instance of face-to-face interaction between a server who is 'officially posted' in some service area and a customer who is present in that service area, that interaction being oriented to the satisfaction of the customer's presumed desire for some service and the server's obligation to provide that service. A typical service encounter is one in which a customer buys something at a store. (1976b: 321)

Merritt's definition focuses on the social interactions occurring in these encounters and covers both their institutionality, characterized by the asymmetric rights and obligations of the categories of the participants involved, and its material ecology. Following Merritt, subsequent studies have further discussed the *types* of service encounters and their differences, as well as the *phases* that characterize their structure or sequential unfolding.

Confronted with the rich array of settings encompassed by commercial encounters, typological attempts to distinguish between different types of commercial encounters are legion (see Félix-Brasdefer 2015: 56ff.). Our aim here is to provide for some useful distinctions, enabling us more to delimit the type of encounters tackled in this book, rather than to provide for a further classification.

The shop encounters defined by Merritt took place face to face, as do all the encounters studied in this book. But of course, commercial transactions do also occur at distance, via phone (for example, Clark et al. 1994; Humă & Stokoe 2020; Lee 2011; Márquez-Reiter 2011), in call centers (Whalen et al. 2002) or increasingly through the internet and various forms of e-commerce (Garcés-Conejos Blitvich 2015), where virtual service agents are increasingly being created (Köhler et al. 2011). The literature on phone and other forms of distant commercial communication is abundant and has not been reviewed here in its specificity, the focus being rather on co-present face-to-face encounters.

Face-to-face encounters take a variety of forms in highly heterogeneous contexts. In a very early linguistic anthropological study of transactions in Cyrenaica, based on fieldwork observations and note-taking, Mitchell (1957) distinguishes between auctions and shop/market transactions, highlighting their organizational differences concerning the way prices are announced, negotiated, and finally decided (for auctions see Heath 2013). Mitchell also considers the practices of haggling, in a context in which prices are not fixed, which is consequential for the way the transaction is conducted and the role of language in it (French 2000; Herrmann 2003, 2004).

Shop encounters, centered in co-present material products, are generally distinguished from *service encounters*, centered in some more abstract type of goods, as in Ventola's distinction (2005: 19) between shop encounters and service encounters providing for different types of commodities, e.g., material goods or information (also referred to as 'linguistic goods'). This useful distinction is nonetheless blurred by the fact that in service encounters some material objects may also be exchanged, typically documents (for example concerning bank or insurance products, or tickets at train counters and travel agencies), and that, conversely, in shop encounters information as service is also provided (as in advice and recommendations). Moreover, other forms of service concern the body of the customer (e.g., hairdressers, Oshima & Streeck 2015) rather than information; others concern products that are ordered and consumed in situ, and provided with the service of preparing and serving them (e.g., food delivery in restaurants and cafés, Kuroshima 2010; Laurier 2013; Richardson & Stokoe 2014; De Stefani 2019). Some are given for free rather than with payment (e.g., at public library desks, Downing 2008; Kidwell 2000; or in the form of offers to taste, Mondada, this volume). All this shows that the difference between material products and immaterial service is not clear-cut (e.g., shoe repair is a service but concerns material objects, Fox & Heinemann, this volume).

The terms *co-present shop encounters* and *service encounters* can also refer to the places where they happen, and their material-spatial and institutional specificities, according to the type of material/immaterial objects they provide. Thus, for example, Félix-Brasdefer (2015: 58–59) lists a series of places (indoor specialized shops, malls, supermarkets and department stores, outdoor markets, etc., along with business vs. public-administrative-institutional counters) describing their specific features, as well as cultural variation; he also lists the places/goods/linguistic and cultural contexts characterizing some of the literature in the field (2015: 61–69).

The spatiality of the encounter – the material environment and its design – matters also for distinguishing encounters at the counter, with a distribution of the participants on both sides of the counter, and free spaces in which the customers can navigate and search for their products (Mondada & Sorjonen 2016; Traverso 2001: 423). In the former case, the product has to be requested and fetched, occasioning sustained interactions between customers and sellers, who can also present, describe, and explain the products (providing for service in the form of advice or expertise). In the latter, like in supermarkets, self-service is the rule, affording other types of actions, such as asking for information, as well as collaborative actions between the customers (De Stefani 2011, 2013) – although there are counters within the supermarket where products are requested from a salesperson (De Stefani, this volume). Different spaces enabling different modes of navigation also distinguish between market stalls in public open space, where the passerby might become a customer or not (Hochuli 2019; Mondada 2022b), and shops constituting a closed space in which the customer is established by the very fact of entering the shop (Harjunpää et al. 2018).

Besides noting differences in the place, goods, and type of commercial encounters, several authors provide for rough models of the shop encounter as articulated in various *phases*. These can be seen from a structural perspective capturing the global organization of the encounter (Ventola 1987; Coupland 1983) or from a sequential perspective, insisting on the subsequent actions and sequences of actions progressing the encounter (Merritt 1976b, 1976c). In his early study of markets and shops in Cyrenaica, Mitchell (1957) is the first to propose a general structure of the encounter: he distinguishes between (1) greetings, (2) request, (3) investigation: examination of the product, (4) establishment of price, and (5) closing. In a similar way, Merritt (1976a), in her study of convenience stores, differentiates between (1) access to the counter and summons, (2) selection of products and decision to buy, (3) exchange of goods and money, and (4) closure (this model has been reused by several authors; see, e.g., Vasquez-Carranza 2017).

From the perspective of Systemic Functional Linguistics, Halliday and Hasan (1980) and Hasan (1985), studying small shops selling fruit, described the generic structure of the shop encounter in terms of obligatory elements (sale request, sale compliance, sale, purchase, and purchase closure). Ventola's structure (1987, 2005) was based on different types of service encounters (at the post, in travel agencies and small shops) and lists greeting, attendance-allocation (e.g., 'who's next?'), service bid (e.g., 'can I help you?'), request and service (e.g., 'could I have ...'), resolution, goods handover, payment, closing, and goodbye (1987: 70–76).

Within the shop encounter, further distinctions are often made between transactional talk, which is functional to the sale, and nontransactional interactions, such as small talk. The latter constitute the sociability of the encounter, rather than the economic aspect of the exchange, although often fully integrated in and supporting the service (Holmes 2000; Raevaara 2011; De Stefani & Horlacher 2018; Mondada & Sorjonen 2016).

This book considers the above distinctions and offers its specific contribution to them: within a perspective relying on conversation analysis, it focuses on face-to-face shop encounters centered on the purchase of material goods at a counter (vs. service encounters in general). The active embodied engagement by the participants in orienting to and manipulating products is seen and examined as constitutive of these encounters, instead of focusing merely on institutional talk between sellers and buyers. For this reason, the studies of this volume deal uniquely with video-recorded data, enabling a full appreciation of the embodied actions and of the multifaceted relations to the materiality of the encounter.

In the following sections we discuss various perspectives that have contributed to the study of diverse aspects of shop encounters. Their sociable and cultural importance beside the economic transactions, especially in traditional markets, has been the focus of sociolinguistic, ethnographic, and linguistic anthropological field studies (Section 1.3). Encounters in shops have been studied in sociolinguistics, discourse analysis, and pragmatics as contexts where social relationships between unacquainted people are nourished in ritual and polite ways (Section 1.4). Finally, shop encounters have been studied by conversation analysts and ethnomethodologists as an ideal setting for the study of action (Section 1.5). We turn to these approaches, which will be briefly discussed before summarizing the contributions of this book (Section 1.6) and offering a conclusion (Section 1.7).

1.3 Markets as Places of Sociability and Culture

Among possible shopping contexts, city markets have attracted the attention of anthropologists, sociologists of public space, and ethnographers of communication, who see them as a locus of sociability (De La Pradelle 2006; Lindenfeld 1990; Watson 2009; Stillerman 2006), and as places where culture and tradition are vividly maintained (see Bestor 2004 about the fish market of Tsukiji in Tokyo), in the midst of economic transactions.

In particular, markets, as well as 'bazaars', have been discussed as unique places for the way they intertwine trading interests and practices with sociocultural practices, relationships, and identities, contributing to both the establishment of value and the negotiation of prices, including the practice of bargaining (Khuri 1968; Geertz 1979; Fanselow 1990). These practices involve language not only in terms of the ability to negotiate but also, often, as a way of self- and other-categorizing the identity of the customer and mobilizing ethnic solidarities. The latter aspect connects anthropological studies of multiethnic markets (Wagner 2015) with linguistic anthropological studies of multilingualism on markets (Calvet 1992; French 2000).

From the perspective of ethnography of communication, the role of language in market practices is conceived as 'ways of speaking' (Hymes 1974) that fuel sociability as well as trade. Combining audio-recordings, ethnography, and interviews, Lindenfeld (1990) studied marketplaces in French towns, with a focus on the sociocultural and communicative competences of the speech community gathering there. She identified several communicative genres or 'ways of speaking', like the vendor calls, the 'vendor spiel' (the advertisement of products), and the interaction between vendor and seller. Moreover, she identified the role of speech as a symbolic practice contributing to the 'generalized sociability' characteristic of the market with small talk and jocular talk, ending with 'verbal dueling'.

Other practices typical of markets have been approached in terms of 'pitching'. Pitching is a practice that shows that selling is first and foremost a sociointeractional accomplishment. On the basis of video-recorded street vendors in open markets, Clark and Pinch (1995) described the pitching routines and rhetorical practices that culminate with what they called the 'sales relevance place', that is, the moment at which the audience buys the product. For instance, the presentation of the product, the preparation and then announcement of its price, dramatized by clapping hands and the construction of the moment as imminent, urgent, and quickly passed, culminate in the response of the customers, deciding to buy.

Selling as an interactional achievement is also embodied, for example, in the practice of street vendors (Llewellyn & Burrow 2008; Mondada 2022a) whose trade is embedded in the urban landscape, melting with and being shaped by the social order of the street. Actions such as offering, agreeing, refusing, and deciding to buy are embodied in actions of vendors and customers, as they accept (or not) engaging in the purchase. More generally, the mobility of customers is a central aspect of markets (Mondada 2022b). Market places constitute a particular social-material environment, being open public spaces, in which passersby walk on the street along the stands. Contrary to shops – in which people entering the door establish themselves as a customer, by initiating an opening in which they interact as customers with sellers (Harjunpää et al. 2018) – the market is an open space in which the passersby are not a priori categorized as customers, but might become so only by engaging with the sellers/products. Mobility has strong membership categorization implications (Sacks 1972): the very recognizability of the category 'passerby' is based on their mobility (Mondada 2009a, 2022b): arrangements and mobile practices of pedestrians in the market categorize them as 'walker-through', 'browser', or 'potential customer' (Lee & Watson 1993: 83). Stands, on the other hand, are organized in such a way that people stop at them and engage as 'customers' in new participation frameworks around them (Hochuli 2019). The fluidity of the market space is related to the practices through which a passerby becomes a customer.

1.4 Social Relations and Politeness in Shops

Pragmatic and sociolinguistic studies of shop encounters have investigated topics related to social relations and stances – politeness, rapport, and relational and transactional roles – and variation in communities, between cultures, and across languages and linguistic varieties.

Regarded as a fundamental social dimension of interaction, politeness has been a key focus in pragmatic studies of shop encounters (see Márquez-Reiter & Bou-Franch 2017 for a recent review). Politeness theory (Brown & Levinson 1987) has been used for analyzing the interplay between the verbal and social dimensions of a central transactional action of shop encounters, requests for product, as well as other verbal practices such as openings and closings, and thanking and apologies. Studies by Kerbrat-Orecchioni (2005, 2006) elaborated on politeness theory through the investigation of shop encounters audio-recorded in France. She argued for a need to revise and expand politeness theory with the concept of Face-Flattering Acts (FFA, e.g., thanking) that enhance the other's face (positive politeness), and to expand the scale of politeness to include 'apoliteness' (a neutral category) and 'hyperpoliteness'. The model became influential, generating studies on shop encounters in several languages and cultures (see, e.g., Kerbrat-Orecchioni & Traverso 2008).

The request for products has been a central object of investigation in shop studies (see Section 1.5.3). The prevalent focus has been on the grammatical design of the request and the degree of politeness exhibited by different grammatical formats. These studies started to call into question the assumption that certain linguistic forms have an intrinsic degree of politeness. For example, Kerbrat-Orecchioni (2005: 36–37, 2006: 91–93) considered the possibility that in commercial encounters requests might not have an inherent threatening component, but could instead be oriented to as Face-Flattering Acts (FFA), which are in the interests of the sellers due to their task of selling, compared to no request by the customer. Further, politeness could not be limited to indirectness, as FFAs are often intensified (e.g., *merci beaucoup* 'thanks very much'), and face-threatening acts (e.g., requests) can be softened in ways other than indirection. In addition, the degree of politeness of all utterances cannot be judged on a grammatical basis, which raises the question whether 'elliptical' requests (e.g., *Une gauloise filtre*, 'a packet of Gauloise filter-tips'), should be taken as 'blunt' acts or as exhibiting some 'sort of politeness'.

Politeness in shop encounters has also been investigated by combining different research perspectives in pragmatics and sociolinguistics. Placencia (2005, 2008) focused on pragmatic variation of requests in audio-recorded corner store (*tiendas de barrio*) encounters between two varieties of Ecuadorian Spanish (Quiteño and Manteño). Both Quiteño and Manteño largely favored direct formats for requests – including imperatives, elliptical utterances such as NPs, 'want'-declaratives (*quiero* 'I want'), and assertions of the shopkeeper's action (*me da* ... 'you give me ...'). Their differences concerned rapport management: requests in Manteño were more task-oriented, whereas in Quiteño requests were more elaborated and had longer preambles (greetings, how-are-yous; teasing and verbal play when requesting; thank-yous in closings). The Quiteños were engaging in the encounter from a more personal point of view, generating more interpersonal work. Tykesson-Bergman (2006) studied Swedish shop encounters from the point of view of *conversational contract* in Fraser's (1990) theory of politeness, using video-recorded data from a supermarket checkout till, a deli counter, and an information desk of a bookshop, finding for example that relational work in the three situations was produced especially by checkout clerks. The study also contains a diachronic investigation of the norms relating to service encounters in shops from the 1940s to the 1990s, based on manuals for the shop employees, interviews, and role playing, and focusing on topics of service over the counter vs. self-service, greetings, and address forms.

Talk and activities considered as not strictly transactional form a long-standing and continuous area of research on shop encounters (e.g., Merritt 1976a; Aston 1988, 1995a, 1995b; Bailey 1997; Ryoo 2005; Félix-Brasfeder 2015; Powell & Placencia 2020). Terminology in discussing them varies, including rapport management, small talk, relational work, and interpersonal work (e.g., Placencia 2004; Kuiper & Flindall 2000; Félix-Brasfeder 2015: ch. 7; Powell & Placencia 2020). While in earlier research transactional and nontransactional talk were clearly distinguished, later studies rather highlighted their intertwining. A good example is the study by Traverso (2007) on customers' 'insistence' in Syrian shop encounters; when sellers claim that the requested product is unavailable, customers commonly respond by asking again, and in so doing challenge the sincerity of the seller. Sellers then restate the impossibility of fulfilling customers' requests, leading to repetitive loops. While these repetitive sequences are clearly transactional, in keeping the sequence initiated with a request for the product open, the repetitions are also treated as teasing, becoming a form of chatting.

Studies of shop encounters have adopted cross-linguistic and cross-cultural perspectives for quite some time. Comparative research between languages was conducted already in early projects, such as PIXI (Pragmatics of Italian/ English Cross-Cultural Interaction, see Aston 1988) on bookstore encounters, with an interest in research outputs for second-language teaching. For example, Aston (1995a) argued that cross-cultural differences in the closings of shop encounters may relate to differences in the preferred ways of local conversational management rather than to different perceptions of the overall situation. Within Systemic Functional Grammar, Ventola (1983) analyzed post office encounters in Australia and Finland as part of testing the flow chart of the schematic structure of service encounters, finding that it worked for both cultures. Comparative interest was also part of the Lyon-based project on shop encounters (see Kerbrat-Orecchioni & Traverso 2008), comparing linguistically and culturally quite different areas (e.g., France and Syria in Traverso 2006; France and the Maghreb in Hmed 2008), highlighting differences in the expression of politeness, related to conversational routines and rituals. A remarkably large number of comparative studies focus on shop encounters in various Spanish-speaking countries and regions (see Placencia 2008 above, and on pragmatic variation below). An early comparative investigation of sales talk in Japan and in the United States was conducted by Tsuda (1984) making use of the approaches of ethnography of communication, interactional sociolinguistics, and conversation analysis.

Intercultural encounters form a further type of studies. Bailey (1997) investigated conflictual situations and issues of respect in video-recorded shop encounters between Korean immigrant shopkeepers and African American customers in the United States, making use of Gumperz's (1982) approach of intercultural communication and Brown and Levinson's (1987) politeness theory. Differences were found in the politeness strategies by the two groups: 'involvement politeness', including compliments, agreement, etc., characterized African Americans, while 'restraint politeness', that is, avoidance of involvement, characterized the Koreans. Interviews then brought up attitudes toward the other group (e.g., arrogance, disdain attributed to Koreans; selfishness, interpersonal imposition attributed to African Americans). Bailey concluded that the groups have different views on the roles of shopkeepers and customers, and on the appropriate conduct in service encounters.

A different perspective on intercultural encounters is provided by Ryoo's (2007) study, in which she analyzes video-recorded encounters between African American customers and Korean immigrant shopkeepers of a beauty supply store in a Midwestern city in the United States, referring to a variety of approaches such as ethnography and interactional sociolinguistics. Interculturality is analyzed as a discursively constructed ongoing process that is made relevant for specific interactional purposes, instead of treating cultural differences and their relevance as predetermined. Ryoo shows that interculturality is invoked only rarely as a relevant issue, and furthermore, is sometimes treated as irrelevant by the participants, for example when the shopkeeper is acting and asked to act as an expert (e.g., on the care of African American hair). In some rare cases, the cultural identities of the participants were evoked and oriented to in the course of interactions, for example, by the shopkeeper to promote sales, make small talk, and create rapport, as well as for recruiting new customers.

A line of research that has developed into a distinctive approach on service encounters is variational pragmatics (Schneider & Barron 2008; Félix-Brasfeder 2015; Félix-Brasfeder & Placencia 2020), with a special focus on varieties of Spanish. Variational pragmatics encompasses a sociolinguistic perspective to service encounters and other types of interactions, especially with respect to macrosocial factors, such as age and gender, but often microsocial and/or situational aspects are investigated at the same time. The methodology refers to the formal, actional, interactional, topic, and organizational levels of (mostly quantitative) analysis (Schneider & Barron 2008), as well as to rapport management at illocutionary, stylistic, participatory, discursive, and nonverbal levels (Spencer-Oatey 2008). These levels of analysis address regional variation, including national variation (pluricentric languages, such as Spanish), subnational variation (internal varieties of a given language, e.g., Mexican Spanish), and (sub)local variation (e.g., between different districts in the same town) (Félix-Brasfeder & Placencia 2020).

As an example of research on pragmatic variation, Félix-Brasdefer and Yates (2020) identified through quantitative and qualitative analyses regional variation in the grammatical format of requests, finding that in small shops in Buenos Aires the range of request formats was most diverse (with mostly elliptical and implicit strategies), whereas in Mexico City the most common strategy was assertion, and in Seville the use of imperative. As an example of variational research on gender, interested in the choice of address forms (T/V pronouns, vocatives), Michno (2020) found that in corner store encounters in Tola in Nicaragua, the selection of the address form was conditioned by the customer's gender, so that *usted* was used significantly more often when the customer was female and *vos* when the customer was male.

There has been a long tradition of research on shop encounters from sociolinguistic, politeness, pragmatic, and variational perspectives, a tradition that has generally focused on rapport management in shop encounters, both in transactional and nontransactional talk, and has largely been based on audio-recorded data in a diversity of languages. More recently, it has included an interest in discourse and social interaction, borrowing from conversation analysis. We now turn to the latter: conversation analytic approaches to shop encounters are a more recent tradition of studies, which highlights the sequential organization of actions constituting the commercial encounter, with a special focus on the format of these actions, both verbal and embodied, from a multimodal approach.

1.5 The Constitutive Actions of Buying and Selling

1.5.1 *Ethnomethodological and Conversation Analytic Studies of Shop Encounters*

The analytical focus of ethnomethodological and conversation analytic (EMCA) approaches is on ways in which situated interactions are accomplished locally and moment by moment through ordered sequences of actions. These sequences of action are methodically organized by the participants mobilizing verbal and embodied practices and resources. Actions are examined as they are produced, formatted, and adjusted to local contingencies, as well as heard and seen, interpreted and responded to by their recipients (Sacks 1992; Schegloff 2007).

This conceptual and methodological approach to action enables EMCA studies to offer an original contribution to the rich literature on shop encounters. EMCA studies recognizes the systematic but also locally occasioned organization of the transaction. In so doing it enables us to understand the routine character of the activity but also its detailed arrangements as locally emerging and accomplished (rather than, e.g., 'scripted', as the models detailing the 'phases' of the transaction often suggest). It also enables us to demonstrate the consequentiality of precise action formats on the progressivity of the interaction and of the economic transaction.

Shop encounters are a form of institutional interaction (Drew & Heritage 1992) in which the organization of turns and sequences of actions brings the specific context into being. They are also a type of workplace interaction (Heath & Luff 2000) in which the spatial and material ecology of activity reflexively shapes opportunities for actions by different participants. As for other topics of EMCA research, an important number of studies have dealt with commercial transactions on the phone (e.g., Mazeland et al. 1995; Rasmussen Hougaard 2008; Lee 2009, 2011), often related to services (e.g., travel agencies). The field has been expanded by taking into account visual, computer and web interfaces mobilized during these transactions, either remotely (e.g., Heinonen et al. 2021) or in person (such as when the transaction at the counter is crucially mediated by the computer). A variety of contexts has been covered, from supermarkets (De Stefani 2011), to markets (Clark & Pinch 1995; von Lehm 2014; Mondada 2022b), from impromptu street sales (Llewellyn & Burrow 2008) to auctions (Heath 2013), from services offered at the counter (Kidwell 2000; Mondada 2018c; Mortensen & Hazel 2014) to a variety of shops (food shops, Mondada 2018a; kiosks, Sorjonen & Raevaara 2014; shoe repair shops, Fox & Heinemann 2015, 2020, 2021).

This book focuses on face-to-face shop encounters (vs. service encounters in general), at the counter (vs. in self-serviced areas), involving the transfer of material objects (vs. dematerialized products, such as, e.g., finance or insurance services). The next sections devoted to EMCA studies are organized by first focusing on openings of the encounter (Section 1.5.2) and typical recurrent actions and sequences initiating the business, such as requests (Section 1.5.3), and then by highlighting the importance of the material ecology of these encounters (Section 1.5.4), whereafter actions when moving to paying and closing will be taken up (Section 1.5.5), also showing how the specific organization of these encounters shapes the economic consequences of the exchange.

1.5.2 Openings

Openings provide for the establishment of an alignment between the relevant categories of the participants, which confer rights and obligations. A basic category is that of seller/service provider vs. customer, which enables for example the seller clearly to frame their action as relative to the institution and not as a personal one (Merritt 1976). Other categories involve expertise (Aston 1995a: 93; Mondada 2019b, 2021), as well as specific responsibility and authority for some area of the business (instead of a general responsibility; expressed, e.g., by variation in the use of personal pronouns, Aston 1995a: 93; Merritt 1976a).

The first mutual coordination in the encounter happens in an embodied way, through the way the person who is not yet a customer enters into the business area and possibly progressively engages in a transaction. While research examining the format of actions in shop encounters has to a large extent focused either on actions in isolation or short sequences of actions (e.g., first greetings, or a greetings pair; requests for a product, or a request and a response to it), studies making use of video-recorded data have started to investigate the temporally emerging multimodal approach by the participants to orient to and dealing with the business early on in market places and shops, in the opening, and even in the pre-opening of the encounter (see Clark & Pinch 2010; Harjunpää et al. 2018; Hochuli 2019; Llewellyn & Burrow 2008; Mondada 2022b).

The gradual, tentative, and contingent process in moving to business in open outdoor markets was demonstrated by Mondada (2022b) in her study on (pre)openings in markets in French-speaking Alsace. The study details the methodic ways in which passersby may orient to the sensory appeal of the products; they may slow down and stop to inspect the products closer (e.g., smell, glance, touch, and taste fruit), and then continue the strolling, or move eventually to initiate interaction with the salesperson or respond to them, becoming then a potential customer (see also Brown 2004 on 'browsing' in covert markets). The study also provides more generally a demonstration of the constitutive relevance of mobility and multisensoriality in moving into a possible (pre)opening of commercial encounters.

An orientation to and projection of selling and buying is displayed more immediately in contexts where people enter the premises of an indoor shop. Examining openings of video-recorded service encounters in bakeries and cheese shops (in Finland, Spain, and Switzerland), Harjunpää, Mondada, and Svinhufvud (2018) showed ways in which from the first moment of the customer entering the shop, the customers and salespersons orient to and project service activities to come. They achieve that by treating their coordinated multimodal actions (mutual gaze, greetings, walking along and toward the counter) not as separate actions or pairs of actions but as relevant in forming a coordinated action trajectory to reach the 'service point'. Instead of being a predefined location and a temporal moment/place, the 'service point' is shown to be situationally achieved and organized, comprising a temporal moment when the participants reach reciprocal positions relative to the counter and when a sequential slot for a request for a product is made relevant. By examining the ways in which salespeople orient to their work as constituted not only by service but also by other, manual, organizational, and accounting tasks, the authors show how salespeople make observable their rights and responsibilities for incoming customers, as well as how customers either adjust to them or manifest their dissatisfaction with a delay in being served (for instance by using double greetings when the salespersons are not available to them).

Once the participants have entered the shop and approached the counter, the first words in the encounter (after the greetings), such as in English *Excuse me* by the customer and *Can I help you?* by the seller, are in service of this alignment of the relative categories (Aston 1995a: 96ff.). The first words also target the type of customer for the type of service or product to offer (for telephone sales see Mazeland et al. 1995; Stokoe et al. 2017). Furthermore, in openings it becomes apparent whether the person coming in is a regular customer (Laurier 2013; De Stefani 2019). Openings also provide for the alignment of the languages of the service in multilingual encounters: the first greeting offers a sample of the linguistic resources that will be available for the transaction and that can be negotiated in the next greeting (Mondada 2018b; Mortensen & Hazel 2014; Varcasia 2010).

1.5.3 Requests

Sequences initiated by requesting a product or practical action verbally and/or with embodied resources form a key transactional and commercial action, the reason for the visit. There has been considerable interest in the grammatical format and pragmatic meaning of requests in shop encounters, in research from perspectives such as politeness theory, and pragmatic and cross-language variation, studied mainly with audio-recorded data. More recently, EMCA studies have foregrounded the sequentially organized character of requests, and video-based studies of face-to-face encounters have demonstrated the fundamentally multimodal character of actions and the ecology of the location, which have been shown to have an impact on the verbal formatting of requests. Furthermore, the relevance of examining larger trajectories of action and activities has begun to be recognized (e.g., Mondada 2022c).

An example showing the relevance of the ecology of the shop and the multimodal character of actions is Sorjonen and Raevaara's (2014) study of requests for tobacco products at convenience store (kiosk) encounters in Finland. They showed that the grammatical format of the request is associated with a temporally progressing trajectory of a larger activity, during which a mutual focus of attention and a joint interactional space between the customer and seller is established (reciprocal sighting, greetings), preparing a sequential slot for initiating and producing the request (see also Harjunpää et al. 2018). In this process, customers treat the seller's greeting as a sequential place for initiating the reason for their visit, that is, to initiate the request for a product. Sorjonen and Raevaara found that the choice of the two formats of the request (phrasal, *punanen Marlboro* 'red Marlboro' vs. clausal) is related to the physical arrangements of space at the kiosk, the location of and the bodily movements by the customer and the seller, as well as to the sequential trajectory of the activity. There is a practical basis for the choice between a phrase (NP) and a clause in formatting the request: the extended verbal format is chosen to manage the time it takes for the customer to reach the transaction point (reaching the counter and achieving a stationary position). Similar kinds of contingencies were found in shoe repair shop encounters by Fox and Heinemann (2020).

The grammatical design of requests can have a central impact on the format of the expected response. In their study of nongranting responses by copy shop employees to customers' requests to have copies made of their documents, Vinkhuyzen and Szymanski (2005) found that the format of the request has a clear impact on whether the nongranting can be done in an affiliative or disaffiliative fashion. This was important for the company as it had a policy of redirecting customers with small copy jobs to the self-service area (DIY, 'do-it-yourself' area) to do the copies themselves. Customers with small copy jobs displayed unhappiness with this policy in various ways, including by manipulating the syntactic format of their request so as to make it problematic for the employees to reject it. Vinkhuyzen and Szymanski showed that a declaratively formatted request (e.g., *I wanna get some quality copies* ...) opened the possibility of treating the turn as a request for advice, which would allow the employees to direct customers to the DYI area to get the copies. Interrogatively formatted yes-no requests (e.g., *can you (.) can you ta:: (.) print up* ...), however, in projecting a confirming response as preferred, made rejecting the request more challenging. The authors of this study, who also had an applied goal, suggested that asking the employees to implement the company's policy put them in a difficult situation, and therefore the charge for copies made by the employees should instead be increased. The impact of the customers' design of the request on the method of formatting a nongranting or dissatisfying response has also been investigated in calls to commercial service providers, for example, to airline companies (Lee 2011) and to telephone services (Varcasia 2007).

The grammatical construction of requests in shop encounters in American English has been recently examined from an interactional linguistic perspective by Fox and Heinemann (2016, 2017, 2021) in a series of studies on video-recorded shoe repair shop encounters in the US. These papers focused on the internal grammatical variation of request formats (e.g., different formats of *can*-interrogatives; *need*- vs. *want*-declaratives; *can*- and *wonder*-initiated requests), showing the interactional relevance of this more low-level grammatical variation, such as differences in the sequential placement of the request formats, the stance to the repairability of the problem, or to the grantability of the request.

Requests may also be formatted in a way that departs from the common, neutral design that is devoid of expressing affect. In their study on video-recorded convenience store encounters in Finland, Haakana and Sorjonen (2011) examined ways in which customers express a playful stance toward buying lottery tickets. They focused on invoking a frame of another type of institutional encounter through interdiscursive lexical elements, most often that of offices (e.g., *pistetään taas anomus sisää* 'let's put the application in again') but also of investment business and hotdog stands. They argued that the parallel between the encounters in the frame shift rests on everyday experiences and is clearly recognizable. Cases where the customers orient to what they are buying as unexpected or dispreferred and accountable are investigated by Raevaara (2011) as part of her study on accounts at convenience stores in Finland (e.g., buying a lottery ticket as one had just won, or buying several chocolate bars so that there is something to offer the grandchildren). Raevaara showed that an account can simultaneously be in some cases designed to launch small talk.

Most previous studies on requests and requesting have concentrated on sequences of single requests and their responses, with possible insert expansions to provide more information about the product or service requested (Merritt 1976b). An exception is a study by Mondada and Sorjonen (2016) on multiple requests as progressively building a global buying project, based on video-recordings of convenience store encounters in France in 1986 and in Finland during 1999–2002. They showed how, in both sets of data, through the use of multimodal practices, requests can be produced and oriented to as simultaneous actions, as well as either contiguously achieved sequences of actions or ones separated by inserted actions. Verbal tying practices are used to indicate the relationship between the requests (Fi *ja* 'and' and Fr *et* 'and' to include two items in a request; Fi *sitte* 'then' and Fr *puis* 'then' to preface a following, separate request). The multimodal formatting and timing of requests is adjusted to the local constraints of the ecology of the buying activity. For example, two sequential organizations were observed for double requests (an embodied request for a picked-up product and a verbal request for a fetched product) issued together: whereas in the more recent Finnish data the seller registers the picked-up product with a barcode-reader, while the customer issues a verbal request for a product, also registered in the same way, in the older French data (without bar-code readers) the seller's registers the picked-up product by a simple glance, while the customer utters their verbal request with a turn-initial *et*.

1.5.4 Manipulating Products: The Relevance of Objects and Materialities

Requests and other actions performed in the face-to-face shop encounters orient to the material ecology of buying and selling, mainly to the products that are exchanged over the counter. Products are verbally named, described, and referred to, but also pointed at and looked at, as well as inspected, grasped, manipulated, and touched, while the customer requests, asks questions, requests advice, etc.

Video-based studies of shop encounters have enabled a new approach to study of the products, not only as discursive objects of reference, but also as material objects. On the one hand, they show how verbal actions of customers and sellers are embodied (e.g., within the embodied organization of requests, including the orientation toward the co-participants and the products), within turns that are multimodally formatted. On the other hand, they also reveal that shop encounters are crucially based on ways in which customers navigate searching for and/or exploring products within the shop silently, as well as ways in which they, possibly with sellers, engage in examining the products in various embodied and sensorial ways (Mondada 2019b). To a large extent, shop encounters as economic transactions focus (often silently) on products and their inspection.

Sellers' and customers' embodied actions make observable the *routinized* character of shop encounters. In these routines, talk is often minimal – as when a request is formatted with just the name of the product – and participants' body orientations, toward each other as well as toward the ecology of the shop and the products, are enough to achieve accountability of the ongoing action and to make it projectable and therefore able to be anticipated. Analyses of routinized ways of entering the shop (Harjunpää et al. 2018), coming closer to the counter (Sorjonen & Raevaara 2014) or to a salesperson (Clark & Pinch 2010), projecting what the request will be (Mondada 2021), and embodying it silently rather than performing it verbally (Mondada 2019c) show the crucial role of embodiment in the material environment for the management of the shop encounter. The encounter cannot be reduced to the first words uttered in the transaction.

Embodied actions also highlight the relevance of *materiality* in shop encounters. Reducing face-to-face shop encounters in which products are being bought to verbal exchanges, and therefore often to issues of social relationships, ignores a fundamental aspect, which is that people go into all kinds of shops and market stands to buy material objects and to inspect them prior to buying them. Products – and, from an EMCA perspective, actions with products – can be mobilized in very different ways: as discursive objects (for instance when informings, explanations, or recommendations are proffered, Moore 2008), as material objects (when they are fetched by the seller and given to the customer), as semiotic objects (when their labels are read by the customer, De Stefani 2011), or as sensorial objects (when they are felt, touched, tasted, etc., Streeck 1996; Mondada 2019a).

The materiality of products as objects has been discussed by De Stefani (2011, 2014) in his studies of shopping in supermarkets, in which customers navigate the shop without any mediation by sellers and engage directly with the products: he showed how they scrutinize them, read the labels, and check them, and finally how the decision to buy them is embodied by putting them in the shopping cart. The manipulation of objects is also important in studies of repair shops where customers display the reason for their visit, either to bring a shoe to be repaired or to pick it up when it has been fixed, orienting bodily and manually to the problem by handling the object in a particular way (Heinemann & Fox 2019). Other objects and products are manipulated depending on the type of shop and the type of actions expected within the transaction, like documents in print shops (Moore et al. 2010), tickets at counters (Lindström et al. 2017), and lottery coupons (Haakana & Sorjonen 2011; Raevaara 2011; Mondada & Sorjonen 2016). The manipulation of objects has contributed to research in elaborating on ways in which multimodal analyses integrate materiality.

This issue of the re-materialization of bodies, identities, objects, and social action has been addressed explicitly within different approaches in the social sciences, which propose moving from a vision based on marketing to one focused on market-things (Cochoy 2007). In this interdisciplinary context, new materialism and actor-network theory (Fox & Alldred 2017; Latour 1996) has revisited the sociology of economic exchanges (Callon 1998), insisting on the relevance of networks of associations between objects, other nonhumans and humans, and the agency of objects and technologies. EMCA's perspective, however, insists instead on the embodied actions that mobilize materiality. The grasping, taking, and moving of objects back and forth have been considered in a multimodal analysis centered on how these manipulations contribute to the progressivity of the encounter.

More recently, a new approach to material objects has been proposed, focusing on how their sensoriality becomes relevant in social interaction and in specific actions with objects (Mondada 2019a, 2021). By manipulating, grasping, fetching, and displacing products, actors engage with objects but do not automatically make their sensorial qualities relevant. Other forms of embodied action engage with sensing them, for the practical purposes of the ongoing transaction. The issue is to take into consideration, document, and analyze the sensorial actions through which participants access, inspect, and feel objects from the perspective of their sensorial qualities, for their relevance within the ongoing course of action. This is not the case for all products sold in shops; it is typically the case for food objects as representative of products to be sensed, which are considered for qualities that can be perceived by the senses, such as consistency, texture, aroma, and taste (Mondada 2019a, 2019b). Attention to these qualities has prompted studies of how products are inspected (Mortensen & Wagner 2019), touched (Mondada 2020; Mondada et al. 2021), tasted (Mondada 2018a, 2019a), and more generally accessed in a multisensorial way (Mondada 2021). These sensorial engagements are fundamental for the assessment of the products and the consequent decision to buy them (Mondada 2022c). In this way, they feature in a sensorial economy, where what is offered to the customer is not just a material object but a sensorial experience.

1.5.5 Moving to Closing

Within the unfolding actions that define the shop encounter, objects are identified and selected, fetched and shown, inspected, given and taken, transiting over the counter back and forth – for instance when a product is fetched by the seller and passed over the counter to the customer, when a lottery ticket is given by the customer to the seller to be checked, or when some money passes back and forth during paying.

The selection of a product can be achieved within the request sequence, but it can also unfold through a range of actions such as offers and recommendations by the seller, questions and discussions of alternative options, closed by a final assessment and decision. Assessments are a crucial action through which both sellers and buyers build a common understanding and (e)valuation of the buyable. Assessments can be the means by which sellers elaborate the value of the product, and seek alignment and even affiliation with the client – although this runs the risk of the client disaffiliating with them (Clark et al. 2003; Mondada 2009b). Producing assessments is a way for the buyer to convey, through the positive evaluation of the product, their decision to buy it: in cheese shops, the simple uttering of a positive assessment can be treated by the seller as attributing decision-making to the customer, made visible by the seller proceeding to the cutting of the cheese, which is an irreversible action closing the purchase (Mondada 2022c).

The progression toward possible closing is typically managed in shop encounters through the initiation of a routine question, affording the opportunity of placing a new order: *Altro?* 'Something else?' / *E' tutto?*, *Basta così?* 'Nothing else?' These two options project different expected responses, orienting to the continuation of the shopping or toward the closing (De Stefani 2006).

The closing of the purchase is achieved by moving to pay. Although the price of a product can be dealt with well before in the transaction, when it is asked for, or even negotiated or established during the encounter (such as in auctions, Heath 2013), it is typically announced toward the completion of the purchase. This completion of the purchase and closing of the encounter is projected and achieved in embodied ways by various practices of the seller, such as packing the requested product, typing the price, etc. (De Stefani 2006), and announcing the price to pay, which is oriented to as initiating closing

(Mondada & Sorjonen 2016). It is also embodied by the customer, who may take their wallet out of their pocket, organize their belongings, and orient toward the till rather than the window-case (De Stefani 2006).

Announcing the price generates various forms of local reasoning and calculation (Halonen & Koivisto, this volume) as well as choice between different types of prices and pricing systems (Llewellyn 2011a, 2014, 2015a). Paying is itself a local accomplishment: it occasions different types of actions, such as occasional gifts (Llewellyn 2011b) and giving and taking change (Llewellyn 2011b). It is achieved through different embodied manipulations of payment means (Mondada et al. 2020), which take not only different shapes but also different interactional trajectories, depending on the system of payment adopted (cash vs. credit card vs. other means) (Llewellyn 2015b). These studies show how a rich array of social, normative, symbolic dimensions are deeply intertwined within the apparently simple action of paying.

Among the actions projecting closing there is thanking (Kipers 1986; Aston 1995b; Zorzi Calò et al. 1990; Koivisto 2009). Studying thanking by two different sellers at Finnish convenience stores, Koivisto (2009) argued that rather than being a conventional practice of politeness, thanking in her data is used as one of the central verbal resources for structuring the encounter, for displaying that a sequence of actions has been brought to conclusion (most frequently uttered by the seller when the customer gives the seller the money, and in the closings of the encounter; see also Mondada 2019c).

Together with thanking, farewell and final greetings definitively achieve the closing – although some late, post-paying and pre-closing last purchases are always possible (Mondada & Sorjonen 2016). This shows how the closing of the encounter is a collaborative and negotiated achievement, which might take time, affording repeated opportunities to add items spotted or remembered at the last moment, as well as a closure of the service and the relationship between the categories involved of customer/client and salesperson.

1.6 The Contributions to This Book

Each contribution to this volume focuses on an action, a practice, or a sequence of actions characteristic of shop encounters. The order of chapters in the book reflects the unfolding organization of the service encounter.

In "Approaching the Counter at the Supermarket: Decision-Making and the Accomplishment of Couplehood," Elwys De Stefani explores the interactional work that two people shopping together do before finally arriving at the counter to make a request, in the context of supermarkets in a Swiss Italian city. While most studies of service encounters have focused on the customer's request as an initial and self-standing object, De Stefani traces the interactional history of requests in a corpus of 'couples' shopping together. While some requests arose from a need that was stated at the very beginning of the shopping expedition (e.g., 'I need cheese') and which then guided the pair to a specific counter at the store, other requests arose from something said or seen in the course of traversing the store, which was treated as 'touching off' or instigating a need. Even needs or wishes that were expressed at the beginning of the interaction undergo transformation, however, as the pair approaches the relevant counter and particular subtypes of the item become visible or otherwise available; for example, a stated need for cheese may become 'Robiola' through verbal and embodied interaction with the partner and through visual inspection of the counter area. Potential purchasable items proffered by one member of the pair may be modified or even rejected by the other, and in this process the pair enacts a particular kind of relationship, namely being a committed couple, in which both parties have a say in food that is to be purchased and prepared for specific meals. In this study we can thus see that requests are not born full-grown out of the head of the speaker but rather emerge incrementally over the course of interactions, and are situated in particular interactional, material, and economy-oriented environments.

While the chapter by De Stefani examines interactions before customers reach the counter and make requests, the next chapter, by Katariina Harjunpää, Lorenza Mondada, and Kimmo Svinhufvud, examines the formatting of initial turns by customers at the counter, in order to decide and select what to buy. In their chapter entitled "Customers' Inquiries about Products: Establishing Grounds for the Decision to Buy," they focus on questions from customers about the identity of a particular product (e.g., 'what is that?'), or about details of a product (e.g., 'what's in it?' or 'does it have lactose?'), before an item is selected for purchase. On the basis of recordings in bakeries in Finland, France, and Switzerland, the authors show how customers may face a range of practical problems in making decisions as to what or whether to purchase, including seeing items that might look appealing but which they do not recognize or for which they do not know the ingredients. Through the design of these questions, drawing on verbal, material, and embodied resources, customers make publicly available to the sellers their epistemic access to the products (for example, they do not know enough about the item to formulate its identity with anything more than a demonstrative pronoun or demonstrative determiner plus 'empty' noun). Through their answers, sellers provide information that may offer immediately useful information for the customer in making their decision ('it's fig bread' → 'no'), or which may need further elaboration. For example, a proper noun which gives no hint to the customer as to its ingredients may get expanded with a list of ingredients: 'there is the Hilde bread, it is wheat based but has millet, corn, soy, groats and flax seed'. Thus, the referential practices employed by both customers and sellers reveal features of items that are locally relevant for the practical purposes of buying, in particular sequential, material, and embodied locations in interaction.

If information and explanations regarding a product provided by the seller are not sufficient to enable a customer to make a decision about purchasing an item, it can in some contexts become relevant for the seller to provide direct sensorial experience to the customer. In Chapter 4, "Offering a Taste in Gourmet Food Shops: Small Gifts in an Economy of Sale," Lorenza Mondada studies sellers offering customers a taste of cheese when a customer has expressed interest in a product but displays some hesitation in making a decision regarding whether to purchase it or not. Hence, such offers to taste, video-documented in gourmet shops in a dozen cities across Europe, clearly pursue sale of the cheese; they are not simple small gifts but are made in 'an economy of sale'. If the offer is made sequentially too late (after the customer has already made the decision to buy) or too early (the person in the shop may not yet have identified themselves as a 'customer'), the offer may be rejected, further underlining the pursuit of sale at work in an offer of a taste. A contrasting environment of offers of a taste is also examined; in these environments a plate of small pre-cut pieces of a particular cheese is on the counter, publicly available for anyone to try, and not directly part of the sequence of the customer purchasing the cheese they have identified as desirable for them. Offers of such cheese are routinely accepted by customers without leading to any sale, contrary to the other, personalized offers. This fact enriches our understanding of the preference organization of offers and requests, and the relationships between benefactor and beneficiary, and further supports the relationship between the offer and the pursuit of the offerer's interests.

Once selection of an item or items has been made by the customer, there must be an interactional and commercial transaction which transforms the selected items from purchasables into possessed objects, that is, from items owned by the shop to possessions of the customer.

The next chapter, by Lorenza Mondada and Marja-Leena Sorjonen, "Embodied Trajectories of Actions in Shop Encounters: Giving or Placing Products on or over the Counter," explores an aspect of this somewhat magical transformation – the transfer of the item(s) from the customer's hands into the hands of the seller. This transfer is a crucial part of many commercial transactions, as the seller must enter the item number into the shop's inventory system, to both learn the price and to subtract the item from inventory. Exploring data from kiosks, or convenience stores, across Europe, Mondada and Sorjonen explore the precise details of this manual transfer of items. There are two general methods by which the transfer is enacted: in the first, the customer gives the item directly into the hand(s) of the seller; in the second, the customer places the item on the counter and the seller picks it up. Which method unfolds depends on a variety of factors, including the seller's physical availability at the moment the customer approaches the counter, the kinds of items purchased, and whether the seller has anticipated the transfer by reaching out their hand, in a shape recognizable as ready to 'take'. These two methods are seen to reveal the moral and commercial nature of the manipulation of objects, and ultimately of the transaction.

After the transformation of the item from a possessable into a possessed, customers and sellers may orient to the need to pack the items so that they can be easily carried away by the customer. Through this process customers and sellers acknowledge that the customer's final destination lies elsewhere and that transporting items may be necessary. Anna Lindström and Barbara Fox, in their chapter "Unpacking Packing," examine normative orientations of packing items at a Farmers Market in Sweden; these orientations to who should pack and under what circumstances reveal the deeply moral and interactional character of packing. While customers are expected to pack most items on their own, bulk items – such as potatoes – are normatively packed by the seller. When these norms are violated, such as when customers ask to pack their own potatoes, moral indignation may result. The study further examines instances in which the seller displays difficulty in packing; customers' careful offers of assistance in these cases display an orientation to the autonomy of the seller and call into question the universal desirability of offers of assistance.

In the chapters so far, the focus has been on the purchase of new items on display at a shop. In Chapter 7, "The Request-Return Sequence: What Can Happen at the Interface between Picking Up a Repaired Item and Paying for It," Barbara Fox and Trine Heinemann analyze sequences in which shoes and other leather items are returned to customers at a shoe repair shop in the USA, having been repaired. Before their final payment for these repairs, customers may be given the chance to inspect the repair work that has been done, and this inspection may lead to assessments, complaints, and so on. Through careful examination of these request-return sequences, the authors find that the staff engage in three different ways of presenting the returned items, each of which opens a space for a different kind of response from the customer: in the first (and most frequent), the staff person simply places the item on the counter and then turns to ring up the sale; in the second, the staff person engages in manual displays of the repair work that has been done; and in the third, the staff person verbally pursues a response through questions. The first type of presentation does not make conditionally relevant any kind of inspection or assessment from the customer, although customers may still inspect and assess; in the second, the pursuit is a bit stronger; and in the third, through questions from the staff such as *good?*, an assessment is made conditionally relevant. The study queries the theoretical implications for the general lack of pursuit of assessment at the shoe shop, compared with, for example, hair salons, in which assessments are typically actively pursued by the stylist.

Shop encounters are closed when payment is made. The final chapter of the volume, "Moving Money: Money as an Interactional Resource in Kiosk Encounters in Finland," analyzes the ways in which the physical presence of money (whether as cash or bank card) shapes the payment phase of the interaction at kiosks in Finland. In this study, Mia Halonen and Aino Koivisto demonstrate that customers orient to payment from the very beginning of the interaction and work to prepare their money and to make it observable to the seller from early on. Moreover, they find that if the customer has made their money observable prior to the price announcement by the seller, the payment phase moves quickly and smoothly to completion. If, on the other hand, the money has not been made observable early in the interaction, payment can be delayed. Conversely, customers can put their money on the seller's side of the counter before payment has been made relevant; in such cases, the seller adjusts his or her actions to speed up the interaction so that the payment phase arrives earlier than is typical. Thus, through money, especially displays of it early in the interaction, customers show their orientation to progressivity.

1.7 Conclusion

The current volume brings together a temporally ordered set of studies that explore a range of theoretical and practical issues in commercial transactions, in Western contexts. Beginning with the emergence of a 'need' for a grocery item before the request to a seller is actually made, all the way through to the payment phase, the volume explores the rich and deeply methodical practices employed by customers and sellers as they go about the apparently mundane work of buying and selling small items (and, in one case, repairing items).

Methodologically, the chapters are all based on video-recorded encounters documented in naturalistic settings, that is, without having been orchestrated by the researchers. This enables the analysts to capture relevant embodied and material details that, together with talk, define the shop encounter. A subtype of encounters has been the focus in this collection, namely those in shops with a counter, where the products have to be requested and fetched by the seller or brought to the counter by the customer to be registered and paid – this makes indispensable, as well as routinizes, the interaction between sellers and customers. Because these short interactions are highly repetitive and routine, all contributors to the volume were able to collect a substantial number of encounters that revealed systematic patterns of specific recurrent key actions, such as requesting, asking questions, transferring objects, packing produce, and paying. Interactions at the counter thus constitute an ideal locus to explore the interplay between situated actions, their formats, and their sequential environments. An important contribution offered by the chapters of the volume can be seen in the systematic study of embodied conducts in these sequential environments: this concerns on the one hand the embodied formatting of actions – requesting, offering, asking questions, assessing, etc. – and on the other hand the manipulations of material objects – gazed at, grasped, moved, inspected, touched, tasted, etc.

Examining how materiality is dealt with in these encounters reveals crucial features of the economic transaction. Objects are present in many different ways: in their multiplicity, they are oriented to as possible buyable options within the surrounding ecology; in their singularity, they are focused on as they are selected, requested, checked, inspected, and manipulated. Moreover, several other material objects feature in the encounter, such as packaging (which might be part of the service offered), and money. The latter is not merely a financial means of exchange, a symbolic and legal equivalent for goods, but also a material thing – a bill, coin, credit card, etc. – that is passed over the counter, back and forth. The book enables a vision of economic encounters that integrates talk and the manipulation of these material objects as performing central tasks in the encounter. The multiplicity of objects that are displayed, offered, and given to look at, smell, and sometimes touch and taste, as well as the ways a product is presented, a plastic bag is handed over, a bill is given, define the transaction in its relevant and consequential details.

These material-embodied details are relevant for a range of practices and actions. The circulation of goods, made recognizable in its specificity by the way they are handled, passed, and received, is deeply intertwined with issues of normativity and legality: they are confronted with, and reflexively shape, the transient ownership of the products and money, the rights and obligations to handle them in determined ways, as well as the definition of what the parties consider as a buyable, a possessable, a free sample, a bought product, or a paid item. The circulation of goods also manifests relations of customership, connoisseurship, and service: they exhibit different forms of knowledge and expertise, as well as desirability; they subsequently show, turn by turn, action by action, who has the right, the ability, the opportunity to appreciate, describe, explain, or taste the product. In this way they emanate from and in return shape a sense of trust in expertise and judgment, which define both good service and good customership. These aspects are fundamental for the situated and endlessly (re)produced definition of these social interactions as social-economic encounters, in which sociability, engagement with materiality, and economy are indissociable. In this sense the book demonstrates both the relevance of multimodal analysis of social interaction for a better understanding of issues related to economic encounters, and the perspicuous character of shop encounters to understand fundamental aspects of social interaction, such as shared attention, common definitions of the value of objects and actions, intersubjectivity, and mutual recognition of normativities.

References

Appadurai, A., ed. (1986). *The Social Life of Things: Commodities in Cultural Perspective*. Cambridge: Cambridge University Press.

Aston, G., ed. (1988). *Negotiating Service: Studies in the Discourse of Bookshop Encounters*. Bologna: CLUEB.

Aston, G. (1995a). In reference to the role of openings in service encounters. *Cahiers de linguistique française*, 16(1), 89–111.

(1995b). Say 'Thank you': Some pragmatic constraints in conversational closings. *Applied Linguistics*, 16(1), 57–86.

Bailey, B. (1997). Communication of respect in interethnic service encounters. *Language in Society*, 26(3), 327–356.

Bestor, T. C. (2004) *Tsukiji: The Fish Market at the Center of the World*. Berkeley: University of California Press.

Brown, B. (2004). The order of service: The practical management of customer interaction. *Sociological Research Online*, 9(4), 28–49.

Brown, P., & Levinson, S. (1987). *Politeness: Some Universals in Language Usage*. Cambridge: Cambridge University Press.

Callon, M., ed. (1998). *The Laws of the Markets*. Oxford: Blackwell.

Calvet, L.-J., ed. (1992). *Les langues des marchés en Afrique*. Paris: Didier Érudition.

Campbell, C. (2021). *Consumption and Consumer Society*. Chur: Springer.

Clark, C., Drew, P., & Pinch, T. (1994). Managing customer "objections" during real-life sales negotiations. *Discourse & Society*, 5(4), 437–462.

(2003). Managing prospect affiliation and rapport in real-life sales encounters. *Discourse Studies*, 5(1), 5–31.

Clark, C., & Pinch, T. (1995). *The Hard Sell: The Language and Lessons of 'Street-Wise' Marketing*. London: Harper & Collins.

(2010). Some major organisational consequences of some 'minor', organised conduct: Evidence from a video analysis of pre-verbal service encounters in a showroom retail store. In N. Llewellyn & J. Hindmarsh, eds., *Organisation, Interaction and Practice: Studies of Ethnomethodology and Conversation Analysis*. Cambridge: Cambridge University Press, pp. 140–171.

Cochoy, F. (2007). A sociology of market-things: On tending the garden of choices in mass retailing. *The Sociological Review*, 55(S2), 109–129.

Cochoy, F., Trompette, P., & Araujo, L. (2016). From market agencements to market agencing: An introduction. *Consumption Markets & Culture*, 19(1), 3–16.

Coupland, N. (1983). Patterns of encounter management: Further arguments for discourse variables. *Language in Society*, 12(4), 459–476.

De La Pradelle, M. (2006). *Market Day in Provence*. Chicago: University of Chicago Press.

De Stefani, E. (2006). Le chiusure conversazionali nell'interazione al banco di un supermercato [Conversational closings in the interaction at a supermarket counter]. In Y. Bürki & E. De Stefani, eds., *Trascrivere la lingua: Dalla filologia all'analisi conversazionale*. Bern: Peter Lang, pp. 369–403.

(2011). "Ah petta ecco, io prendo questi che mi piacciono." Agire come coppia al supermercato. Un approccio conversazionale e multimodale allo studio dei processi decisionali *["Oh wait here, I'm getting these, cos I like them." Acting as a couple at the supermarket. A conversational and multimodal approach to the analysis of decision-making]*. Rome: Aracne.

(2013). The collaborative organisation of next actions in a semiotically rich environment: Shopping as a couple. In P. Haddington, L. Mondada, & M. Nevile, eds., *Interaction and Mobility: Language and the Body in Motion*. Berlin: De Gruyter, pp. 123–151. https://doi.org/10.1515/9783110291278.123

(2014). Establishing joint orientation towards commercial objects in a self-service store: How practices of categorisation matter. In M. Nevile, P. Haddington, T. Heinemann, & M. Rauniomaa, eds., *Interacting with Objects: Language, Materiality, and Social Activity*. Amsterdam: John Benjamins, pp. 271–294. https://doi.org/10.1075/z.186.12ste

(2019). Ordering and serving coffee in an Italian café: How customers obtain 'their' coffee. In D. Day & J. Wagner, eds., *Objects, Bodies and Work Practice*. Bristol: Multilingual Matters, pp. 113–139. https://doi.org/10.21832/9781788924535-008

De Stefani, E., & Horlacher, A.-S. (2018). Mundane talk at work: Multiactivity in interactions between professionals and their clientele. *Discourse Studies*, 20(2), 221–245. https://doi.org/10.1177/1461445617734935

Douglas, M., & Isherwood, B. (1979). *The World of Goods*. New York: Basic Books.

Downing, A. (2008). *Requesting in Library Reference Service Interactions*. Doctoral dissertation, Rutgers University.

Drew, P., & Heritage, J., eds. (1992). *Talk at Work: Interaction in Institutional Settings*. Cambridge: Cambridge University Press.

Fanselow, F. S. (1990). The bazaar economy or How bizarre is the bazaar really? *Man*, 25(2), 250–265.

Félix-Brasdefer, J. (2015). *The Language of Service Encounters: A Pragmatic-Discursive Approach*. Cambridge: Cambridge University Press. https://doi.org/10.1017/CBO9781139565431

Félix-Brasfeder J. C., & Placencia, M. E., eds. (2020). *Pragmatic Variation in Service Encounter Interactions across the Spanish-speaking World*. London: Routledge.

Félix-Brasdefer, J. C., & Yates, A. B. (2020). Regional pragmatic variation in small shops in Mexico City, Buenos Aires, and Seville, Spain. In J. C. Félix-Brasfeder & M. E. Placencia, eds., *Pragmatic Variation in Service Encounter Interactions across the Spanish-speaking World*. London: Routledge, pp. 15–34.

Fox, B., & Heinemann, T. (2015). The alignment of manual and verbal displays in requests for the repair of an object. *Research on Language and Social Interaction*, 48(3), 342–362. https://doi.org/10.1080/08351813.2015.1058608

(2016). Rethinking format: An examination of requests. *Language in Society*, 45(4), 499–531. https://doi.org/10.1017/S0047404516000385

(2017). Issues in action formation: Requests and the problem with x. *Open Linguistics*, 3(1), 31–64.

(2020). Spatio-temporal contingencies for making a request at the shoe repair shop. *Journal of Pragmatics*, 167, 20–67.

(2021). Are they requests? An exploration of declaratives of trouble in service encounters. *Research on Language and Social Interaction*, 54(1), 20–38.

Fox, N. J., & Alldred, P., eds. (2017). *Sociology and the New Materialism*. London: Sage.

Fraser, B. (1990). Perspectives on politeness. *Journal of Pragmatics*, 14, 219–236.
French, B. M. (2000). The symbolic capital of social identities: The genre of bargaining in an urban Guatemalan market. *Journal of Linguistic Anthropology*, 10(2), 155–189.
Garcés-Conejos Blitvich, P. (2015). Setting the linguistics research agenda for the e-service encounters genre: Natively digital versus digitized perspectives. In M. de la O Hernández-López & L. Fernández Amaya, eds., *A Multidisciplinary Approach to Service Encounters*. Leiden: Brill, pp. 13–36.
Geertz, C. (1979). The bazaar economy in Sefrou. In C. Geertz, H. Geertz, & L. Rosen, *Meaning and Order in in Moroccan Society*. Cambridge: Cambridge University Press, pp. 123–244.
Goffman, E. (1961). *Encounters: Two Studies in the Sociology of Interaction*. Indianapolis: Bobbs-Merrill.
 (1963). *Behavior in Public Spaces: Notes on the Social Organization of Gatherings*. New York: The Free Press.
Gumperz J. (1982). *Discourse Strategies*. Cambridge: Cambridge University Press.
Haakana, M., & Sorjonen, M. -L. (2011). Invoking another context: Playfulness in buying lottery tickets at convenience stores. *Journal of Pragmatics*, 43(5), 1288–1302. https://doi.org/10.1016/j.pragma.2010.10.029
Halliday, M. A. K., & Hasan, R. (1980). Text and context: Aspects of language in a social-semiotic perspective. *Sophia Linguistica (Working Papers in Linguistics)*, 6, 4–91.
Harjunpää, K., Mondada, L., & Svinhufvud, K. (2018). The coordinated entry into service encounters in food shops: Managing interactional space, availability, and service during openings. *Research on Language and Social Interaction*, 51(3), 271–291. https://doi.org/10.1080/08351813.2018.1485231
Hasan, R. (1985). The structure of a text. In M. A. K. Halliday & R. Hasan, eds., *Language, Context and Text: Language in a Social-Semiotic Perspective*. Oxford: Oxford University Press, pp. 52–69.
Heath, C. (2013). *The Dynamics of Auction: Social Interaction and the Sale of Fine Art and Antiques*. Cambridge: Cambridge University Press. https://doi.org/10.1017/CBO9781139024020
Heath, C., & Luff, P. (2000). *Technology in Action*. Cambridge: Cambridge University Press.
Heinemann, T., & Fox, B. (2019). Dropping off or picking up? Professionals' use of objects as a resource for determining the purpose of a customer encounter. In D. Day & J. Wagner, eds., *Objects, Bodies and Work Practice*. Bristol: Multilingual Matters, pp. 143–163. https://doi.org/10.21832/9781788924535-009
Heinonen P., Niemi. J., & Kaski, T. (2021). Changing participation in web conferencing: The shared computer screen as an online sales interaction resource. *Applied Linguistics Review*, June 2021. https://doi.org/10.1515/applirev-2021-0056
Herrmann, G. M. (2003). Negotiating culture: Conflict and consensus in US garage-sale bargaining. *Ethnology*, 42(3), 237–252.
 (2004). Haggling spoken here: Gender, class, and style in US garage sale bargaining. *Journal of Popular Culture*, 38(1), 55–81.
Hmed, N. (2008). Analyse comparative d'interactions dans des petits commerces français, tunisiens et franco-maghrébins [Comparative analysis of interactions in

small French, Tunisian, and Franco-North African shops]. In C. Kerbrat-Orecchioni & V. Traverso, eds., *Les interactions en site commercial: invariants et variations [Interactions in Commercial Sites: Invariants and Variations]*. Lyon: ENS Éditions, pp. 254–276.

Hochuli, K. (2019). Turning the passer-by into a customer: Multi-party encounters at a market stall. *Research on Language and Social Interaction*, 52(4), 427–447. https://doi.org/10.1080/08351813.2019.1657288

Holmes, J. (2000). Doing collegiality and keeping control at work: Small talk in government departments. In J. Coupland, ed., *Small Talk*. Harlow: Pearson, pp. 32–61.

Humă, B., & Stokoe, E. (2020). The anatomy of first-time and subsequent business-to-business "cold" calls. *Research on Language and Social Interaction*, 53(2), 271–294. https://doi.org/10.1080/08351813.2020.1739432

Hymes, D. H. (1974). Ways of speaking. In R. Bauman & J. Sherzer, eds., *Explorations in the Ethnography of Speaking*. Cambridge: Cambridge University Press, pp. 433–452.

Kerbrat-Orecchioni, C. (2005). Politeness in France: How to buy bread politely. In L. Hickey & M. Stewart, eds., *Politeness in Europe*. Bristol: Multilingual Matters, pp. 29–44.

(2006). Politeness in small shops in France. *Journal of Politeness Research*, 2(1), 79–103.

Kerbrat-Orecchioni, C., & Traverso, V. (2008). *Les interactions en site commercial: invariants et variations*. Lyon: ENS Éditions.

Khuri, F. (1968). The etiquette of bargaining in the Middle East. *American Anthropologist*, 70(4), 698–706.

Kidwell, M. (2000). Common ground in cross-cultural communication: Sequential and institutional context in front desk service-encounters. *Issues in Applied Linguistics*, 11 (1), 17–37. https://doi.org/10.5070/L4111005024

Kipers, P. (1986). Initiation and response in service encounter closings. *Working Papers in Educational Linguistics*, 2(2), 1–16. https://repository.upenn.edu/wpel/vol2/iss2/2

Koivisto, A. (2009). Kiitoksen paikka. Kiittäminen kioskiasiointia jäsentämässä [Time to say thank you: Thanking in organizing the kiosk encounter]. In H. Lappalainen & L. Raevaara, eds., *Kieli kioskilla: tutkimuksia kioskiasioinnin rutiineista [Language at the Kiosk: Studies on Routines of Kiosk Encounters]*. Helsinki: Suomalaisen Kirjallisuuden Seura, pp. 174–200.

Köhler, C. F., Rohm, A. J., de Ruyter, K., & Wetzels, M. (2011). Return on interactivity: The impact of online agents on newcomer adjustment. *Journal of Marketing*, 75(2), 93–108.

Kuiper, K., & Flindall, M. (2000). Social rituals, formulaic speech and small talk at the supermarket checkout. In J. Coupland, ed., *Small Talk*. Harlow: Pearson, pp. 32–61.

Kuroshima, S. (2010). Another look at the service encounter: Progressivity, intersubjectivity, and trust in a Japanese sushi restaurant. *Journal of Pragmatics*, 42(3), 856–869. https://doi.org/10.1016/j.pragma.2009.08.009

Labov, W. (1972). *Sociolinguistic Patterns*. Philadelphia: University of Pennsylvania Press.

Lappalainen, H., & Raevaara, L., eds. (2009). *Kieli kioskilla: tutkimuksia kioskiasioinnin rutiineista* [*Language at Kiosk: Studies on Routines of Kiosk Encounters*]. Helsinki: Suomalaisen Kirjallisuuden Seura.

Latour, B. (1996). On interobjectivity. *Mind, Culture and Activity*, 3(4), 228–245.

Laurier, E. (2013). Encounters at the counter: The relationship between regulars and staff. In P. Tolmie & M. Rouncefield, eds., *Ethnomethodology at Play*. Farnham: Ashgate.

Lee, J. R. E., & Watson, R. (1993). *Interaction in Urban Public Space*. Paris: Plan Urbain.

Lee, S.-H. (2009). Extended requesting: Interaction and collaboration in the production and specification of requests. *Journal of Pragmatics*, 41, 1248–1271. https://doi.org/10.1016/j.pragma.2008.09.013

(2011). Managing nongranting of customers' requests in commercial service encounters. *Research on Language and Social Interaction*, 44(2), 109–134. https://doi.org/10.1080/08351813.2011.567091

Lindenfeld, J. (1990). *Speech and Sociability at French Urban Marketplaces*. Amsterdam: John Benjamins.

Lindström, J., Norrby, C., Wide, C., & Nilsson, J. (2017). Intersubjectivity at the counter: Artefacts and multimodal interaction in theatre box office encounters. *Journal of Pragmatics*, 108, 81–97. https://doi.org/10.1016/j.pragma.2016.11.009

Llewellyn, N. (2011a). The delicacy of the gift: Passing donations and leaving change. *Discourse & Society*, 22(2), 155–174. https://doi.org/10.1177/0957926510392126

(2011b). The gift in interaction: A study of 'picking-up the bill'. *The British Journal of Sociology*, 62(4), 718–738. https://doi.org/10.1111/j.1468-4446.2011.01388.x

(2014). "He probably thought we were students": Age norms and the exercise of visual judgement in service work. *Organization Studies*, 36(2), 153–173. https://doi.org/10.1177/0170840614546151

(2015a). Microstructures of economic action. *The British Journal of Sociology*, 66, 486–511. https://doi.org/10.1111/1468-4446.12143

(2015b). 'Money talks': Communicative and symbolic functions of cash money. *Sociology*, 50(4), 796–812. https://doi.org/10.1177/0038038515585475

Llewellyn, N., & Burrow, R. (2008). Streetwise sales and the social order of city streets. *The British Journal of Sociology*, 59, 561–583. https://doi.org/10.1111/j.1468-4446.2008.00208.x

Márquez-Reiter R. (2011). *Mediated Business Interactions. Intercultural Communication Between Speakers of Spanish*. Edinburgh: Edinburgh University Press.

Márquez-Reiter R., & Bou-Franch P. (2017). (Im)politeness in service encounters. In J. Culpeper, M. Haugh, & D. Kádár, eds., *Handbook of Linguistic Impoliteness*. London: Palgrave Macmillan, pp. 661–687.

Mazeland, H., Huisman, M., & Schasfoort, M. (1995). Negotiating categories in travel agency calls. In A. Firth, ed, *The Discourse of Negotiation: Studies of Language in the Workplace*. Oxford: Pergamon, pp. 271–297.

Merritt, M. (1976a). *Resources for Saying in Service Encounters*. Unpublished dissertation manuscript, Department of Linguistics, University of Pennsylvania.

(1976b). On questions following questions in service encounters. *Language in Society*, 5(3), 315–357. https://doi.org/10.1017/S0047404500007168

(1976c) On the use of OK in service encounters. In R. W. Shuy & A. Shnukal, eds., *Language Use and Uses of Language*. Washington, DC: Georgetown University Press, pp. 162–172.

Michno, J. (2020). Gender variation in address form selection in corner-store interactions in a Nicaraguan community. In J. C. Félix-Brasfeder & M. E. Placencia, eds., *Pragmatic Variation in Service Encounter Interactions across the Spanish-speaking World*. London: Routledge, pp. 77–98.

Miller, D. (1998). *A Theory of Shopping*. Cambridge: Polity.

Mitchell, T. F. (1957). The language of buying and selling in Cyrenaica: A situational statement. *Hesperis*, 44, 31–71.

Mondada L. (2009a). Emergent focused interactions in public places: A systematic analysis of the multimodal achievement of a common interactional space. *Journal of Pragmatics*, 41, 1977–1997. https://doi.org/10.1016/j.pragma.2008.09.019

(2009b). The embodied and negotiated production of assessments in instructed actions. *Research on Language and Social Interaction*, 42(4), 329–361. https://doi.org/10.1080/08351810903296473

(2018a). The multimodal interactional organization of tasting: Practices of tasting cheese in gourmet shops. *Discourse Studies,* 20(6), 743–769. https://doi.org/10.1177/1461445618793439

(2018b). Multiple temporalities of language and body in interaction: Challenges for transcribing multimodality. *Research on Language and Social Interaction*, 51(1), 85–106. https://doi.org/10.1080/08351813.2018.1413878

(2018c). Greetings as a device to find out and establish the language of service encounters in multilingual settings. *Journal of Pragmatics*, 126, 10–28. https://doi.org/10.1016/j.pragma.2017.09.003

(2019a) Contemporary issues in Conversation Analysis: Embodiment and materiality, multimodality and multisensoriality. *Journal of Pragmatics*, 145, 47–62. https://doi.org/10.1016/j.pragma.2019.01.016

(2019b). Participants' orientations to material and sensorial features of objects: looking, touching, smelling and tasting while requesting products in shops. *Gesprächsforschung*, 20, 461–494. www.gespraechsforschung-online.de/fileadmin/dateien/heft2019/si-mondada.pdf

(2019c). Transcribing silent actions: A multimodal approach of sequence organization. *Social Interaction. Video-Based Studies of Human Sociality*, 2(1), https://doi.org/10.7146/si.v2i1.113150

(2020). Sensorial explorations of food: How professionals and amateurs touch cheese in gourmet shops. In A. Cekaite & L. Mondada, eds., *Touch in Social Interaction. Touch, Language, and Body*. London: Routledge, pp. 288–310.

(2021). *Sensing in Social Interaction*. Cambridge: Cambridge University Press.

(2022a). Adjusting step-by-step trajectories in public space: The microsequentiality of approaching and refusing to be approached. *Gesprächsforschung*, 23, 36–65.

(2022b). Appealing to the senses: Approaching, sensing and interacting at the market's stall. *Discourse & Communication*, 16(2), 160–199.

(2022c). Attributing the decision to buy: Action ascription, local ecology, and multimodality in shop encounters. In A. Deppermann & M. Haugh, eds., *Action Ascription*. Cambridge: Cambridge University Press, pp. 105–132.

Mondada, L., Bänninger, J., Bouaouina, S. A., Gauthier, G., Hänggi, P., Koda, M., Svensson, H., & Tekin, B. S. (2020). Doing paying during the Covid-19 pandemic. *Discourse Studies*, 22(6), 720–752. https://doi.org/10.1177/1461445620950860

Mondada, L., Bouaouina, S. A., Camus, L., Gauthier, G., Svensson, H., & Tekin, B. S. (2021). The local and filmed accountability of sensorial practices: The intersubjectivity of touch as an interactional accomplishment. *Social Interaction. Video-based Studies on Human Sociality*, 4(3), https://doi.org/10.7146/si.v4i3.128160

Mondada, L., & Sorjonen, M.-L. (2016). Making multiple requests in French and Finnish convenience stores. *Language in Society*, 45(5), 733–765. https://doi.org/10.1017/S0047404516000646

Moore, R. J. (2008). When names fail: Referential practice in face-to-face service encounters. *Language in Society*, 37(3), 385–413. https://doi.org/10.1017/S004740450808055X

Moore, R., Whalen, J., & Gathman, C. (2010). The work of the work order: Document practice in face-to-face service encounters. In N. Llewellyn & J. Hindmarsh, eds., *Organization, Interaction, and Practice: Studies in Ethnomethodology and Conversation Analysis*. Cambridge: Cambridge University Press, pp. 172–197. https://doi.org/10.1017/CBO9780511676512.009

Mortensen, K., & Hazel, S. (2014). Moving into interaction: Social practices for initiating encounters at a help desk. *Journal of Pragmatics*, 62, 46–67. https://doi.org/10.1016/j.pragma.2013.11.009

Mortensen, K., & Wagner, J. (2019). Inspection sequences: Multisensorial inspections of unfamiliar objects. *Gesprächsforschung*, 20, 399–343.

Oshima, S., & Streeck, J. (2015). Coordinating talk and practical action: The case of hair salon service assessments. *Pragmatics and Society*, 6(4), 538–564. https://doi.org/10.1075/ps.6.4.04osh

Placencia, M. E. (2004). Rapport-building activities in corner shop interactions. *Journal of Sociolinguistics*, 8(2), 215–245.

(2005). Pragmatic variation in corner store interactions in Quito and Madrid. *Hispania*, 88(3), 583–598.

(2008). Requests in corner shop transactions in Ecuadorian Andean and Coastal Spanish. In K. Schneider & A. Barron, eds., *Variational Pragmatics*. Amsterdam: John Benjamins, pp. 307–332.

Powell, H., & Placencia, M. E. (2020). Interpersonal work in service encounters in Mercado Libre Argentina: A comparison between buyer and vendor patterns across two market domains. In J. C. Félix-Brasfeder & M. E. Placencia, eds., *Pragmatic Variation in Service Encounter Interactions across the Spanish-speaking World*. London: Routledge, pp. 209–229.

Raevaara, L. (2011). Accounts at convenience stores: Doing dispreference and small talk. *Journal of Pragmatics*, 43, 556–571. https://doi.org/10.1016/j.pragma.2010.01.02

Rasmussen Hougaard, G. (2008). Membership categorization in international business phonecalls: The importance of 'being international'. *Journal of Pragmatics*, 40(2), 307–332. https://doi.org/10.1016/j.pragma.2007.08.011

Richardson, E., & Stokoe, E. (2014). The order of ordering. In M. Nevile, P. Haddington, T. Heinemann, & M. Rauniomaa, eds., *Interacting with Objects: Language, Materiality, and Social Activity*. Amsterdam: John Benjamins, pp. 31–56.

Ryoo, H. K. (2005). Achieving friendly interactions: A study of service encounters between Korean shopkeepers and African-American customers. *Discourse & Society*, 16(1), 79–105.

(2007). Interculturality serving multiple interactional goals in African American and Korean service encounters. *Pragmatics*, 17(1), 23–47. https://doi.org/10.1075/prag.17.1.03ryo

Sacks, H. (1972). On the analyzability of stories by children. In J. J. Gumperz & D. Hymes, eds., *Directions in Sociolinguistics: The Ethnography of Communication*. New York: Rinehart & Winston, pp. 325–345.

(1992). *Lectures on Conversation, Vols 1 & 2*. Ed. by G. Jefferson. Oxford: Basil Blackwell.

Schegloff, E. A. (2007). *Sequence Organization in Interaction: A Primer in Conversation Analysis, Vol. 1*. Cambridge: Cambridge University Press. https://doi.org/10.1017/CBO9780511791208

Schneider, K., & Barron, A. (2008). *Variational Pragmatics: A Focus on Regional Varieties in Pluricentric Languages*. Amsterdam: John Benjamins.

Simmel, G. (1900). *The Philosophy of Money*. London: Routledge.

Sorjonen. M.-L., & Raevaara, L., eds. (2006). *Arjen asiointia. Keskusteluja Kelan tiskin äärellä* [*Everyday Service Encounters. Interactions in Offices of the Social Insurance Institution*]. Helsinki: Finnish Literature Society.

Sorjonen, M-L., & Raevaara, L. (2014). On the grammatical form of requests at the convenience store: Requesting as embodied action. In P. Drew & E. Couper-Kuhlen, eds., *Requesting in Social Interaction*. Amsterdam: John Benjamins, pp. 243–268. https://doi.org/10.1075/slsi.26.10sor

Spencer-Oatey, H. (2008). Face, (im)politeness and rapport. In H. Spencer-Oatey, ed., *Culturally Speaking. Culture, Communication and Politeness Theory*, 2nd Ed. London: Continuum, pp. 11–47.

Stillerman, J. (2006). The politics of space and culture in Santiago Chile's street markets. *Qualitative Sociology*, 29(4), 507–530.

Stokoe, E., Sikveland, R. O., & Huma, B. (2017). Entering the customer's domestic domain: Categorial systematics and the identification of 'parties to a sale'. *Journal of Pragmatics*, 118, 64–80.

Streeck, J. (1996). How to do things with things: Objects trouvés and symbolization. *Human Studies*, 19(4), 365–384. https://doi.org/10.1007/BF00188849.

Svinhufvud, K. (2018). Waiting for the customer: Multimodal analysis of waiting in service encounters, *Journal of Pragmatics*, 129, 48–75. https://doi.org/10.1016/j.pragma.2018.03.002

Traverso, V. (2001). Syrian service encounters. A case of shifting strategies within verbal exchange. *Pragmatics*, 11(4), 421–444.

(2006). Aspects of polite behaviour in French and Syrian service encounters: A data-based comparative study. *Journal of Politeness Research: Language, Behaviour. Culture*, 2(1), 105–122.

(2007). Insisting: a goal-oriented or a chatting interactional practice? One aspect of Syrian service encounters. *Intercultural Pragmatics*, 4(3), 377–398.

Tsuda, A. (1984) *Sales Talk in Japan and the United States. An Ethnographic Analysis of Contrastive Speech Events*. Washington, DC: Georgetown University Press.

Tykesson-Bergman, I. (2006) *Samtal I butik. Språklig interaktion mellan biträden och kunder. Acta Universitatis Stockholmiensis. Stockholm Studies in Scandinavian Philology. New Series*, 41.

Varcasia, C. (2007). English, German and Italian responses in telephone service encounters. In P. Seedhouse & H. Bowles, eds., *Conversation Analysis and Language for Specific Purposes*. Bern: Peter Lang, pp. 217–244.

(2010). L'apertura degli incontri di servizio in una realtà plurilingue. In M. Pettorino, A. Giannini, & F. Dovetto, eds., *La comunicazione parlata 3. Atti del terzo Congresso Internazionale del Gruppo di studio sulla Comunicazione Parlata, Vol. I.* Naples: Università degli studi di Napoli L'Orientale, pp. 655–670.

(2013). *Business and Service Telephone Conversations. An Investigation of British English, German and Italian Encounters*. London: Palgrave Macmillan.

Vasquez-Carranza, A. (2017). "If vegetables could talk . . .": A structural and sequential analysis of buying and selling interactions in a Mexican fruit and vegetable shop. *Discourse Studies*, 19(6), 711–731.

Ventola, E. (1983). Contrasting schematic structures in service encounters. *Applied Linguistics*, 4(3), 242–258.

(1987). *The Structure of Social Interaction: A Systemic Approach to Semiotics of Service Encounters*. London: Pinter.

(2005). Revisiting service encounter genre: Some reflections. *Folia Linguistica*, 39(1–2), 19–43.

Vinkhuyzen, E., & Szymanski, M. (2005). Would you like to do it yourself? Service requests and their non-granting responses. In K. Richards & P. Seedhouse, eds., *Applying Conversation Analysis*. New York: Palgrave Macmillan, pp. 91–106. https://doi.org/10.1057/9780230287853_6

vom Lehn, D. (2014). Timing is money: Managing the floor in sales interaction at street-market stalls. *Journal of Marketing Management*, 30(13–14), 1448–1466. https://doi.org/10.1080/0267257X.2014.941378

Wagner, L. B. (2015). 'Tourist price' and diasporic visitors: Negotiating the value of descent. *Valuation Studies*, 3(2), 119–148.

Warde, A. (2017). *Consumption: A Sociological Analysis*. London: Palgrave Macmillan.

Watson, S. (2009). The magic of the market place: Sociality in a neglected public space. *Urban Studies*, 46(8), 1577–1591.

Whalen, J., Whalen, M. R., & Henderson, K. (2002). Improvisational choreography in teleservice work. *The British Journal of Sociology*, 53(2), 239–258.

Zorzi Calò, D., Ruey, B., Gavioli, L., & Aston, G. (1990). Opening and closing service encounters: Some differences between English and Italian. In C. De Stasio, M. Gotti, & R. Bonadei, eds., *La rappresentazione verbale e iconica: valori estetici e funzionali*. Milan: Guerini, pp. 445–458.

2 Approaching the Counter at the Supermarket
Decision-Making and the Accomplishment of Couplehood

Elwys De Stefani

2.1 Introduction

Studies on interaction at the point of sale have traditionally conceived of service encounters as discrete interactional events delimited by an opening and a closing (for early accounts see Mitchell 1957; Merritt 1976; for recent developments see Chapter 1 of this book). Accordingly, data were generally collected with fixed recording devices placed in close proximity to market stalls or at the counters of shops where customers are served. This setup reifies the conception of service encounters as events that start *at* the point of sale, with the beginning of the verbal interaction between a seller and a buyer. However, research on the mobile conduct of interacting individuals has shown that they mutually adjust their bodies before or while engaging in conversation with each other, thereby initiating a face-to-face encounter (Mondada 2009; De Stefani & Mondada 2010, 2018). How customers entering small shops adapt their talk to their movement toward the counter has recently been studied (Sorjonen & Raevaara 2014; Harjunpää et al. 2018; De Stefani 2019). Service counters, however, can also be found in supermarkets, where they are generally located far away from the entrance. Hence, in this setting, the customers' approach to the counter is different from what has been observed for small grocery shops: it takes more time, it is generally preceded by repeated orientation to products available in the self-service area of the supermarket, or it may never happen at all since customers may buy only freely accessible products.

In this chapter, I analyze the approach to supermarket counters from the customers' perspective. For this purpose, I use video data collected by following couples as they navigate through a supermarket as publicly recognizable *participation units* (Goffman 1963: 91). I have followed three couples on their tour through a supermarket located in the Italian-speaking part of Switzerland. Two couples interacted with the service personnel (five different shop assistants) at three different counters (fish, meat, and cheese).[1] Participants

---

[1] Customers order and receive goods in the requested quantity at the counter and pay for them at a checkout, together with the products picked up in the self-service area.

engaging in joint shopping alternate mobile episodes of interaction – e.g., moving through the aisles – with occasions of stationary interaction, e.g., when they establish a common focus of attention toward a specific product (located on a shelf, in a refrigerator, etc.) or when they request some item at the counter.[2] In joint shopping, participants not only cooperatively work out their navigation through space, but they also continuously engage in negotiating and refining their buying projects, which are situatedly emerging.[3] Consequently, grocery stores offer an extraordinary opportunity for observing how decision-making is contingent on progressively emerging and altering *semiotic fields* (Goodwin 2000) to which participants orient as they move through the aisles of the supermarket. They also offer the occasion to examine how co-shoppers constitute different kinds of *couplehood* through their decision-making practices. In this chapter, I examine the interaction between co-shoppers from the first mention of a *potentially purchasable item* (De Stefani 2014: 273) to the actual request for that item at a served counter.[4]

In my data, vocal requests at the counter are typically shaped as follows:

Excerpt 2.1 (cons42271, 15:09–15:12)

```
01 CAR:     vorrei un^eh::: (.) robiola matura.
            I'd like an^uh::: (.) ripe Robiola.
```

Excerpt 2.2 (cons42271, 31:52–31:55)

```
01 CAR:     eh:: vorrei: dodici pezzet- (0.2) pezzi di:: sardine.
            uh:: I'd like:: twelve piece- (0.2) pieces of:: sardines.
```

Excerpt 2.3 (cons42271, 25:25–25:28)

```
01 CAR:     eh: vorrei del^eh:: dello spezzatino di vitello.
            uh: I'd like some^uh:: some veal stew.
```

Excerpt 2.4 (cons45111, 07:02–07:07)

```
01 MAR:     eh:::m mezzo chilo di:: sbrinz. (.)
            uh:::m half a kilo of:: Sbrinz. (.)
02          me lo grattugia per piacere?
            do you grate it for me please?
```

---

[2] This *stop-and-go* pattern (De Stefani 2013) of mobile activity is similar to the way in which guided tours are organized (Stukenbrock & Birkner 2010; De Stefani 2010; Best 2012; Mondada 2012; Pitsch 2012). In guided tours, however, one participant takes the lead as a *guide* by organizing the alternation between stationary and mobile episodes of interaction and by deciding which objects are of interest (but see De Stefani & Mondada 2014).

[3] Hence, my use of the phrase *project* is different, e.g., from Linell's (2009) understanding of communicative projects.

[4] For analyses of how customers refer to and select products available in the self-service areas of the supermarket see De Stefani (2011, 2013, 2014).

Excerpt 2.5 (cons45111, 08:42–08:46)

```
01 TER:    mi dà u:na fettina di gorgonzola col mascarpone
           (do you) give me a: slice of Gorgonzola with mascarpone
02         per favore.
           please.
```

All of these instances occur immediately after the opening of the encounter, i.e., after an exchange of greetings between the service assistant at the counter and one member of the couple.[5] These requests exhibit certain similarities, such as a turn-initial *əh(m)* 'uh(m)'[6] (Excerpts 2.2–2.4), lengthening of the article (*un^eh::* 'an^uh::', Excerpt 2.1; *u:na* 'a:', Excerpt 2.5) and/or partitive (*di::* 'of::', Excerpts 2.2 and 2.4; *del^eh::* 'some^uh::', Excerpt 2.3) preceding lexical reference to the requested item (Excerpts 2.1–2.5), the use of the conditional verb form *vorrei* 'I'd like' (Excerpts 2.1–2.3), and others. Remarkably, in all the excerpts, the lexical reference form allowing for the identification of the requested item is delivered in a clear-cut way, without any hitches, lengthenings, or hesitation. Also, it is systematically placed in TCU-final position (Sacks et al. 1974), possibly followed by a *politeness token* (Antaki & Kent 2012), as in Excerpt 2.5.[7]

Shoppers may order more than one item at the counter, and they do so by articulating follow-up requests. Such subsequent requests occupy a different sequential position. Excerpt 2.6 occurs after the shop assistant has produced an 'anything else?' question,[8] which is routinely present in interactions at the counter (see also Halonen & Koivisto, this volume). The fragment reproduces the words that Carmine uses when ordering lamb chops, after having requested 'veal stew' (Excerpt 2.3):

---

[5] For a conversation analytic account of openings in service encounters, see Aston (1995).

[6] This use recalls Schegloff's (2010) analysis of *uh(m)* occurring in turn-initial position of turns with which speakers produce the reason for the call. Similarly, in the excerpts analyzed here, the *əh(m)* 'uh(m)' can be seen to *mark* (Schegloff's term) the reason for the encounter.

[7] From a grammatical point of view, the requests for the product are shaped as clauses (Excerpts 2.1–2.3, 2.5–2.7) or as noun phrases (Excerpt 2.4). Sorjonen and Raevaara (2014) have observed the same formats in Finnish kiosk requests, whereas De Stefani (2019) has found these formats in orders at Italian cafés. Vinkhuyzen and Szymanski (2005) draw a distinction between *self-oriented declaratives* (Excerpts 2.1–2.3) and *other-oriented interrogatives* (Excerpts 2.5–2.7) on the basis of supposedly different degrees of knowledge with regard to the actual availability of a specific product (see also Fox & Heinemann 2015: 343). Excerpt 2.4 is other-oriented with respect to the customer's inquiry into the shop assistant's ability to grate the cheese, but not with respect to the request for the product per se, which is done without any verb (*əh:::m mezzo chilo di:: sbrinz.* 'uh:::m half a kilo of:: Sbrinz.'). For a discussion see also Fox and Heinemann (2016).

[8] Shop assistants use different recurrent formats for this purpose, such as *altro* 'anything else', *(l')è tutto?* 'is that all?', and *basta così?* 'is that enough?' For an analysis of these resources as possible pre-closing devices see De Stefani (2006).

Excerpt 2.6 (cons42271, 26:10–26:12)

```
01 CAR:    əh:: costolette d'agnello voi ne avete?
           uh::   lamb chops         do you have any?
```

In this case, the lexical reference[9] to the product is placed in turn-initial position, whereas the verb phrase occupies the end of the turn. The following request is produced by Teresa's shopping companion Maria. Teresa has just ordered 'a slice of Gorgonzola with mascarpone' (Excerpt 2.5) and now Maria orders the same product:

Excerpt 2.7 (cons45111, 09:22–09:24)

```
01 MAR:    al dà anca^a mi^n::: tochett iscì per piacere.
           (do you) also give me a::: piece like this please.
```

In this turn, which is produced in a Lombard dialect, Maria makes use of deictic reference. She embodies the dimension of the piece of cheese she is ordering with a hand gesture that is co-occurring with *iscì* 'like this', thereby offering an iconic representation (Goodwin 2003) of the requested item. She formats her turn as a declarative request.[10]

All of these requests – whether they are *first* or *subsequent* requests – are produced as one single turn.[11] For shop assistants, such requests are brand new because in this specific setting they cannot foresee what a customer is going to ask. For shoppers, such requests consolidate consecutive, previous spates of interaction devoted to deciding what to buy. In the remainder of this chapter, I track the episodes of interaction between the shoppers that precede and are related to the requests above. I start by analyzing the circumstances under which shoppers orient, for the first time, to a product (or product category) that can be bought at the counter (Section 2.2). I then examine how, at a later moment, generally in proximity to the counter, participants reintroduce a reference to that product (category) (Section 2.3). Finally, I look at how buying

---

[9] I use *lexical reference* for expressions comprising words that are part of the Italian lexicon (such as *costolette d'agnello* 'lamb chops') as opposed, e.g., to *deictic reference*, accomplished through pointing gestures and vocal deictics.

[10] In Italian, polar questions share the same syntactic structure as declarative constructions, and prosody plays a central role in distinguishing declaratives from interrogatives. Furthermore, a wide regional variety in the prosodic patterning of questions has been observed (see Rossano 2010 for a detailed discussion). This is why the English translations of Excerpts 2.5 and 2.7 offer both a declarative and an interrogative reading.

[11] The formats participants use for requesting a product at the counter show how turn-constructional features are reflexively and contingently tied to the (multiple) actions, social categorizations, and settings that participants make relevant as they produce a request. Hence, the requests found in these data differ in format and accomplished action from what Rossi (2015: 5) observes in what he calls "informal interaction among adults" (and elsewhere).

projects are refined, challenged, and modified as the shoppers approach the counter and wait to be served (Section 2.4). By doing so, I piece together the *interactional history* (De Stefani et al. 2016) of what ends up as a request for a product that a customer addresses to a shop assistant in a single turn. Consequently, this chapter widens the scope of recent research on requests at the counter (Sorjonen & Raevaara 2014; Fox & Heinemann 2015, 2016) by showing how, in this setting, requests at the counter are shaped by prior interaction: what ends up being uttered as a simple and straightforward request is in fact the outcome of a complex adjustment to shared or individual shopping trajectories. Hence, the analysis of these decision-making practices allows me, additionally, to show how the participants display different kinds of *couplehood*. Indeed, couples can be seen to shop 'for the couple' because they share the same household or a momentary common activity (see the couple composed of Carmine and Piero). But members of a couple can also have individual shopping projects, for instance, because each of them is buying things for their own household, as is the case for Maria and Teresa, who each shop for their respective families.[12]

2.2 Introducing a Next Purchasable Item

Members of a couple engaged in joint shopping repeatedly make buying proposals or announcements to each other. In the data under examination, participants may do so (a) by displaying their orientation toward an otherwise undisclosed 'shopping list', which becomes relevant in displays of a need for a specific item (e.g., 'I need cheese', Excerpt 2.10); (b) by categorizing the surrounding environment on the basis of the locally available products (e.g., as the 'dairy area'), hence introducing specific items related to that category; (c) by making plans concerning the subsequent days' meals, hence introducing items that they need to buy in order to prepare those meals (Excerpts 2.12, 2.16, and 2.17). In this section, I focus on *when* (with respect to the overall shopping activity) and *where* such buying proposals or announcements occur. Supermarkets, which Lave (1988) describes as *arenas* where shoppers navigate and pick up items, pose a complex navigational and organizational problem for shoppers. Indeed, customers have to move to specific areas to get particular items. Hence, commercial products are frequently used as landmarks for spatial orientation (De Stefani 2011, 2013, 2014). Moreover, the

---

[12] The different kinds of couplehood are displayed also by the fact that Carmine and Piero use only one shopping cart, whereas Maria and Teresa move through the shop, each with their own shopping cart; however, they do so as a couple, thereby displaying their togetherness for the specific activity in which they are engaged (see De Stefani 2011 for a detailed discussion).

spatial extension of these shops (as opposed to small stores; see Sorjonen & Raevaara 2014; Mondada & Sorjonen 2016) provides for a different temporal organization of actions, and participants may orient to potentially purchasable items at diverse moments of their shopping tour.

2.2.1 Coordinated Transition from a Previous to a Next Action

One recurrent moment in which shoppers refer to potentially purchasable items arises when a previous activity (e.g., the selection of a product, the interaction at the counter) has been closed down (see De Stefani 2006, 2013). This is visible in the following excerpt, which starts with an exchange of thank yous and greetings between Maria and a shop assistant (SHO) at the cheese counter:

Excerpt 2.8 (cons45111, 10:38–10:44)

```
01 MAR:    gra[zie mille arrivederci buo[na giornata
           tha[nks a lot good bye have [a nice day
02 SHO:        [grazie arrivederci.
               [thanks   good bye.
03 TER:                                 [poi ti fa niente se
                                        [then you don't mind if
04         guardo le: le: hm: marmellate quelle robe li?
           I look at the: the: uhm: jams those things there?
```

At line 3, Teresa manifestly orients to the sequence reproduced at lines 1–2 as closing down the service encounter. By introducing a new potentially purchasable item, *marmellate* 'jams' (line 4), Teresa establishes the relevance of orienting to a subsequent action (see the turn-initial *poi* 'then', line 3) at this precise moment. As I have shown elsewhere (De Stefani 2013, 2014), couples generally organize their shopping tour on the basis of a locally emerging and transformable list of potentially purchasable items. Hence, by introducing *marmellate* 'jams' at this moment, Teresa launches the ensuing trajectory of the couple, where the referent *marmellate* 'jams' appears as a landmark that may be more or less easily locatable in the supermarket. Teresa shapes her turn as doing a proposal that projects agreement and presents the new item as related to a personal project (*ti fa niente se guardo* 'you don't mind if I look', lines 3–4). In this way, Teresa displays a specific kind of couplehood, in which each member appears to orient toward individual buying projects that need to be coordinated in order to shop *as a couple*. Compare this procedure with the following excerpt. Carmine and Piero have just chosen a milk carton (line 1, *va bene questo.* 'this one is fine.'), which Piero is putting in the cart during the subsequent pause (line 2). As in the previous example, as soon as the choice of the prior item (milk) has been completed, one participant introduces a next potentially purchasable item, *formaggi* 'cheese' (line 3).

Excerpt 2.9 (cons42271, 12:10–12:31)

```
01 CAR:    va bene questo.
           this one is fine.
02         (1.8)
03 PIE:    tsk (fe- di) formaggi non ne prendo perché con te
                        cheese  I'm not getting because with you
04         non ci ho mai avuto bisogno- non ho mai avuto
           it's never been the need- I have never
05         bisogno di for°maggi.°
           needed ch°eese.°
06 CAR:    perché no?
           why not?
07         (2.5)
08 CAR:    prendi^i^ioghurt tu hai detto che
           get the yogurt you  said    that
09         volevi^i^[ioghurt io non ne  vogl]io.
           you wanted yogurt I don't want any.
10 PIE:              [°sì  prendo-  è  vero.°]
                      °yes I get-  it's true.°
11         (10.0)
```

Piero's action at lines 3–5 is somewhat paradoxical: on the one hand he refers to a so-far-unmentioned product category, 'cheese', thereby orienting to a potentially purchasable product; on the other hand he explicitly presents it as something that he is not going to buy. He shapes his turn as displaying a decision that he took individually (*non ne prendo* 'I'm not getting', line 3) and for which he accounts by saying that he has 'never needed' (*non ho mai avuto bisogno*, lines 4–5) cheese with Carmine (*con te* 'with you', line 3). Carmine challenges this unilateral announcement by asking *perché no?* 'why not?' (line 6), thereby treating Piero's assertion as in need of an account. This question remains unanswered (line 7), and talk about 'cheese' is momentarily coming to an end. However, the participants' orientation toward a next possible product (category) is visible at lines 8–9, where Carmine introduces an alternative item ('yogurt'), which Piero is going to get during the subsequent pause (line 11).

Carmine and Piero's ways of introducing a next potentially purchasable item differ from what we have observed in Excerpt 2.8. Both participants orient toward the needs and wishes of the other member of the couple (*con te* 'with you', line 3; *tu hai detto che volevi* 'you said that you wanted', lines 8–9), thereby unveiling their knowledge about the other's habits and needs and displaying to each other their being a *committed couple*.

2.2.2 Concurrent Actions

While in many cases participants introduce new potentially purchasable items right after the end of some prior activity, on occasion they do so while some other action is still ongoing. The subsequent excerpt occurs while Maria and Teresa are walking in the area in which fruit and vegetables are on display. At line 1, Maria asks Teresa whether she needs to buy fruit. After having replied negatively (line 2), Teresa explains that now she needs to buy a lot of things 'for the house' (lines 10–11), which appears to be a second residence that Teresa owns.[13]

Excerpt 2.10 (cons45111, 05:09–05:21)

```
01 MAR:    te hai bisogno frutta?=
           do you need fruit?=
02 TER:    =io mi son presa la rucola no: (.) °perché° quella noi
           =I got rocket for myself no: (.) °because° we have
03         la dobbiamo prendere su dal ((business [n+ame))
           to get that up at ((business name))
04 MAR:                                            [si?#
                                                   [really?
    fig                                            #fig.2.1
```

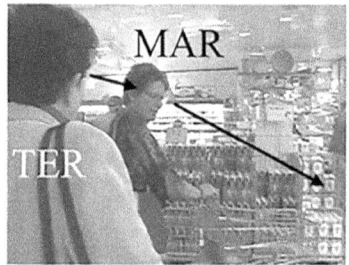

Figure 2.1 Diverging gaze orientation

```
05         (0.3)
06 MAR:    awah
           ((idiomatic sound))
07         (1.0)
08 TER:    sai^desso io #tan[ta spesa
           you know^now  a l[ot of shopping
    fig                     #fig.2.2
```

---

[13] When saying that she 'needs to do a lot of shopping for the house' (lines 8–11), Maria appears to refer to 'general shopping' she has to do for the house, not to something particular she has to buy during the current shopping tour.

Figure 2.2 Maria looks toward the dairy area

```
09 MAR:                [ah io ho bisogno [formaggio,
                       [oh I need [cheese,
10 TER:                           [la: (.) la devo fare
                                 [I (.) I have to do
11          per la casa.
            for the house.
```

Teresa's account of why she does not need to buy any fruit (lines 2–3) is progressively transformed into a topic of conversation (lines 8–11). Maria initially participates in the development of that talk (sì? 'really?', line 4) but then initiates a different action as she comes in with the words *ah io ho bisogno formaggio*, 'oh I need cheese' (line 9). By producing her turn in overlap with Teresa's talk, Maria not only discloses her involvement in a concurrent action but also presents her turn as having some local relevance. She initiates her turn with an *ah* 'oh', a resource that can be described as a *change-of-state token* (Heritage 1984). At first glance, Maria's use of this resource could be analyzed as a display of remembering,[14] especially since she makes relevant a personal buying project, highlighted by the subject pronoun *io* 'I' (line 9), which is not mandatory in Italian.[15] Introductions of this kind – occurring while some other action is ongoing – require more interactional work between the participants, who have to coordinate diverging concurrent action trajectories and transform them into serially organized converging actions (see Mondada 2014 on the organization of multiactivity). However, they generally do not occur out of

---

[14] See Poggi (1981: 120) on Italian *ah* as displaying remembering, and Jefferson (1978: 221–222), who observes similar uses for the 'disjunct marker' *oh* (see also Heinemann & Koivisto 2016).
[15] Because in Italian conjugated verbs are inflected for time and person, co-occurring subject pronouns are not necessary from a normative, grammatical point of view, hence Chomsky's (1981) understanding of Italian as a *pro-drop* language. This notion establishes the use of subject pronouns as the default case, while the nonuse is seen as the 'absence' of an element that has been 'dropped'.

the blue: in fact, they make visible the participants' continuous monitoring of the environment in which the interaction takes place. This excerpt occurs as the couple is moving away from the vegetable and fruit area (lines 1–2). Figure 2.1 shows the participants' divergent gaze orientation:[16] Teresa is looking at Maria while answering her interlocutor's question, whereas the latter orients her gaze to an area situated in close proximity. The participants display diverging orientations also in their talk: Teresa is engaged in further developing topic talk (lines 2–11), whereas Maria only minimally contributes to that course of action (line 4–6).

A few seconds later, Maria (and Teresa) can be seen to orient her gaze toward the end of the area, where packaged dairy products are visible in a refrigerator to the left, whereas cheese wheels are exposed to the right, in proximity to the cheese counter (Figure 2.2). It is on the basis of the visual assessment of the environment that Maria articulates the words *ah io ho bisogno formaggio*, 'oh I need cheese' (line 9). Hence, with her words, Maria is not only 'doing remembering' as explained above, but she is also displaying an *environmental noticing* (Sacks 1992 vol. II: 87–97; *noticing* in Heritage 1984: 300), that is, the fact that she has just spotted the dairy area (and possibly the cheese counter).

The following excerpt provides a similar case in point. Piero and Carmine have just closed down their interaction with the butcher at the meat counter and are now walking in an aisle of the supermarket.

Excerpt 2.11 (cons42271, 29:16–29:24)

```
01        #(0.2)    # (1.8)
   fig    #fig.2.3 #fig.2.4
```

Figure 2.3 Carmine's and Piero's gaze

---

[16] One reviewer suggested indicating the temporal progression of gaze reorientations with respect to talk in an additional line of the transcript. Given that the data have been collected by shadowing the couples, i.e., by following them with a video camera, gaze behavior is not visible in detail (since the recordings often show the back of the participants' heads, not their eyes) and a precise rendering of gaze in the transcript is impossible.

Figure 2.4 Carmine looking toward the fish shop

```
02 PIE:    pisellini sei sic[uro che li abbiamo?
           peas      are you  s[ure that we have them?
03 CAR:                       [ca:-ˆaspetta che volevo vedere, p- sai
                              [ca:-ˆwait I wanted to see, p- you know
04         che non riesco a trovare le sardi:ne
           that I can't     find the sardi:nes
05         [né alla ((business name))
           [neither at ((business name))
06 PIE:    [senti perché non fai la pasta invece quella di:
           [listen why don't you make pasta instead the one of:
07         di ((name)) quella con le triglie?
           of ((name)) the one with the red mullet?
```

The couple is monitoring the immediate environment during the pause at line 1. While at first both participants orient their gaze to the right side of the aisle (Figure 2.3), one moment later Carmine looks to the left, where the fish counter is located and where the writing *pescheria* 'fish shop' is visible (Figure 2.4).

At this moment, both participants introduce some potentially purchasable item. While Piero mentions *pisellini* 'peas' as a product that the couple might buy, Carmine overlaps his partner's talk in a disruptive way, as is visible in the initial and abandoned *ca:-* and the subsequent *aspetta* 'wait'.[17] He announces that he 'wants to see' whether he can find sardines, which he has been unable to find for a while (lines 3–4). Just as in the previous excerpt, here too one participant initiates a concurrent action based on the visual monitoring of the environment that he just performed. Similarly, Carmine relates his (not overtly displayed) noticing of the fish counter to some personal project that he is admittedly pursuing, namely buying sardines. Note that Piero orients to Carmine's mentioning of the sardines as he proposes that his partner might make pasta 'with the red mullet' (lines 6–7). Indeed, he refers to another

---

[17] Keisanen, Rauniomaa, and Haddington (2014) describe 'wait' as a resource by which participants *suspend* an ongoing action. In this case, Carmine will never provide an answer to Piero's question (line 2), and the sequence is eventually abandoned.

product ('red mullet') that is conventionally seen as pertaining to the same object category as sardines, i.e., fish.[18] A few moments later, the couple is going to order fish at the counter (see Excerpt 2.2).

So far, I have described one specific course of action that can lead to initiating interaction at the counter: shoppers are monitoring the environment as they move through the supermarket while introducing potentially purchasable items. One participant orients to a visually accessible counter and displays that orientation through a noticing (Excerpt 2.10) by disrupting some ongoing action and by introducing reference to an item that is expectedly available at that counter (Excerpts 2.10–2.11).

2.2.3 Locating the Counter

Another recurrent activity leading to interactions at the counter consists of discussions about future events for which the purchase of a specific product is necessary. Piero's proposal in Excerpt 2.11 (lines 6–7) already hinted at how this couple decides what to buy: Carmine and Piero repeatedly discuss during their shopping tour what they are going to eat in the following days. The subsequent excerpt provides a further illustration of this practice. The couple is facing a refrigerator with packaged poultry (Figure 2.5) while discussing what they are going to have for lunch on Sunday.

Excerpt 2.12 (cons42271, 19:52–20:22)

```
01 CAR:    a- s- (0.3) okay per sabato- per sabato sera
           a- s- (0.3) okay for Saturday- for Saturday evening
02         quindi c'è la roba. per domenica mezzogiorno c'è
           then there is stuff. for Sunday noon there is
03         la pasta col sugo tu il sugo non ci vuoi niente
           pasta with sauce you don't want anything in the sauce
04         dentro (la) ca[:rne [(   )
           inside      mea[:t
05 PIE:                [no. [no no a me piace così come lo
                       [no. [no no I like it the way you make
06         fai sempli[ce.
           it  simpl[e.
07 CAR:              [semplice okay. .h e per secondo? (.) eh:
                     [simple okay. .h and as a second? (.) uh:
08         °t-° la c- eh ti andrebbe del- della carne?#
           °t-° the m- uh would you like som- some meat?
   fig                                                  #fig.2.5
```

---

[18] This is reminiscent of Sacks's (1972) *Membership Categorization Device*. In the case discussed here, the *object categories* 'sardines' and 'red mullet' can be seen to belong to the common *collection* 'fish'. For other uses of the notion of *object categories*, see Jayyusi (1984: 36) and De Stefani (2014: 284, 2019).

Figure 2.5 Carmine and Piero at the refrigerator

```
09 PIE:    allora (guarda) fa lo spezzatino allora.
           well (look) make stew then.
10         (0.2)
11 PIE:    che ti viene bene.
           since you make it well.
12 CAR:    nel sug- (0.2) ah quindi vuoi il sugo allo spezzatino.
           in the sauc- (0.2) oh so you want the sauce with stew.
13 PIE:    tsk va beh sì (.) però non: non lo fai con la carne
           tsk well yes (.) but not: you don't make the sauce with
14         macinata il sugo lo fai con lo spezzati:no.
           mincemeat you make it with stew.
15         e va bene così.
           and it's fine like that.
16         (0.7)
17 CAR:    eh::#::  (0.4) e allora lo f- la car#ne lo compro lì
           uh::::  (0.4) well then I d- the meat I buy it there
   fig           #fig.2.6                       #fig.2.7
```

Figure 2.6 Carmine orienting to the aisle

Figure 2.7 Carmine pointing

```
18         in macelleria non prendo questa qui perché lo
           at the butcher's I don't get this one because
19         spezzatino mi sa che si compra solo lì.
           the stew I think one buys it only there.
20 PIE:    allora prendila lì °sì.°
           then get it there °yes.°
```

After observing that 'there is stuff' to eat for 'Saturday evening' and 'Sunday noon' (lines 1–2), Carmine asks Piero how he should prepare the pasta sauce that the couple will have for Sunday noon (lines 3–4). They reach an agreement that the sauce should be 'simple' (lines 5–7), and Carmine asks Piero what they should have as a second course (line 7)[19] and proposes 'meat' as an option (line 8). Piero responds with *fa lo spezzatino allora* 'make stew then' (line 9), a turn that Carmine treats as an alternative proposal rather than as an agreement to have meat as a second course. Indeed, at line 12, Carmine articulates his understanding of Piero's turn (*quindi vuoi il sugo allo spezzatino.* 'so you want sauce with stew.'), and Piero subsequently affiliates with that project (lines 13–15). At this point, the members of the couple have reached an agreement to buy stew. Shortly after, Carmine turns his body away from the refrigerator and embodies a 'searching' posture while at the same time pronouncing a prolonged *eh::::* 'uh:::::' (Figure 2.6).

In his ensuing turn, Carmine makes recognizable the object of his visual search. Indeed, while pointing to the area ahead (Figure 2.7), he explains that he is going to buy the meat 'there at the butcher's' (lines 17–18), thereby

---

[19] Traditionally, in Italian cuisine pasta is regarded as a first course (*primo*), whereas a second course (*secondo*) typically consists of meat or fish.

referring to the meat counter that is located in proximity to where the couple is currently standing. Carmine accounts for his project by saying that stew is an item that 'one buys only there' (at the counter) (line 19). Piero aligns with this project (line 20), and the couple heads toward the meat counter.

The analysis of how shoppers first introduce reference to a potentially purchasable item has shown that they can do it in a convergent way (Excerpts 2.8, 2.9, and 2.12), i.e., with both members of the couple engaged in jointly organizing the subsequent (buying) action, or they may display divergent orientations (Excerpts 2.10–2.11), which are observable when participants make reference to two different potentially purchasable items. Also, shoppers strongly orient to the visual accessibility of the counters: as they continuously monitor the surroundings, shoppers categorize the different areas in which they are moving. In many cases (Excerpts 2.9–2.11), the introduction of a potentially purchasable item is grounded in an analysis of the immediate environment. In other cases, shoppers first introduce a potentially purchasable product and then try to locate it in the supermarket (Excerpts 2.8 and 2.12).

2.3 Reintroducing a Purchasable Item

I have looked so far at the spatial environments and interactional circumstances under which participants orient their attention to supermarket counters. In the excerpts discussed above, when they first introduce verbal reference to a product available at a counter, participants are standing at a distance from the respective counter. They may subsequently orient toward other items located in their proximity, or they may engage in topic talk. Hence, as they move closer to the counter, they make relevant their previously mentioned buying project again. Both Carmine and Piero (Excerpt 2.9) and Maria and Teresa (Excerpt 2.10) have displayed orientation toward cheese in the prior excerpts. The following analyses focus on how both couples reorient toward buying cheese as they approach the counter.

2.3.1 The Counter as a Locus of Additional Service

In supermarkets, many items are available both in the self-service area and at service counters. Some cheese varieties, for instance, can be bought either as packaged products available in the refrigerators or, alternatively, at a counter. The added value of buying products at the counter is made relevant in the following excerpt, which occurs about 80 seconds after Maria has first mentioned her project of buying cheese (Excerpt 2.10). The couple is walking alongside the refrigerator displaying packaged cheese (Figure 2.8) as Maria announces that she is going to get Sbrinz cheese:

Excerpt 2.13 (cons45111, 06:32–06:48)

```
01 MAR:      io vado a prendere^il^eh
             I go and get^the^uh
02           (3.6)
03 MAR:      vado a #prendere lo sbrinzo sbrinzo ma::=
             I go and get the Sbrinzo Sbrinzo but::=
   fig              #fig.2.8
```

Figure 2.8 Teresa and Maria at the refrigerator

```
04 TER:      =°ah° no ma prendilo in pe#zzi allora.
             =°oh° no but get it in pieces then.
   fig                                 #fig.2.9
```

Figure 2.9 Maria grabbing a cheese package

```
05           (0.2)
06 MAR:      me #lo faccio ta-# ah[: gratt]ugiare.#
             I'm having it cu-  ah[: grat]ed.
   fig          #fig.2.10    #fig.2.11       #fig.2.12
```

Approaching the Counter at the Supermarket 53

Figure 2.10 Maria gazing at the cheese package

Figure 2.11 Maria gazing toward the cheese counter

Figure 2.12 Maria and Teresa move away from the refrigerator

```
07 TER:                          [˘eh:   ]
                                 [right:]
08 TER:    a pezzi ti conviene.
           in pieces it's better.
```

```
09            (0.2)
10 MAR:       ˇeh
              yes
11            (0.8)
12 TER:       te lo tagliano loro.
              they cut it for you.
```

While walking behind Teresa, Maria utters the words *io vado a prendere^il^eh* 'I'm gonna get^the^uh' (line 1). By starting the turn with the subject pronoun *io* 'I' (see note 15), she displays personal responsibility for the projected action. By using the construction *vado a prendere* 'I go and get', she displays that spatial movement will be necessary to accomplish that action. Maria's turn is recognizably incomplete at the end of line 1, with the definite article *il* 'the' strongly projecting a noun phrase as the next syntactic element. After a 3.6 second pause, Maria produces a restart (line 3) and introduces the referent *sbrinzo sbrinzo*.[20] An obvious difference with respect to Maria's first orientation to the counter earlier (see Excerpt 2.10) is visible in the choice of the referent. While earlier she was referring to the general category 'cheese', she now introduces a specific member of that category. She thus formulates an upcoming activity and relates that activity to a specific referent. This contrasts with other buying decisions that Maria makes tacitly. For instance, while this interaction unfolds, Maria grabs a package of Grana cheese (Figure 2.9), which she subsequently places in her shopping cart. Such tacit and unilateral decision-making shows, once again, that each member of this couple is pursuing their own shopping project, which does not need to be ratified by the other member. By articulating her decision to buy Sbrinz cheese, Maria manifests instead that her decision will be consequential for the couple's movement in space. Indeed, one way in which Maria and Teresa display 'togetherness' is by moving through space as a couple (see De Stefani 2013). In other words, announcing that she will buy Sbrinz cheese allows Maria to organize the practical problem of jointly moving to the counter with her friend.

Maria suspends her turn with a prolonged *ma::* 'but::' (line 3), which makes expectable a specifying continuation of her turn-in-progress. At this point, Teresa produces advice suggesting getting the cheese 'in pieces' (line 4). After a brief pause (line 5), Maria completes her suspended turn by saying that she is having the cheese 'grated' (line 6). While she is producing this turn, Maria withdraws her gaze from the package of cheese she is holding in her hands and orients it to the cheese counter (Figures 2.10 and 2.11).

---

[20] *Sbrinzo sbrinzo* appears to be a locally emerging form of the commonly used proper name *Sbrinz*, which Maria also uses, e.g., in her interaction with the shop assistant at the counter (see Excerpt 2.4).

It is with this turn that Maria plainly displays her project to buy cheese at the counter, on the one hand by using a causative construction (*farsi grattugiare* 'to have (the cheese) grated'), hence presupposing that someone else will carry out this task, and on the other hand by bodily orienting toward the cheese counter. At line 7, Teresa aligns with Maria's project, and by the end of Maria's turn, the couple is walking away from the refrigerator toward the counter (Figure 2.12).

This excerpt illustrates a case in which a member of the couple orients to the 'same' supermarket counter not only for the second time, but also in closer proximity to that counter. In this case, the referent is specified as *sbrinzo sbrinzo*, rather than simply 'cheese' (Excerpt 2.10). The closer the couple gets to the counter, the more precisely they appear to orient to their buying project. Moreover, the decision to get the cheese at the counter (rather than from the refrigerator with packed cheese) is accounted for with additional service that Maria expects from the personnel at the counter, namely that they grate her cheese.[21] Similarly, Teresa also makes additional service relevant very early in the interaction: as soon as Maria mentions that she is going to buy Sbrinz cheese, Teresa suggests getting it 'in pieces' (line 4), whereas later she explicitly formulates an action carried out by third persons (*te lo tagliano loro* 'they cut it for you', line 12).[22] Hence, Maria and Teresa not only display to each other their engagement in joint shopping, but they also exhibit their expertise with regard to what can be expected from buying cheese at the counter rather than in its packaged form from the refrigerator.

2.3.2 Negotiating the Purchasability of an Item

With Maria and Teresa, the purchasability of a product is never at stake. In other words, there is no joint decision about whether Maria needs to buy Sbrinz cheese or any other product. This is one way in which Maria and Teresa exhibit their couplehood: they are two friends with individual buying agendas, who shop together for their respective families. By contrast, Carmine and Piero buy products for themselves as a couple, and this is visible in the way in which they reorient toward cheese as a potentially purchasable item.

---

[21] Indeed, grated Sbrinz cheese would also be available in the refrigerator the couple is passing. By getting the cheese from the counter – rather than in its packaged form – Maria can benefit from different advantages, such as deciding the quantity she is going to buy, being served, etc. Maria is going to buy half a kilo of cheese (see Excerpt 2.4), whereas the packaged versions of grated Sbrinz cheese contain smaller amounts.

[22] Both participants strongly align in the projected activity of buying cheese at the counter, regardless of the diverse formulations relative to the 'treatment' of the cheese: Whereas Maria expects the shop assistant to 'grate' (*grattugiare*) the cheese, Teresa is speaking of 'cutting the cheese in pieces' (lines 4, 8, 12). Note, however, Maria's self-repair at line 6 (*ta-* 'cu-*) putatively interpretable as an abandoned *tagliare* 'cut'.

56   E. De Stefani

The following fragment occurs about two minutes after the end of Excerpt 2.9. Piero and Carmine are walking and reaching the area where the cheese counter is located (Figure 2.13). They come to a halt right next to the counter, where Carmine visibly monitors the environment while listing the items the couple already 'has' (Figure 2.14, lines 2–7).

Excerpt 2.14a (cons42271, 14:18–14:30)

```
01           #(3.2)
   fig       #fig.2.13
```

Figure 2.13 Approaching the cheese area

```
02 CAR:      il #burro mi sa che ce l'abbia:mo il əh::
             the butter I guess that we have it the uh::
   fig       #fig.2.14
```

Figure 2.14 Piero and Carmine stopping at the counter

```
03           (1.5)
04 CAR:      [il:^əh::
             [the: uh::
05 PIE:      [ma io formaggio ( )
             [but I cheese ( )
```

```
06            (0.5)
07 CAR:       parmigiano reggiano a:nche
              Parmigiano Reggiano t:oo
08            (1.4)
09 PIE:       io l'əh:
              I the uh:
10            (0.6)
```

As they are scanning the area around them, both participants manifestly orient toward the cheese that is visible from where they are standing and detectable both in the refrigerator and at the counter (Figure 2.13). Carmine suspends his turn at line 2 after having produced the definite masculine article *il* 'the', which strongly projects a noun phrase as a next possible item. While at line 4 Carmine repeats the final items of his turn-in-progress, Piero initiates a turn with the contrastive *ma* 'but', followed by *io* 'I' and reference to 'cheese' (line 5). On the one hand, with this uncompleted turn Piero identifies a possible referent that Carmine might putatively introduce (i.e., *formaggio* 'cheese'), and on the other hand he displays his opposition to buying cheese (see also Mazeland & Huiskes 2001 on Dutch *maar* 'but' as a resumption marker). Subsequently, Carmine completes his turn with the words *parmigiano reggiano a:nche* 'Parmigiano Reggiano t:oo' (line 7), thereby introducing a further product that the couple does not need to buy. Given that so far Carmine has not detected any potentially purchasable product in the environment at hand and that Piero has displayed opposition to buying cheese, this is a moment in which the couple could resume walking. Indeed, Piero starts moving away, just before Carmine draws his attention to the cheese counter (Figure 2.15).

Excerpt 2.14b (cons42271, 14:30–14:36)

```
11 CAR:   tsk e #p:er i formaggi dici proprio nulla?
          tsk and f:or the cheese you say really nothing?
   fig          #fig.2.15
```

Figure 2.15 Piero starts moving away

```
12         (0.7)
13 PIE:    no io non prendo nul[la.
           no I'm not getting anyth[ing.
14 CAR:                      [perché no?#
                             [why not?
   fig                                    #fig.2.16
```

Figure 2.16 Carmine and Piero facing the counter

```
15         (1.4)
```

At line 11, Carmine orients to 'cheese' as a potentially purchasable item. He produces a first pair part that projects the preference of a negative response by Carmine – at least with regard to turn-design, whereas with respect to action, a conceding response appears to be projected (see Schegloff 2007: 76–78 on "cross-cutting preferences"). On the one hand, this resource, together with his tipping Piero's arm (Figure 2.15), allows Carmine to reorient his partner's attention to the cheese counter. On the other hand, the format that Carmine chooses takes into account Piero's previous displays of reluctance to buy cheese (see line 5 and Excerpt 2.9, line 3). Piero aligns with this projection and provides a negative answer at line 13 in which he uses the pronoun *io* 'I', thereby opening up the possibility of pursuing two different buying projects. Note that Carmine subsequently recasts the question *perché no?* 'why not?' (line 14), which he had already addressed to Piero, just after Piero's announcement that he was not going to buy any cheese (Excerpt 2.9, line 6). As with that first occurrence, this second occurrence of the question remains unanswered (line 15). However, both participants are now facing the cheese counter (Figure 2.16).

Excerpt 2.14c (cons42271, 14:36–14:45)

```
16 PIE:    quando (li) facciamo possiamo prendere un- un
           when do we make (them) we can get a- a
17         əh: forma:ggio per: domani a pranzo,
           uh: chee:se for: tomorrow at lunch,
```

Approaching the Counter at the Supermarket   59

```
18              (0.9)
19 CAR:     #a [me piacciono::
                I [like::
    fig     #fig.2.17
```

Figure 2.17 Carmine and Piero scan the counter

```
20 PIE:     [se tu vuoi prendere una di queste formaggelle
            [if you want to get one of these small cheeses
21          prendi una formaggella.
            get a small cheese.
22          (0.3)
23 CAR:     #[la robiola matura [voglio.
            [the ripe Robiola   [I want.
    fig     #fig.2.18
```

Figure 2.18 Carmine looks at the Robiola cheese

Not having provided an answer to Carmine's previous question, Piero first sketches an explanation (*quando (li) facciamo* 'when do we make (them)', line 16) that conveys the idea that there is no appropriate moment for eating cheese. He then identifies 'tomorrow at lunch' (line 17) as a possible mealtime. The couple then moves forward along the front side of the counter while scanning the kinds of cheese that are on display (Figure 2.17). Carmine initiates a turn, announcing the type of cheese he 'likes'[23] (line 19) while Piero simultaneously suggests getting a *formaggella* 'small cheese' (lines 20–21). With the word *formaggella*, Piero is referring to different kinds of small loaves of cheese that he is seeing. He uses it as a generic term, whereas Carmine's visual assessment of the counter allows him to identify a specific cheese he 'wants', namely the 'ripe Robiola' (line 23, Figure 2.18).

While Carmine accounts for his choice of Robiola cheese by saying that he 'likes' and 'wants' it (lines 19, 23), thereby presenting it not only as a personal decision but also displaying that he is going to be the unique beneficiary of this acquisition, Piero is now oriented toward accounting for the buying decision in a way from which both members of the couple can benefit. At lines 24–25, he suggests making salad with *tomini* (another kind of cheese that comes in small loaves).

Excerpt 2.14d (cons42271, 14:45–15:01)

```
24 PIE:    [possiamo fare-    [possiamo fare (.) l'insalata
           [we can make-      [we can make (.) salad
25         con i tomini e riscaldiamo i tomini.
           with the tomini and we heat the tomini.
26         (0.9)
27 PIE:    ti va:? te lo mange[resti?
           is tha:t okay? would you [eat that?
28 CAR:                       [no: no: no: voglio il robiola
                              [no: no: no: I want the ripe
29         maturo >ma ma mangiarlo così non ho- non lo vo-
           Robiola >but eat it like that I don't ha- I don't
30         (    ) con il to[mino ma non lo voglio.<
           want (    ) with the to[mino but I don't [want it.<
31 PIE:                    [allora prendi il robiola.
                           [get the Robiola then.
32         (8.0)
```

Carmine vigorously rejects his partner's proposal (*no: no: no:*, line 28). He repeats that he 'wants' to buy the Robiola cheese and then explicitly says that he does 'not want' the *tomini* (line 30). Piero finally aligns with this explanation and encourages Carmine to get the Robiola cheese (line 31). A few seconds later, Carmine is going to start interacting with the server at the counter.

---

[23] In a previous study on decision-making between couples shopping in a supermarket (De Stefani 2011: 351–357), I have shown that participants use 'liking' or 'not liking' a specific item as a robust account for making a buying decision.

I have used this excerpt as a further illustration of how participants reorient toward a previously mentioned referent. Just as in the preceding excerpt (Excerpt 2.13), in this fragment they do so in proximity to the area in which the product in question is on display; however, at least two differences are worth mentioning. Whereas in Excerpt 2.13 Maria introduces a specific kind of cheese (*Sbrinz*) and accounts for her decision to buy it at the counter by saying that she is having it 'grated' (Excerpt 2.13, lines 3–6) *before* actually moving toward the counter, in Excerpt 2.14 Carmine first reintroduces the product category 'cheese', but discovers the specific kind of cheese he is going to get (*Robiola*) only *while approaching* the counter. Furthermore, Maria displays individual responsibility for buying Sbrinz cheese at the counter, and her shopping partner immediately aligns with that project. Conversely, Piero and Carmine exhibit contrasting projects (buying or not buying cheese) but eventually work toward a collaborative buying decision. Hence, buying decisions appear to be an ideal locus for studying how participants actively constitute and renegotiate their identity as a couple. Whereas Maria and Teresa negotiate 'stopping points' on their shopping tour by articulating what either of them needs to buy, Carmine and Piero, in addition to organizing their movement through space, negotiate the purchasability of products that they will consume, use, etc., together.

2.4 Being a Couple at the Counter

The last analytical part of this chapter zooms in on how participants refine, renegotiate, and account for their buying projects: while on some occasions these are unchallenged, on other occasions they give rise to vivacious sequences of negotiation, during which the participants account for the necessity to buy a specific item, the most solid accounts being reference to a specific purpose (why this product?) or to a specific beneficiary (for whom?); see De Stefani (2011).

The following fragment illustrates an unchallenged buying decision that Teresa articulates at the counter. It occurs about one minute after Excerpt 2.13. Maria and Teresa have reached the cheese counter and Maria has just asked the shop assistant to prepare grated Parmesan cheese for her. Maria's talk at lines 1–3 is still directed to the shop assistant, who has just placed a knife on a loaf of cheese and is now waiting to hear where she should cut the cheese.

Excerpt 2.15 (cons45111, 07:33–07:50)

```
01 MAR:    eh:: f- əh: mi dia la parte un po' più granda.
           uh:: f- uh: give me the part that is a bit larger.
02         (0.4)
03 MAR:    ecco. (.) così grazie.
           that's it. (.) like that thank you.
04         (1.9)
```

```
05 MAR:     poi così lo lo:#
            so then  I I:
   fig                     #fig.2.19
```

Figure 2.19 Teresa looks at the counter

```
06          (0.6)
07 TER:     io prendo un po' di
            I'm getting a bit of
08          gor[gonzola col mascarpone. QUEllo è dietetico a- sai?#
            Gor[gonzola with mascarpone. THAT one's dietetic a- you know?
   fig                                                        fig.2.20#
```

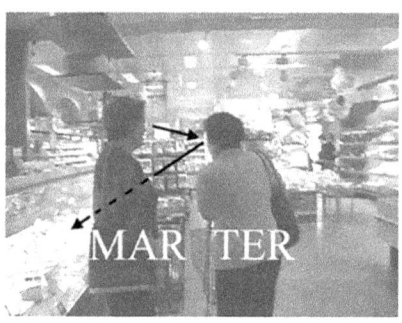

Figure 2.20 Maria follows Teresa's repositioning

```
09 MAR:     [°faccio-° faccio dei pezzi e poi lo lo: (0.3)
            [°I make-° I make pieces and then I I: (0.3)
10          lo congelo.
            freeze it.
11 MAR:     ((laughs))[((laughs))
12 TER:               [guardalo là.#
                      [look at it there.
   fig                            #fig.2.21
```

Approaching the Counter at the Supermarket 63

Figure 2.21 Maria and Teresa looking at the Gorgonzola with mascarpone

```
13          (0.6)
14 MAR:     .hhh
15          (1.7)
16 MAR:     prendo anch'io.
            I'm getting (it) too.
```

After having provided the expected information to the shop assistant, Maria thanks her (line 3) and then reorients her body toward Teresa, who is standing beside her. She initiates a turn (line 5), and gazes at Teresa while the latter is looking at the cheese on display (Figure 2.19). The participants thus display diverging orientations: while Maria is engaging in talk about the cheese she has just ordered (see also line 9), Teresa is assessing the cheese on display. After a brief pause (line 6), Teresa articulates the result of that assessment by announcing that she is getting some 'Gorgonzola with mascarpone' (lines 7–8). Simultaneously with the initiation of her turn, Teresa moves past Maria while the latter follows that repositioning with her gaze and body reorientation (Figure 2.20). In overlap, Maria ends her previously initiated turn by explaining how she will store the cheese that she has just ordered (lines 9–10).

In this excerpt, Teresa can be seen to *discover* a potentially purchasable item at the counter. Indeed, whereas Maria repeatedly articulated her wish to buy cheese (see Excerpts 2.10 and 2.13), thereby presenting her buying decision as previously planned, Teresa here displays her orientation toward buying cheese for the first time. Teresa presents her announcement to buy 'Gorgonzola with mascarpone' as a highly contingent buying decision that she has just made. The format Teresa employs (*io prendo un po' di gorgonzola col mascarpone.* 'I'm getting a bit of Gorgonzola with mascarpone.', lines 7–8) discloses a decision for which she alone is responsible as the first person form and the declarative format show. By introducing a potentially purchasable item in this specific way, rather than by questioning each other's buying decisions, Maria and Teresa constitute their common activity of shopping together as taking place *among friends*, where each one is responsible for their own decisions. However, as the continuation of this excerpt shows, both monitor each other's buying decisions. At line 12, Teresa, who has reached a stationary position at the counter, says *guardalo là.* 'look at it there.', thereby inviting Maria to inspect the area at which Teresa is looking. Maria responds to this directive by orienting her gaze toward that area (Figure 2.21).

Teresa's use of the lexical reference 'Gorgonzola with mascarpone' and the joint monitoring of the same area of the counter allow Maria to identify the item her partner is going to buy. Based on this circumstance, Maria subsequently announces that she is also going to buy the same cheese (line 15).

The way in which Maria and Teresa make buying decisions contrasts with how the other couple observed in this study, Piero and Carmine, achieve joint buying decisions. The following excerpt is the continuation of Excerpt 2.12. Piero and Carmine have just decided that they are going to buy stew and are now walking toward the butcher's counter. While they are walking, Piero asks his partner whether they should buy beef or veal stew (line 2). Carmine immediately replies (line 3), opting for veal.

Excerpt 2.16 (cons42271, 20:31–20:54)

```
01            (0.5)
02 PIE:       ma di manzo^o di vitello?=
              but of beef^or of veal?=
03 CAR:       =no di vitello di vitello.
              =no of veal of veal.
04            (12.0) ((interactions hearable between other customers;
05            someone is mentioning "horse meat"))
06 PIE:       senti perché invece (0.4) non compri: due fettine di
              listen why instead (0.4) don't you buy: two slices of
07            di cavallo e le facciamo: la:: la sera domenica
              horse and we make them: the:: the evening on Sunday
08            sera?
              evening?
09            (0.9)
10 CAR:       da oggi a domenica [vanno a maliss:imo.
              from today until Sunday [they spoi:l rotten.
11 PIE:                          [cosa vuoi fare domenica sera?
                                 [what do you want to make on Sunday evening
```

While Piero initiates the enquiry about which kind of stew they are going to buy (line 2), Carmine imparts a decision (line 3) that is not questioned further as the subsequent long pause shows (line 4). During that pause, both participants reach a stationary position at the counter. They manifestly overhear co-occurring talk between other customers as well as between the butcher and the person currently being served: at lines 6–8, Piero utters a proposal to buy 'two slices of horse', a lexical referent that the butcher has just mentioned while talking to another customer. Again, this potentially purchasable item is introduced, as in Excerpt 2.12, along with a specific time at which the couple could eat it, namely 'Sunday evening' (lines 7–8). It is precisely on the basis of that specific day that Carmine however rejects his partner's proposal in line 10 (*da oggi a domenica vanno a maliss: -imo.* 'from today until Sunday they spo:il rotten.').

In this excerpt, Piero uses interrogative formats when introducing a specification of a previously agreed-on product (line 2) or a new potentially purchasable item (lines 6–8). This practice contrasts with the way Maria and Teresa introduce new purchasable items (i.e., by producing their buying decision in an assertive way). By using an interrogative format, Piero displays his orientation toward achieving jointly ratified buying decisions.

While they are still waiting to be served, Piero and Carmine continue talking about their meal plans. In reply to Piero's question about what they are having on Sunday evening (Excerpt 2.16, line 11), Carmine has just proposed tortellini with ham and cream. Piero now rejects that proposal on the basis that it is not necessary to have pasta in the evening if they are already having pasta for lunch on the same day (lines 1–2):

Excerpt 2.17 (cons42271, 21:10–21:30)

```
01 PIE:    se mangiamo pasta a mezzogio:rno, la sera non
           if we eat pasta at noo:n, in the evening it is not
02         è necessario mangiare di nuovo pasta.
           necessary to eat pasta again.
03         (0.4)
04 PIE:    [conviene fare qualcos'altro.
           [it is better to make something else.
05 CAR:    [e allora ti va al forno: əh patate
           [well then would you like from the oven: uh potatoes
06         [e: e agnello?
           [and: and lamb?
07 PIE:    [patate bravo.
           [potatoes good.
08         (1.5)
09 PIE:    ma quindi non la fai a pranzo (col)lo spezzatino.
           but then you don't make it for lunch (with) the stew.
10         (0.8)
11 CAR:    oh:: ma che fa- non fa niente che mangiamo carne: sia-
           oh:: but what do- it doesn't matter if we eat meat: both-
12 PIE:    ma no se mangio a pranzo- se mangio a pranzo la carne
           but no if I eat for lunch- if I eat meat for lunch
13         perché la devo mangiare anche la sera. .h
           why should I eat it also in the evening. .h
14         allora fallo- compralo soltanto per te lo spezzatino.
           then make it- buy the stew only for yourself.
```

Responding to Piero's objection to having tortellini for dinner on Sunday (lines 1–2) and to his proposal to prepare 'something else' (line 4), Carmine suggests a different dish composed of potatoes and lamb (lines 5–6), and produces his turn with an interrogative prosody. Piero positively assesses Carmine's mentioning of *patate* 'potatoes' right away, in overlap with his partner's talk (*bravo*[24] 'good', line 7). However, a noticeable pause occurs at line 8. Whereas Carmine's question (lines 5–6) projects a positive or negative answer, Piero responds to that question in a different way, namely by first positively assessing Carmine's proposal (line 7) and then by voicing the consequences of the proposal: in Piero's view, if the couple is to have potatoes and lamb for dinner on Sunday, then they would not need to have stew for lunch on the same day (line 9). At line 11, Carmine articulates his understanding of the problem that Piero is exhibiting as relating to the fact that they would eat meat twice on the same day. Whereas Carmine holds that 'it doesn't matter' (line 11), Piero first substantiates his opposition (lines 12–13) and then ends his turn by saying that Carmine should buy the stew only for himself (line 14).

In this case, the members of the couple display diverging criteria for deciding not only what kind of meat they are going to buy (Excerpt 2.16) but also how they are going to use it, i.e., when they should eat it (Excerpt 2.17). These diverging orientations resolve as Piero ratifies the purchase of 'stew' as an acquisition that his partner will make for himself rather than for the couple. Without further discussion between them, Carmine is going to order 'veal stew' and 'lamb chops' (Excerpts 2.3 and 2.6).

2.5 Discussion and Conclusions

In this chapter, I have tracked the interactional history of the requests customers address to shop assistants at the counter (Excerpts 2.1–2.7). The straightforwardness of the requests, which shoppers deliver in single turns-at-talk contrasts with the complex and successive renegotiation and refinement of the buying decisions that account for these requests. This finding problematizes openings of service encounters (Aston 1995) by showing that shoppers prepare such encounters in advance. Requests that end up being uttered at the counter and that the shop assistants comprehend as brand new are in fact prepared: they condense the preceding interaction between co-shoppers and eventually materialize as single turns in which the requested product is named with a lexical reference form.[25] Table 2.1 provides an overview of the temporal succession of the excerpts analyzed in this chapter (the excerpts with requests that customers address to service personnel are framed).

---

[24] *Bravo*, a very common assessment in Italian, is applied to persons (not to objects) and could thus be translated as 'good boy', 'well done' in English.
[25] This holds true for the first requests (Excerpts 2.1–2.5) observed in my data. However, deictic reference (e.g., *one of these please*) is also imaginable – especially in cases in which the product represents a buyable unit (and does not need to be weighed, grated, etc., as in the cases analyzed here).

Table 2.1. *The temporal succession of the excerpts*

Product category	Couple	Excerpts
Fish	Carmine and Piero	11 → ②
Meat	Carmine and Piero	12 → 16 → 17 → ③ → ⑥
Cheese	Carmine and Piero	9 → 14 → ①
Cheese	Maria and Teresa	10 → 13 → ④ → 15 → ⑤ → ⑦ → 8

The table shows that the requests may follow more or less elaborate preparatory actions, which start, in my analysis, with the first mention of a potentially purchasable product category. Early orientations toward the counters are not haphazard but rely on the continuous monitoring of the environment, which is in constant transformation as the shoppers move through the aisles of the supermarket. Whether shoppers present the purchase of an item as 'planned' (Excerpt 2.10), as a mutually agreed-upon and locally emerging project (Excerpt 2.12), or as a discovery (Excerpt 2.15), in all the cases analyzed here, shoppers orient to visually or acoustically[26] available semiotic resources. In many cases, shoppers first refer to specific potentially purchasable items when they have visual access to areas or counters where those items are putatively available (Excerpts 2.9–2.11). Alternatively, shoppers may first mention a potentially purchasable item and then locate the place where that item is supposedly available (Excerpts 2.8 and 2.12). Finally, shoppers may discover products while they are standing at the counter (Excerpts 2.15–2.16).

The analysis has also shown how shoppers progressively transform the item to be purchased as they approach the counter. Shoppers may first orient toward a specific group of products and refer to them by using general (food) categories (such as 'cheese', Excerpts 2.9–2.10). As they approach the counter, shoppers may use more specific categories: whereas 'general' categories (e.g., 'meat', Excerpt 2.12) are found early on, they are progressively replaced by more specific categories (e.g., 'stew', Excerpt 2.12, and finally 'veal stew', Excerpt 2.16), which will eventually be instantiated during the service encounter. On some occasions, shoppers specify the product to be purchased while they are still at a distance from the counter. This is the case for Maria, who explains to her friend that she is going to get 'grated Sbrinz cheese' before actually moving to the counter (Excerpt 2.13). By doing so, Maria presents this buying decision as planned beforehand, as emerging from a pre-established (immaterial) shopping list, whereas none of the three couples recorded use material shopping

---

[26] As Excerpt 2.16 has shown, overhearing a service encounter occurring nearby (or any kind of conversation) allows interactants to spot potentially purchasable products (here, horse meat).

lists. On other occasions, the specification is achieved *at* the counter: this is the case for Carmine, who decides to buy a 'ripe Robiola cheese' only after having visually assessed the products on display (Excerpt 2.14). A striking aspect of the way in which Carmine exhibits his buying decision is that he repeatedly treats Robiola cheese as an item he 'wants' (Excerpt 2.14, lines 23, 28) just after having discovered it in the display. 'Wanting' a product is, indeed one way of displaying the non-negotiability of a buying project for which one can be held responsible (see De Stefani 2011). Shoppers may thus present such buying projects as rooted in a (not overtly exhibited) shopping list, as emerging from local discoveries, or as emanating from a collaborative planning of future activities, such as the organization of meals for subsequent days. With regard to the latter practice, the analyses have shown that the organization of Carmine and Piero's common meals is reflexively tied to the transformation of the potentially purchasable items. It appears then that shoppers work toward assigning a *legitimate history* (Garfinkel 1967: 114) to their buying projects and that they may do so in different ways.

Buying decisions appear to be ideal loci for displaying the specific relationship that ties co-shoppers to each other: through practices of shared decision-making and planning, participants are recognizably acting as members of a committed couple, with 'the couple' being the beneficiary of these buying decisions. By contrast, shoppers who engage in unilateral decision-making take full responsibility for their buying decisions and display orientation toward a 'just friends' kind of couplehood.

Buying decisions materialize at the service encounter as requests that a customer addresses to a shop assistant. In the case of the couple formed by Carmine and Piero, the specific request format observed in Excerpts 2.1–2.7 appears to be an economical solution for transferring what has (laboriously) been agreed upon in one specific *participation framework* (Goffman 1981), i.e., the couple, to another participation framework, where one member of the couple interacts with the shop assistant at the counter. Incidentally, in this couple, it is always Carmine who acts as a spokesperson for the couple. In Maria and Teresa's couple, the person interacting with the shop assistant is also the one who is responsible for that individual buying project. Hence, at the cheese counter, Maria first requests 'half a kilo of:: Sbrinz' (Excerpt 2.4), and then Teresa asks for 'Gorgonzola with mascarpone' (Excerpt 2.5), after which Maria will also request a 'piece like this [of Gorgonzola with mascarpone]' (Excerpt 2.7). Clearly, their requests are much more tied to individual buying decisions that may be based on (materially or cognitively available) shopping lists, on monitoring and discovering purchasable items on the spur of the moment, etc.

The observation according to which requests (may) have a long interactional history that is initiated much earlier than in pre-beginning position (see Keisanen & Rauniomaa 2012) opens up an interesting analytical problem: at what point should the analysis start? Determining the precise moment at which a social encounter begins is a challenging endeavor (see De Stefani & Mondada 2018), and it appears that customers may take more time to 'prepare' the service encounter than shop assistants, who have to identify the 'next' customer recognizably waiting to be served. Data analysis is always perspectival: the focus on the interactional history of requests at the counter was only possible because customers were shadowed on their shopping tour, whereas orienting a stationary video camera toward the counter enables researchers to study other conduct relevant for such service encounters, e.g., how shop assistants 'wait' for customers to place their order (Svinhufvud 2018). In other words, the method of data collection shapes the ensuing analytical possibilities. In this chapter, I have only been able to focus on the interactional history of requests as observed in two different couples shopping in the supermarket. Further research is needed to reveal how such preparatory negotiations are done in other kinds of couples or groups (e.g., families with children) and also how service personnel categorize the couples they serve.[27] Moreover, research on different kinds of businesses (small specialized shops vs. supermarkets) with different spatial dimensions and arrangements is needed to show how participants deal with environmental aspects and how these impact their interaction.

References

Antaki, C., & Kent, A. (2012). Telling people what to do (and, sometimes, why): Contingency, entitlement and explanation in staff requests to adults with intellectual impairments. *Journal of Pragmatics*, 44(6–7), 876–889. https://doi.org/10.1016/j.pragma.2012.03.014

Aston, G. (1995). In reference to the role of openings to service encounters. *Cahiers de linguistique française*, 16(1), 89–111.

Best, K. (2012). Making museum tours better: Understanding what a guided tour really is and what a tour guide really does. *Museum Management and Curatorship*, 27(1), 35–52. https://doi.org/10.1080/09647775.2012.644695

Chomsky, N. (1981). *Lectures on Government and Binding*. Dordrecht: Foris. https://doi.org/10.1515/9783110884166

De Stefani, E. (2006). Le chiusure conversazionali nell'interazione al banco di un supermercato [Conversational closings in the interaction at a supermarket counter]. In Y. Bürki & E. De Stefani, eds., *Trascrivere la lingua: Dalla filologia all'analisi conversazionale*. Bern: Peter Lang, pp. 369–403.

(2010). Reference as an interactively and multimodally accomplished practice: Organizing spatial reorientation in guided tours. In M. Pettorino, A. Giannini,

---

[27] For instance, Carmine and Piero could be categorized as a committed couple, as a couple of two friends who accidentally shop together, etc. Maria and Teresa, who use two shopping carts, appear to be treated as a couple of friends, not as a committed couple.

I. Chiari, & F. Dovetto, eds., *Spoken Communication*. Newcastle: Cambridge Scholars, pp. 137–170.

(2011). "Ah petta ecco, io prendo questi che mi piacciono." Agire come coppia al supermercato. Un approccio conversazionale e multimodale allo studio dei processi decisionali [*"Oh wait here, I'm getting these, cos I like them." Acting as a couple at the supermarket. A conversational and multimodal approach to the analysis of decision-making*]. Rome: Aracne.

(2013). The collaborative organisation of next actions in a semiotically rich environment: Shopping as a couple. In P. Haddington, L. Mondada, & M. Nevile, eds., *Interaction and Mobility: Language and the Body in Motion*. Berlin: De Gruyter, pp. 123–151. https://doi.org/10.1515/9783110291278.123

(2014). Establishing joint orientation towards commercial objects in a self-service store: How practices of categorisation matter. In M. Nevile, P. Haddington, T. Heinemann, & M. Rauniomaa, eds., *Interacting with Objects: Language, Materiality, and Social Activity*. Amsterdam: John Benjamins, pp. 271–294. https://doi.org/10.1075/z.186.12ste

(2019). Ordering and serving coffee in an Italian café: How customers obtain 'their' coffee. In D. Day & J. Wagner, eds., *Objects, Bodies and Work Practice*. Bristol: Multilingual Matters, pp. 113–139. https://doi.org/10.21832/9781788924535-008

De Stefani, E., & Mondada, L. (2010). Die Eröffnung von sozialen Begegnungen im öffentlichen Raum. Die emergente Koordination der räumlichen, visuellen und verbalen Handlungen [Opening social encounters in open space. The emerging coordination of spatial, visual and verbal actions]. In L. Mondada & R. Schmitt, eds., *Situationseröffnungen. Zur multimodalen Herstellung fokussierter Interaktion*. Tübingen: Narr, pp. 103–170.

(2014). Reorganizing mobile formations: When 'guided' participants initiate reorientations in guided tours. *Space and Culture*, 17(2), 157–175. https://doi.org/10.1177/1206331213508504

(2018). Encounters in public space: How acquainted versus unacquainted persons establish social and spatial arrangements. *Research on Language and Social Interaction*, 51(3), 248–270. https://doi.org/10.1080/08351813.2018.1485230

De Stefani, E., Sambre, P., & Van De Mieroop, D. (2016). The interactional history of examples and parentheses: Note-taking practices in multiparty interaction among attendees of a mutual-help group for Chronic Fatigue Syndrome (CFS) sufferers. *Language and Dialogue*, 6(1), 110–139. https://doi.org/10.1075/ld.6.1.04des

Fox, B., & Heinemann, T. (2015). The alignment of manual and verbal displays in requests for the repair of an object. *Research on Language and Social Interaction*, 48(3), 342–362. https://doi.org/10.1080/08351813.2015.1058608

(2016). Rethinking format: An examination of requests. *Language in Society*, 45(4), 499–531. https://doi.org/10.1017/S0047404516000385

Garfinkel, H. (1967). *Studies in Ethnomethodology*, Englewood Cliffs: Prentice-Hall.

Goffman, E. (1963). *Behavior in Public Spaces: Notes on the Social Organization of Gatherings*, New York: The Free Press.

(1981). *Forms of Talk*, Philadelphia: University of Pennsylvania Press.

Goodwin, C. (2000). Action and embodiment within situated human interaction. *Journal of Pragmatics*, 32(10), 1489–1522.

(2003). Pointing as a situated practice. In S. Kita, ed., *Pointing: Where Language, Culture, and Cognition Meet*. Mahwah: Lawrence Erlbaum, pp. 217–241. https://doi.org/10.4324/9781410607744

Harjunpää, K., Mondada, L., & Svinhufvud, K. (2018). The coordinated entry into service encounters in food shops: Managing interactional space, availability, and service during openings. *Research on Language and Social Interaction*, 51(3), 271–291. https://doi.org/10.1080/08351813.2018.1485231

Heinemann, T., & Koivisto, A. (2016). Indicating a change-of-state in interaction: Cross-linguistic explorations. *Journal of Pragmatics*, 104, 83–88. https://doi.org/10.1016/j.pragma.2016.09.002

Heritage, J. (1984). A change of state token and aspects of its sequential placement. In J. M. Atkinson & J. Heritage, eds., *Structures of Social Action*. Cambridge: Cambridge University Press, pp. 299–345. https://doi.org/10.1017/CBO9780511665868.020

Jayyusi, L. (1984). *Categorization and the Moral Order*, Boston: Routledge.

Jefferson, G. (1978). Sequential aspects of storytelling in conversation. In J. Schenkein, ed., *Studies in the Organization of Conversational Interaction*. New York: Academic Press, pp. 219–248. https://doi.org/10.1016/B978-0-12-623550-0.50016-1

Keisanen, T., & Rauniomaa, M. (2012). The organization of participation and contingency in prebeginnings of request sequences. *Research on Language and Social Interaction*, 45(4), 323–351. https://doi.org/10.1080/08351813.2012.724985

Keisanen, T., Rauniomaa, M., & Haddington, P. (2014). Suspending action: From simultaneous to consecutive ordering of multiple courses of action. In P. Haddington, T. Keisanen, L. Mondada, & M. Nevile, eds., *Multiactivity in Social Interaction: Beyond Multitasking*. Amsterdam: John Benjamins, pp. 109–133. https://doi.org/10.1075/z.187.04kei

Lave, J. (1988). *Cognition in Practice*, Cambridge: Cambridge University Press. https://doi.org/10.1017/CBO9780511609268

Linell, P. (2009). *Rethinking Language, Mind and World Dialogically: Interactional and Contextual Theories of Human Sense-Making*, Charlotte: Information Age Publishing.

Mazeland, H., & Huiskes, M. (2001). Dutch 'but' as a sequential conjunction: Its use as a resumption marker. In M. Selting & E. Couper-Kuhlen, eds., *Studies in Interactional Linguistics*. Amsterdam/Philadelphia: John Benjamins, pp. 141–169. https://doi.org/10.1075/sidag.10.08maz

Merritt, M. W. (1976). *Resources for Saying in Service Encounters*. PhD dissertation, University of Pennsylvania.

Mitchell, T. F. (1957). The language of buying and selling in Cyrenaica: A situational statement. *Hesperis*, 44, 31–71.

Mondada, L. (2009). Emergent focused interactions in public places: A systematic analysis of the multimodal achievement of a common interactional space. *Journal of Pragmatics*, 41(10), 1977–1997. https://doi.org/10.1016/j.pragma.2008.09.019

(2012). Garden lessons: Embodied action and joint attention in extended sequences. In H. Nasu & F. Chaput Waksler, eds., *Interaction and Everyday Life*. Lanham: Lexington Books, pp. 293–311.

(2014). The temporal orders of multiactivity: Operating and demonstrating in the surgical theatre. In P. Haddington, T. Keisanen, L. Mondada, & M. Nevile, eds., *Multiactivity in Social Interaction: Beyond Multitasking*. Amsterdam: John Benjamins, pp. 33–75. https://doi.org/10.1075/z.187.02mon

Mondada, L., & Sorjonen, M.-L. (2016). Making multiple requests in French and Finnish convenience stores. *Language in Society*, 45(5), 733–765. https://doi.org/10.1017/S0047404516000646

Pitsch, K. (2012). Exponat – Alltagsgegenstand – Turngerät: Zur interaktiven Konstitution von Objekten in einer Museumsausstellung [Exhibit – everyday object – gym equipment: On the interactive constitution of objects in a museum exhibition]. In R. Schmitt, L. Mondada, & H. Hausendorf, eds., *Raum als interaktionale Ressource*. Tübingen: Narr, pp. 233–273.

Poggi, I. (1981). *Le interiezioni. Studio del linguaggio e analisi della mente* [*Interjections. The analysis of language and the analysis of the mind*]. Turin: Boringhieri.

Rossano, F. (2010). Questioning and responding in Italian. *Journal of Pragmatics*, 42(10), 2756–2771. https://doi.org/10.1016/j.pragma.2010.04.010

Rossi, G. (2015). *The Request System in Italian Interaction*, Nijmegen: Ipskamp Drukkers.

Sacks, H. (1972). An initial investigation of the usability of conversational data for doing sociology. In D. Sudnow, ed., *Studies in Social Interaction*. New York: The Free Press, pp. 31–74.

(1992). *Lectures on Conversation, Vols 1 & 2*. Ed. by G. Jefferson. Oxford: Basil Blackwell.

Sacks, H., Schegloff, E. A., & Jefferson, G. (1974). A simplest systematics for the organization of turn-taking for conversation. *Language*, 50(4), 696–735. https://doi.org/10.2307/412243

Schegloff, E. A. (2007). *Sequence Organization in Interaction: A Primer in Conversation Analysis, Vol. 1*. Cambridge: Cambridge University Press. https://doi.org/10.1017/CBO9780511791208

(2010). Some other "uh(m)"s. *Discourse Processes*, 47(2), 130–174. https://doi.org/10.1080/01638530903223380

Sorjonen, M.-L., & Raevaara, L. (2014). On the grammatical form of requests at the convenience store: Requesting as embodied action. In P. Drew & E. Couper-Kuhlen, eds., *Requesting in Social Interaction*. Amsterdam: John Benjamins, pp. 243–268. https://doi.org/10.1075/slsi.26.10sor

Stukenbrock, A. & Birkner, K. (2010). Multimodale Ressourcen für Stadtführungen [Multimodal resources for city tours]. In M. Costa & B. Müller-Jacquier, eds., *Deutschland als fremde Kultur: Vermittlungsverfahren in Touristenführungen*. Munich: Judicium Verlag, pp. 214–243.

Svinhufvud, K. (2018). Waiting for the customer: Multimodal analysis of waiting in service encounters. *Journal of Pragmatics*, 129, 48–75. https://doi.org/10.1016/j.pragma.2018.03.002

Vinkhuyzen, E., & Szymanski, M. (2005). Would you like to do it yourself? Service requests and their non-granting responses. In K. Richards & P. Seedhouse, eds., *Applying Conversation Analysis*. New York: Palgrave Macmillan, pp. 91–106. https://doi.org/10.1057/9780230287853_6

3 Customers' Inquiries about Products
Establishing Grounds for the Decision to Buy

Katariina Harjunpää, Lorenza Mondada, and Kimmo Svinhufvud

3.1 A Customer's Practical Problem: How to Identify Products to Buy

In shops where products are requested by the customer and fetched by the salesperson at the counter, like bakeries, as opposed to self-service baking shelves in supermarkets, the customer is often confronted with several practical problems. How to identify and/or name what they want? How to determine whether a product they spotted is actually something available to buy? And consequently, how to gather information that will constitute the basis on which to decide whether or not to buy it? These practical problems are addressed by customers and sellers together within the practices of identification, differentiation, characterization, and specification of products.

This chapter studies how customers look for information about the products they are about to buy by asking the sellers questions before making their final decision. These questions open up a sequence in which the product is identified, differentiated from some other products, and described by the seller. By analyzing these questions, we show how customers engage in an inquiry about the detailed features of bakery products and establish their relevance within their personal perspective.

Such a focus contributes to a better understanding of the practices that constitute the building blocks of commercial encounters and establish the value and meaningfulness of products in these interactions. It also contributes to broader discussions about how reference, information, and knowledge are dealt with in institutional interactions, including how questions are shaped for and serve larger activities. Furthermore, the analysis casts some light on issues of interactional semantics – that is, on the practices through which speakers engage in ad hoc situated semantic work by making specific features of the objects handled in the interactions relevant.

3.2 Issues Addressed and State of the Art

3.2.1 Designing Actions in Commercial Encounters

Commercial encounters have been specifically studied within conversation analysis (CA) by focusing on the actions constitutive of these exchanges. For instance, customers' requests are crucial to achievement of the buying activity (Fox & Heinemann 2015, 2016; Kuroshima 2010; Mondada & Sorjonen 2016). Customers' turns formatted as questions can function as requests for products, but also as requests for information, which can serve as a preliminary to the actual request (Merritt 1976). Sellers use question-formatted turns to organize the progression of the activity (*how can I help you? anything else?* see Halonen & Koivisto, this volume), as well as to specify the kinds of products requested.

CA work on requests and questions in general has been interested in their formatting, displaying degrees of entitlement (Curl & Drew 2008; Heinemann 2006; Lindström 2005), and the epistemic positioning they reflect (Heritage 2012). Comparatively, the material and other kinds of objects targeted by these actions and the way they are described has attracted less attention (but see De Stefani 2011, 2014; Moore 2008). Excerpt 3.1 illustrates how an object becomes described in a request sequence expanded by a question. At line 8, the seller (SEL) asks a question in order to specify further the product requested by the customer (CUS) (Merritt 1976; Mondada & Sorjonen 2016).

Excerpt 3.1 (Swiss German, BAK_CH_BAS_111505_1.25.22)

```
01 SEL:    guede da:g
           good morning
02         (0.2)
03 CUS:    guede dag
           good morning
04         (1.0)
05 CUS:    e:hm: (0.5) ich probier mal so e dinkelbro::tsch=
           e:hm:       I try once such a spelt bread
06 SEL:    =sehr gärn
            with pleasure
07         (0.5)
08 SEL: →  a grosses oder [a chlises?]
           a big      or  a small?
09 CUS:                   [ne e    kl]eines
                           no a small
```

The seller asks a question of specification to match the customer's request for a 'spelt bread' by offering the relevant options: the question narrows down the choice by specifying subclasses of the type of bread requested. Features treated as gradual in some other contexts, such as small and big, may in this commercial setting rather correspond to a standard description, categorization, and

Customers' Inquiries about Products   75

distribution of products within the shop. In other words, they are relevant as 'standard' features from the seller's perspective.

This chapter expands on the analytic interest in how questions characterize the products asked about, but in contrast to sellers' questions, it focuses on how questions asked by customers progressively specify the product. The features targeted by these questions are relevant for that customer at that moment. Therefore, they do not necessarily correspond to 'standard' features. The following is a case in point.

Excerpt 3.2 (Swiss German, BAK_CH_BS_260515_03.32.03)

```
01            (2.0)
     cus      >>looks at the showcase->
02 SEL:       grüezi:
              hello
03            (1.0) * (0.4) * (1.7) • (0.4)
     cus           ->*at  SEL*at showcase->
                                    •points->
04 CUS:  → sind das gmüeswähe?•=
            are these vegetable pies
                             -->•
05 SEL:     =>jä<
            yes
06          (0.6)
07 CUS:  → häts dört pe*peroni dinne?
            is there peppers inside
                      -->*looks at SEL-->
08          (1.2)
09 SEL:     oh‡je::.hh‡ gue*ti fro‡:g
            oh::    .hh good question
            ‡.......‡approaches-‡leans over showc looking at prod->
     cus                  ->*looks at showcase->

((SEL redirects the Q to a colleague - 8 lines omitted))

18 SE2:     >nei.< peperoni ‡nid nää
            no     peppers   not no
                          ->‡turns to CUS-->>
19          (0.3)
20 CUS:  → •denn häti gärn eins von• (   )=
            then I would like one of
            •points----------------•walks to till--->>
```

After greetings, the customer asks a question about a pie, pointing to it (line 4). The question displays an assumption that the pie has vegetable filling, and could manifest a preference for vegetarian food. After the seller confirms the assumption (line 5), the customer makes a follow-up query about a particular ingredient, peppers (line 7). The seller redirects the question to a colleague (omitted part after line 9), who reassures the customer that there are no peppers inside. As the customer receives this answer, she announces her decision to buy the pie (line 20). Retrospectively, this shows that the presence of peppers could have been an obstacle to the purchase (as shown by the connective *denn* 'then').

In this chapter, we deal with questions (highlighted in grey) like the ones in Excerpt 3.2, where customers explore personal relevancies in a process of discovery of products, forming the basis of the decision to buy (marked with a fat arrow) (in contrast to questions addressing the availability of the products, like 'do you have/sell x?'; Merritt 1976, not addressed here). The questions targeted are either WH questions (Fox & Thompson 2010; Thompson et al. 2015) that make it relevant for the seller to provide specific information, or they are polar questions that, in most cases, make confirmation relevant (de Ruiter 2012; Raymond 2000, 2003; Sorjonen 2001a, 2001b; Stivers et al. 2010). The information given in the responses provides grounds for the customers' decision to buy. As will be shown, the information can be treated as sufficient or can be expanded, either by the customer or by the seller: in this way, they both show their orientation in relation to the relative transparency/opaqueness and sufficiency of the answer as a characterization of the product for the customer. The identification and establishment of the object inquired about thus bears on the expansion-relevance of the answers and the unfolding of the sequence.

More broadly, this chapter discusses how the ways of referring to the products in the customers' questions and the sellers' responses build the institutionality of the exchange in terms of manifesting the expertise of the seller and disclosing the epistemic stance of the customer, as well as other situated and personal relevancies. Additionally, these referential practices may manifest the prestige and quality of the shop, reveal complementary rights and obligations between the participants, and contribute to specific types of rapport in the institutional encounter.

3.2.2 Referring to Products in Commercial Encounters

Shops are environments densely populated with objects to be bought. The objects can be diversely referred to in the actions implemented by customers – as being known in advance or as being newly discovered, as having a recognizable shape and content or as difficult to recognize and interpret, and as having specific sensorial characteristics (De Stefani 2011, 2014; Mondada 2021).

Studying how customers identify and describe products contributes to the understanding of how reference is achieved through language and the body in specific social interactional and institutional settings. Within the CA literature, issues of reference were addressed early on by Sacks (1963; see also Schegloff 1972) in terms of the relevance (vs. vericonditionality) of descriptors and descriptions. Further studies have primarily addressed issues of reference to persons, in terms of a double preference for minimization and recognition (Sacks & Schegloff 1979). In formulating persons and places, the use of proper names has been regarded as the preferred way to introduce a new referent, as names are both minimal and recognitional (Enfield & Stivers 2007; Sacks & Schegloff 1979; Schegloff 1972). That is, they achieve identification with the least interactional effort and the greatest accuracy. As such, they rely on shared knowledge about the referred to entity: they are successful if the referent is "expectably recognizable" by the co-participants (Schegloff 1972: 92). However, the choice of reference forms can also do "more than referring," such as indicate why the person is being talked about at this moment (Schegloff 1996).

Here, we are interested in reference to objects in the shop context, where the issues of reference relate to commercial labeling and the branding of products for selling. For instance, bakeries sell traditional and standard products that can be found in most shops, but they also sell products that are unique to that bakery (signature products). People entering the bakery might be regular customers, who regularly buy familiar items, but also one-time customers who pass by and enter the shop without exactly knowing what to buy. The products as such are more or less familiar and recognizable by their appearance and their names (given in written labels or mentioned by the seller), being fully transparent ('wheat bread roll'), somewhat transparent ('sesame square'), or opaque (*le dessert de la marquise*) – that is, they can provide more or less inferable hints concerning the type of product and its ingredients.

Referring practices also reveal the epistemic stances of the participants. Shops, like other institutional settings, are characterized by an asymmetry of knowledge: the seller is supposed to know the products they sell, whereas the customer can possess variable knowledge (Moore 2008), and yet the customer is the one who makes decisions about buying. These features occasion negotiations about the resources to secure the identification, recognition, and characterization of the products.

In asking questions, customers can use a variety of resources to refer to the products, and these do not always correspond to their official labels. The linguistic expressions that customers use reveal their (previously existing and inferred) knowledge about the product while also indicating what piece of relevant information is missing ('what is the flan in the bottom over there?', 'what kind of flan?'). Even the use of product names ('groat bread', 'Hilde bread') in customers' questions is multifaceted. On the one hand, using a product name reveals some kind of recognition and knowledge (they can also be just read on the written labels on the products), while on the other hand, asking the question indicates that the customer has not sufficiently identified the properties of the product to make a decision about buying it. In fact, the bakery's product names (e.g., 'Hilde bread') are not the primary way that the customers refer to the products. In formulating their questions, they make use of visibly available, familiar, and inferable features of the products, mobilizing resources such as deictic expressions and common nouns, accompanied by various kinds of ad hoc descriptors, together with pointing.[1] This shows that customers display their own situated perspective in choosing products rather than their alignment with standards and brands.

Even though linguistic forms are crucial for establishing reference, referential practices in face-to-face interaction are generally multimodal: they are articulated with verbal and embodied resources, comprising pointing gestures, glances, sustained gaze, and visual inspection, as well as body orientation. These embodied resources have been extensively studied by CA literature on reference (e.g., Eriksson 2009; Goodwin 2003; Hindmarsh & Heath 2000; Mondada 2014, 2016), including in relation to practices of assessing, noticing, and exploring products in commercial settings (De Stefani 2011, 2014 on supermarkets; Mondada 2012 on car showrooms; Sorjonen & Raevaara 2014 on kiosks).

The use of embodied resources is organized with respect to both the physical environment and the accessibility and identifiability of the products. In shops like the bakeries in our data, customers' access to the products is constrained by the fact that they are separated by a window, sometimes even far away on the back shelves, and they have to be fetched by the seller. Moreover, the location of the products is relevant for their categorization and typology in terms of commercial strategies. These spatial and material characteristics of the ecology of the shop encounter are oriented to in the customer's multimodal formatting of both requests and questions. The questions examined in this chapter, which display knowing the product only partially, are all accompanied by pointing. In comparison, requests in similar settings that are made by naming the products and without pointing at them show that the customers are familiar with the object, that they expect the shop to sell it, and that the purchase has been planned ahead (Mondada 2019). The current set of examples shows that pointing is not only used to accompany deictic expressions in establishing a shared focus of attention, but relates in more complex ways to activities that involve identifying and specifying the targeted objects in the shop encounter.

The locally negotiated and emergent classification of shop products is also an example of the participants' endogenous orientation to semantic dimensions in interaction (Deppermann 2011, 2019; Hakulinen & Selting 2005). In the question-answer sequences in our data, the participants establish and orient to the local meaning of the linguistic resources they are using in activity-relevant ways. Their

---

[1] The distinction between appellatives and proper nouns in reference to bakery products is often not straightforward, as the same lexeme may be used as a classifying appellative (e.g., 'groat bread') or as a product name (or part of one). Product names are by definition proper names, yet they can be used rather as appellatives or in combination with them (Ainiala & Paukkala 2012: 210–249). What we call 'transparent' product names are typically composed of common nouns descriptive of the product's composition, whereas 'opaque' ones contain name elements from other sources (e.g., 'Hilde bread'). Such naming may be more typical of signature products.

semantic work is observable in the forms they choose to refer to the products, selected among sets of possible alternatives, from stand-alone deictic elements to ones accompanied by further characterization with adjectives or adverbs, to common nouns and proper nouns with and without further characterization. Moreover, the way customers identify, differentiate, and specify the objects in terms of ingredients and other features reveals the participant's conception of the items as belonging to a class or a subclass (see Sacks 1992 vol. II: 499–503; also Bilmes 2015) of products. These are not necessarily known beforehand nor shared between the interactants; the properties of an object are characterized and elaborated in service of the unfolding activity (see Harjunpää et al. 2021).

These practices allow us to provide a respecification (Garfinkel 1991) of semantics as a member's problem. This chapter shows how customers identify, point at, and formulate generic or specific properties of the products as locally relevant for them. We describe how participants raise and solve these tasks as a basis for making a decision.

3.3 The Data and Outline of Analysis

This study is based on video data collected in bakeries in four countries – Finland, Switzerland, Germany, and France – with interactions in English as a lingua franca, Finnish, Finland Swedish, Swiss German, German, and French. For each site, 3 to 5 hours were video-recorded, with the collaboration of the sellers and the informed consent of the customers.

The analyses focus on practices through which the customers establish what it is for all practical purposes when facing a product they might decide to buy. The practices studied here are implemented in the form of questions that mobilize a range of multimodal resources, including gazing, leaning closer to the showcase, and, in all cases, pointing. The questions occur in two sequential positions: either preliminary to a request, or inserted after a request has already been initiated but is cut off to ask something about the product.

The questions asked by customers range from very general to more specific inquiries about the products. In the analysis, we distinguish two broad sets of general and specific scopes of questions: questions about the generic type of product (Section 3.4) and those that target its specific properties, typically ingredients (Section 3.5). Moreover, within each set, we divide the cases according to the generic and specific ways of formatting questions. The analysis proceeds from plain WH questions that display least knowledge about the products ('What is that?', 'What is in that one?') to polar questions that display the questioner as assuming more detailed knowledge about the product ('Is that x?', 'Does it contain x?'). In each section, we also examine the use of common nouns compared with product names and descriptive elements that identify and characterize the products, and their consequences. With these analyses, we aim to show how the referential practices used within different question formats invoke locally relevant features of the objects and thereby serve the mutual process of establishing shared meaning and building specific accountability of actions in the shop encounter.

3.4 Inquiring about the Type of Product

In this section, we explore inquiries about the type, or class, of product, going from the most unspecified, plain questions (Section 3.4.1), to ones that involve more identifying elements (Section 3.4.2), and to requests for confirmation using polar questions (Section 3.4.3). By using the first format, the customers reveal that they have little knowledge of the product, whereas by using the third format, they display that they know or assume quite a bit about the product. These questions manifest not only the customer's knowledge, but also the customer's emergent visible and epistemic access to the product.

3.4.1 *Generic, Plain WH Questions about Products*

The least knowledge customers may exhibit about a product with their questions is manifested with a plain 'what's that?' question (see also Lindström & Fox, this volume). These WH questions contain a reference to the product with a demonstrative only, possible pronominal or demonstrative determiners, and pointing. The seller's response typically provides the name of the product, which can turn out to be either transparent or rather opaque, and consequently possibly expanded by a description.

On some occasions, the standard name of the product provided by the seller is treated by the customer as sufficient information for deciding to buy. Whether the provision of a name is sufficient depends on either its familiarity to the customer or on how much it reveals about the product – that is, its relative transparency or opaqueness in terms of ingredients or other relevant properties. In Excerpt 3.3, the name *feigenbrot* 'fig bread' (line 8) is treated as enough information for declining the product, whereas in Excerpt 3.4, the name *maggiabrot* 'Maggia bread' (line 4) is treated as needing further explanation.

Excerpt 3.3 (German, BAK_D_LOR_170415_46–32_CLI2/SEL2_V)

```
01        ‡(0.3) ‡ (0.7) • (1.0)
    sel   ‡nods--‡
    cus                  •1 step fwd--->
02 CUS:   °ich nehme gerne°
          I take please
03        (2.5) • #(0.4)
    cus         ->•points--->
    fig             #fig.3.1
```

Customers' Inquiries about Products

Figure 3.1

```
04 CUS:     ich nehme gerne °was- ‡ (0.2) •was is• es?°        ‡
            I take please    what-         what is it
                                        ->•,,,,,,•
     sel                             ‡turns twds pointed at dir‡
05          ‡(0.2)
     sel    ‡walks and pts twd the pointed at direction->
06 CUS:     (fä-)
            (fä-)
07          (0.4)
08 SEL:     ein fei‡genbro[::t?]
            a    fig-bread
                 ->‡turns to CUS--->>
09 CUS: →                [nei]:n=
                          no
```

The customer initiates a request (line 2) and progressively points at the product (line 3, Figure 3.1), but encounters a problem in naming and/or identifying it. She converts her action into a question, with the plain demonstrative reference *es* 'it' (line 4). The sustained pointing gesture supporting the emergent turn guides the seller in the identification of the targeted item, which she then names (line 8). *Feigenbro::t?* is a transparent, descriptive name, built on a particular ingredient. That the customer treats it as informative is shown by her quick responsive decision not to buy the bread (line 9).

Alternatively, the name given as a response to the question can be treated as opaque, shown by the absence of uptake by the customer and oriented to by the seller by providing further product description. This is the case in the following excerpt, in which the question, as in the previous one, emerges out of an initially projected request.

Excerpt 3.4 (Swiss German, BAK_CH_BS_260515_02.20.12_CLI88-SEL1)

```
01 SEL:     sunnscht no e wunsch?=
            otherwise still another desire
02 CUS:     =sone•:: (0.6) was isch das für *eins?
            a              what is this for one
              •points---->
                                              *looks at SEL->

03          (0.6)
04 SEL:     maggia+brot. •+da*s meine si?=
            Maggia bread  that do you mean
                 +.......+points---->
   cus                 ->•holds his arm twd bread-->
   cus                 ->*looks at the bread-->
05 CUS:     =jä+*
            =yes
              ->*looks at SEL->
   sel      ->+
06          (0.6)
07 SEL:     maggia. *das •wär us rogge und wie[ze
            Maggia   that would be rye and   wheat
08 CUS: →                                    [ich nehm•e *eins•
                                              I take one
              ->*looks at bread---------------------*
              ->•points again straight to bread•,,,,,,•
```

Here, too, a request is projected (by *sone::*, line 2) but then converted into a generic question within the same trajectory of pointing (line 2), using the construction *was isch das für eins?* 'what is this for one?', in which the pronoun *eins* stands as a placeholder for the class to which the object belongs to (see also Excerpt 3.8). The seller answers with the name, *maggiabrot*, a combination of the common noun 'bread' and a place name. She also produces an understanding check, made with a similar pointing gesture to the product, and confirmed by the customer (lines 4–5). It is only after an absence of response (line 6) that she expands the name (line 7), repeated in a shorter form, into a list of ingredients of the product. This enables the customer to recognize it for all practical purposes, and, consequently, decide to buy the product. So here, the alignment with the naming of the product (*ja* 'yes', line 5) is not treated as closing the sequence: the seller orients to the completion of the sequence only when the buying decision is announced (line 8), after her provision of extra information at line 7. The customer's buying decision is based on the specification of the ingredients of the product. Here, the ingredients of the product are listed, uttered as further specifications, whereas in Excerpt 3.3, the ingredient-based name itself revealed specific enough properties.

3.4.2 WH Questions with Identifying and Descriptive Elements

While with the previous, generic questions the customer does not predicate anything about the product, other types of WH question display some access to it. These questions contain common nouns or product names, demonstrative determiners, and descriptive elements, such as adjectives and locative adverbs. For instance, in combination with a demonstrative reference form and pointing gestures, the customers may use visibly available features, such as shape and location of the product, to identify it further.

Excerpt 3.5 (Finnish, BAK_FIN_HEL 210415_0.28.50-CLI10.1/2)

```
01 SEL:     s•itte=
            then
            >>looks at CUS-->
   cus      •....-->
02 CUS:     =mi•täs    noi     +•pit•kä- (.) +pitkulaiset ‡leivät ( ).
            what.CLI   DEM2.PL long          oblong       bread.PL
            what are those long               longish breads
            ->•points-------•,,,•adjusts scarf--->
   sel                     -->+turns--------+looks at breads-->>
   sel                                                 ‡........-->
03 SEL:     (n)‡ää.
            these
            ->‡points-->
04 CUS:     [ni.
            yes
05 SEL:     [tää o rouhe‡lei‡pä.
            this is groat bread
                        -->‡,,,‡
06          (0.3)
07 CUS:->   ↑sehän näyttää hyvältä.=otetaa semmone mukaa.
            it looks good=let's take one to go
08 SEL:     joo •( )
            yes
   cus         -->•
```

The customer's question concerns the third purchase in the same encounter. The customer begins by already pointing at the breads on the other side of the counter during the seller's turn, inviting a request for the next item (line 1) with *sitte* 'then' (Halonen & Koivisto, this volume; Mondada & Sorjonen 2016; Svinhufvud 2011). The customer's pointing reaches its apex during the interrogative pronoun and the demonstrative determiner *noi* 'those' (see Etelämäki 2009). It is retracted as the characterization of the product begins (line 2). She does not withdraw the hand completely, but rests it on her scarf, lightly adjusting it until the seller grants the request (line 8). The verbal description further identifies the pointed-at product among other nearby breads. The customer characterizes the items by the adjective ('longish') that describes a visibly available feature and by using a noun for their generic category ('breads'). In responding to her question, the seller first checks the reference, also pointing at the bread, and then gives the name (line 5). The name contains the type of grain used for the bread ('groats'). This, together with the visual appearance, is treated as sufficient: the customer assesses the object positively and decides to buy (line 7).

Similarly, the following cases of preliminary questions mention a generic name (*flan*, *bröd* 'bread') and the location of the product in the window display, further indicated by pointing and gaze direction. Location is a visible feature that grounds the shared identification of the referent.

We join the next excerpt as the seller prepares a sliced bread requested by the customer, while the customer inspects the counter displaying pastries.

Excerpt 3.6 (French, BAK_F_STL_100415_ap24.45=25.27_CLI15_V)

```
01 SEL:     avec ceci?
            with that?
02          (0.9)
03 CUS:     bon •alors déj•à:    (1.9) •  c'est quoi le# flan
            well so already            what is the pudding
                •........•self-touch•points---->
   fig                                              #fig.3.2
04          au fond là-bas?•
            in the bottom over there
                     ->•
```

Figure 3.2

```
05          (.)
06 CUS:     [c'est
            it's
07 SEL:     [ça ‡c'est l'flan >feuilleté crème pâtissi‡ère pépites
            this it's the flan puff pastry cream       nuggets
                 ‡points--------------------------------‡grasps tong->
08          de chocolat<
            of chocolate
09          (1.4)
10 CUS:  →  non‡ j'veux pas d'chocolat
            no I don't want any chocolate
   sel         ->‡lowers tong->>
11          (0.6)
```

The customer refers to the object as a generic type of product (*flan*) and locates it both gesturally and verbally, with a locative adverb (*au fond là-bas* 'in the bottom over there') (lines 3–4, Figure 3.2). After a micro-pause, the seller answers the question (in overlap with the customer probably initiating a guess, line 6), referring to the item with the deictic *ça*, possibly contrasting with other pastries, followed by a complex description/list of ingredients: it is prosodically delivered in a fast and compact way, treating the ingredients almost as a compound name. The customer, in uttering her negative decision (line 10), orients only to one ingredient, which she picks out as unwanted, and as grounds for declining the product. Earlier, the seller was grasping the pastry tongs, projecting an imminent purchase, but now, as a consequence of the customer declining to buy, she lowers them.

While in the previous case, the question was answered with just the name (*rouheleipä*), in this case, a series of lexical items elaborately revealing both the type and ingredients are packaged into a continuous prosodic unit. This is a relatively rare case in which the customer makes explicit the grounds for declining, in a negative form. The uptake shows that the question/answer concerning the product aims at crafting the decision to buy. The negative account also vividly shows how the seller's description is selectively used to isolate one particular relevant item as personally disliked by the customer.

In contrast to responding with a densely descriptive name-like unit, like in Excerpt 3.6, a brief and opaque name given in response to a question is expanded in Excerpt 3.7 into a description of the ingredients.

Excerpt 3.7 (Finnish, BAK_FIN_ESP_210415_2.20.15_CLI72.1/2)

```
01 CUS:    *mmmm,
           *looks at left shelf-->
02         (1.2)*(0.4)
   cus       -->*looks at right shelf-->
03 CUS:    mites•   tuol*la      yl*häällä+ on
           how.CLI  DEM2.LOC.ADE up         is.3SG
           how about up there
                   -->*..........*looks at left shelf---->
                   •...........................................->
   sel                                  +looks at point-->
04         mitäs    +säm•py[löitä_
           what.CLI roll.PL.PAR
           what bread rolls
05 SEL:                    [siel on hilde-sämpylät se ov
                            there are the Hilde bread rolls it is
           -->+looks at shelf---->
   cus             -->•points at left shelf-->
06         vehnäpo*hjane mut siin on si•tä, (0.4) •hirssiä
           wheat based but it has the              millet
   cus       -->*looks at SEL-->
   cus                                 ->•,,,,,,,,,,,•hands folded-->>
```

```
07  SEL:      ma+issia*  soijarouhetta  [pellavansie+mentä.
              corn       soy groats     flax seed
              ->+looks at CUS--------->
    cus              -->*looks at left shelf-->
08  CUS:                                [joo:.
                                         yes
09  SEL:      no nii. ↑no?
              so well  so
              (0.3)
10  CUS:   →  otetaan nyv vaikka_
              let's take say
11            (0.6)*
    cus              -->*looks at middle shelf-->>
12  CUS:   →  kaks semmos‡ta ja     ‡kaks tommost kaurasämpy[lää.
              two of that kind and   two of those oat bread rolls
    sel                             ‡turns head‡walks-->>
13  SEL:                                                   [joo.
                                                            yeah
```

At the onset of the sequence, the customer is scrutinizing the shelves (lines 1–2). She utters the question while gradually extending the pointing. The customer first identifies the product(s) only by location, using the locative expression *tuolla ylhäällä* 'up there' (line 3), and then expands the question to include the generic type 'bread rolls' (line 4). The seller first gives the product name (*hildesämpylät* 'Hilde bread rolls', line 5) that consists of the same common noun in combination with the proper name Hilde. This product name is not very informative, and in contrast to treating it as possibly recognizable (as in Excerpt 3.4, *maggiabrot*), the seller immediately expands her response to a detailed list of ingredients (lines 6–7), during which the customer retracts the pointing (line 6). Using the name while treating it as not allowing recognition makes visible the participants' different positions with regard to the product; sellers sometimes 'teach' the standard name to the customers (Moore 2008). The customer announces the decision to buy after a moment's contemplation (lines 10–12).

In the next case, a request is transformed into a question about the product.

Excerpt 3.8 (Finland Swedish, BAK_FIN_ESP_210415_2.00.28_CLI58)

```
01            (0.8)
    cus       >>looks at shelf-->
02  SEL:      ‡får det vara något an↑nat?
              would you like to have something else
              ‡........................-->
03  CUS:      ja‡ j#ag  skulle  ‡ha     et- et-‡+ et•t brö-
              yes 1SG   AUX      have ART  ART    ART  bre-
              yes I would like to have a- a- a brea-
                                               •.....-->
    sel       ->‡bag to counter‡,,,,,,,,,,,,,‡
    sel                                      -->+looks at shelf-->
    fig       #fig.3.3
```

Figure 3.3

```
04        vad är•     det där+ för   ett bröd+‡#
          what be.3SG DEM      PREP ART bread
          what is that         for a (type of) bread
   cus       -->•points at shelf----------------------->
   sel                -->+look at CUS---+looks at shelf-->
   sel                                  ‡......-->
   fig                                  #fig.3.4
```

Figure 3.4

```
05        det där som är      där# nere.•‡
          DEM   REL be.3SG   DEM  down
          that  that is there below
                                        ->•,,,,,->
   sel                                  ->‡pointing at shelf-->
   fig                           #fig.3.5
```

Figure 3.5

```
06 SEL:    det är* sån dän•‡ jäst‡br+öd.*
           it is one of those yeast bread
                                  -->+looks at CUS-->
                          -->‡,,,,,‡
    cus        -->*looks at SEL---------*looks at shelves-->>
    cus             -->•hand on counter-->>
07         (.)
08 CUS:    ja.
           yes
09         (0.5)‡+(0.3)
    sel        ‡................->
    sel        -->+looks at bags-->
10 CUS:    och,‡
           and
    sel    -->‡grabs a bag-->>
11 SEL:    de e med +lite råg och jästbröd+svetemjöl
           they are with a little rye and yeast bread wheat flour
                      -->+looks at shelf-------+looks at CUS-->
12 SEL:    och +[( ) lite rypsolja.+
           and ( )    a little rapeseed oil
                -->+looks down---------+looks at CUS-->>
13 CUS:         [ja
                 yes
```

Here, the request for information occurs in the second purchase in the encounter. As the seller is packing the previous purchase and inquiring about further requests (lines 1–3, Figure 3.3), the customer is already gazing at a shelf on the back wall. As a response to the seller's inquiry (line 2), the customer begins a request, which is cut off and converted into a WH question (lines 3–5). Before the request is transformed into an inquiry, the customer starts to point, indicating the location of the product gesturally and verbally, with the demonstrative (*det där*) and a relative clause 'that is there below' (lines 4–5, Figures 3.4 and 3.5). At this point, the seller has already started moving toward the product and pointing at it. The customer withdraws her gesture as a shared focus is established.

The question *vad är det där för ett bröd* 'what is that for a (type of) bread' (line 4) refers very generically to the overall class of products ('bread') (cf. Excerpt 3.4, line 2). The seller's initial answer (line 6), mentioning the type of bread (*sån dän jästbröd* 'one of those yeast bread') provides some description of the product, which is nevertheless treated as insufficient. It is followed by a slightly delayed uptake from the customer and a longer silence (lines 8–9). During the pause, the seller grabs a new paper bag, so as to prepare for giving the product, anticipating a positive decision (see Lindström & Fox, this volume). However, as in Excerpt 3.4, the seller treats the customer's simple uptake as insufficient for closing the sequence and instead as inviting further information; consequently, she expands her response in a list of ingredients. Later on, after this exchange, the customer will reject the product to look for another one more similar to her favorite bread that was not available that day. Thus, retrospectively, the information received constitutes the basis for declining to buy.

The excerpts in this section show that customers draw on a number of resources available to them to identify products: they use generic nouns, and they describe the products by their outward appearance and by their location, pointing at them during their question and often until the completion of the sequence. The customers' WH questions formally project an answer with a noun. In responding, the sellers may first provide a name, which can be either transparently built on a particular ingredient (*rouheleipä* 'groat bread' in Excerpt 3.5) or an opaque product name based on, for example, a proper name ('Hilde roll' in Excerpt 3.7). Transparent and opaque names legitimize the formatting of the answer and its possible expansions in quite different turn and sequence trajectories, in which the sufficiency and relevance of the names is implicitly negotiated. The seller can treat names as opaque, and thereby as insufficiently identifying the product, by immediately expanding them into more detailed descriptions of the ingredients, even though the customers' plain questions have not specifically requested information on the ingredients. After giving only a name as an answer, sellers often orient to a third position in the sequence as a slot for the customer to announce their decision to buy; if this is not done, the sellers engage in providing more detailed information about the product, typically ingredients. This shows that both parties orient to the informativeness of the answer in terms of what basis it provides for making the decision and as making a decision relevant.

The progressive expansion of the turns constituting these sequences shows the emergent character of establishing what the product is. The customer might begin with a request but convert it into a question when they face the problem of not knowing what the product is actually made of. The seller might respond in a minimal way, but immediately expand the response, offering more information for the decision to be taken.

3.4.3 Polar Questions about the Type of Product

In the previous cases, the customer produced a WH question that described the product by its visible features, sometimes using the generic name of the product ('bread'), and thus displayed few assumptions or only little knowledge about the product (minimally distinguishing it, for example, from 'pastry' or 'pie'). By comparison, and as shown in this section, when the customer makes a polar question concerning the product – even its generic type – they claim more specialized knowledge about the item. These questions involve common nouns or product names, demonstratives, and, to a lesser extent, other descriptive elements. They are mostly formatted as interrogative, but as they already express the type or characteristic of the product, they include candidate answers and work to invite confirmation of these assumed features, thereby displaying a positive epistemic stance (Heritage 2012; Pomerantz 1988).

A first instance of polar questions was seen in Excerpt 3.2, in which a vegetable pie was inspected for the presence of peppers. In Excerpt 3.9, the customer asks about bread rolls.

Excerpt 3.9 (Finnish, BAK_FIN_ESP_210415_2.19.02_CLI72.1_CLI72.2)

```
01 CU1:     onks           noi_• (0.3) sä•#mpylä•t ni  se•mmosia:_
            be.3SG.Q.CLI DEM2.PL       roll.PL    PRT DEM3.ADJ.PL.PAR
            are those                  rolls sort of:
            >>looks at shelf on left--------->
                                  •.........•points•,,,,,,,,•
    fig                                       #fig.3.6
02 CU1:     (1.1) * •mo#nivilja_•
                    multigrain
                    multigrain
                  -->*looks at SEL-->
                    •shakes hand•
    fig               #fig.3.7
```

Figure 3.6

Figure 3.7

```
03            (0.3)
04   SEL:     .h on joo. ‡mul on täs*sä *vehnä kaura ‡kurpitsansiämen.
              are yes   I have here  wheat oat  pumpkinseed
                           ‡.........................‡touches roll-->
     cu1                      -->*...*gaze follows SEL hand-->
05            (0.2)‡
     sel      -->‡,,,,>
06   SEL:     *tai ‡sitte vähän* tummempi‡ vehnä ruis*
              or  then a bit darker      wheat rye
              ,,->‡....................‡grabs roll-->
     cu1      *...............*looks at SEL hand----*at left shelf->
07            [pellava ja   [auringonkukansiämen.
               flax and      pumpkinseed
((repair sequence omitted))
16   SEL:     tässä olis +semmost *tummarouheis+*ta.
              here there's sort of with dark groat
                          -->+looks at CU1---------+looks at CU2-->
     cu1                         -->*looks SEL hand*looks at shelf-->>
17   CU2:     mm[m.:+ joo. .hjoo.
              mmm    yeah .hyeah
18   CU1:       [joo ne oli hyviä.
                 yeah they were good
     sel      -->+looks at CU2-->
19   CU2:  → ote+‡taa erilaisia sämpylöitä niit
              let's take different kinds of rolls so they ((continues))
     sel      -->+looks at rolls-->>
     sel      -->‡...............-->>
```

Here, customer 1 requests confirmation for the recognition of the object as multigrain bread rolls (lines 1–2), only quickly pointing at the shelf while removing his gloves and opening his jacket (Figures 3.6 and 3.7). He treats the type of bread, *sämpylät* 'rolls', as known, inquiring about its ingredient-based subclass by using the compound noun *monivilja* 'multigrain'. However, instead of achieving confirmation of whether 'those' indicated bread rolls are, in fact, multigrain (which they are not), the question ends up designating the wrong object, as it draws the seller's attention to the rolls that actually are multigrain. That is, the inquired feature 'multigrain' comes to work as an erroneous identifier of the object, and as inviting a specification: after first confirming with *joo*, the seller lists the multiple grains and seeds (lines 4–7). Moreover, the response shows that the seller has understood the question as concerning two distinct products.

During the omitted repair sequence, the customer multimodally locates the right object, a third type of bread roll, which the seller reveals to be simple wheat rolls. She then introduces a fourth option (line 16). Here she gives an adjectival description of the bread as made of dark groats. 'Groats' means coarse flour, not a mix of grains. However, customer 1 displays recognition of the product as familiar, one that he has already tasted, and assesses it positively (line 18). The excerpt shows that the asked-about property ('multigrain') indicates general desirability (of something close to it) instead of concerning only the asked-about item. When the initial item does not match this property, the pair of customers abandon the search for a single bread and decide to buy the dark groats as well as a selection of bread rolls – anything but the wheat rolls.

Even with polar questions, both sellers and customers orient to the relevance of not simply confirming the type of product but to detailing what the product is made of. The type of product mentioned in the question may initially characterize the product as familiar and (un)desirable, but the discovery of further details is treated as determining the decision to buy.

Within the set of questions formatted as inquiries about the type of product, we see a cline from plain questions of what something is to questions that characterize the product in terms of simple visual aspects, used to identify the indicated object, and finally to naming characteristics that are indicative of specific edible features. In the two former sets of questions (Sections 3.4.1–3.4.2), the decision to buy is displayed as dependent, in an ad hoc manner, on the newly acquired information about the product, which may reveal its potential (non)desirable properties. In the last set (Section 3.4.3), some assumptions are manifested already in the naming of the option to be confirmed, allowing the seller to orient to them in responding. Moreover, the available ways of referring to the product vary in their transparency with regard to its characteristics, leading to different sequential trajectories, such as the seller's immediate unpacking of a name or a confirmation versus the projection of the customer's decision.

Customers' Inquiries about Products 93

3.5 Inquiring about Specific Edible Properties of the Product

Instead of a inquiring about the generic type of the product (Section 3.4), customers may ask directly about the ingredients (filling, topping, etc.). This can be done, again, either with plain or more descriptive WH questions (Sections 3.5.1–3.5.2), or with polar questions (Section 3.5.3). While the former questions often index the discovery of a new product, the latter convey a more knowledgeable inspection of specific (non)desirable features of the product. In turn, they reveal how customers appreciate the specialties of the shop and voice their own personal taste.

3.5.1 WH Questions about Ingredients

By asking what there is in the product, the customer poses a question about ingredients in the most generic way. In their plainness, these questions are similar to the questions in Section 3.4.1, but they have a more detailed scope of inquiry in asking what is 'in' a product. The questions contain demonstrative and other pronominal elements.

In the following excerpt from a Finnish bakery, customers use English as a lingua franca and display their lack of knowledge about many of the products on display.

Excerpt 3.10 (English, BAK_FIN_HEL 210415_0.44.53-CLI15.1&CLI15.2/SEL1)

```
01 CU2:    •what's •in these +ones? +
           •........•points------>
   sel                          +at CU2+..->
02         (0.1)+(0.3)
   sel           ->+looks at products-->
03 SEL:    eh:::: øit's #uhø app+le.
                              --->+at CU2->
   cul             øpoints--ø
   fig                      #fig.3.8A/3.8B
```

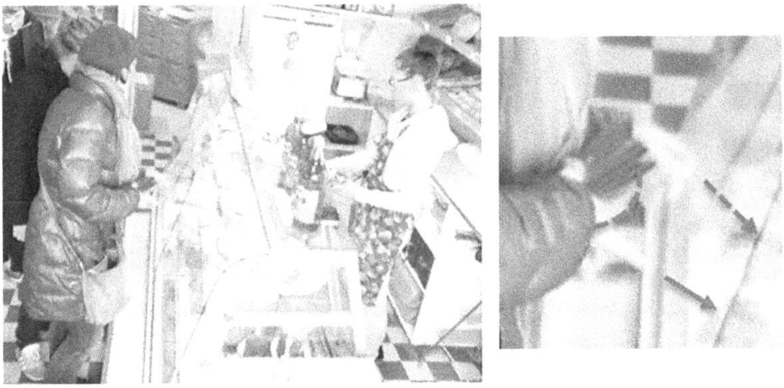

Figure 3.8

```
04         (0.2) •* (0.5)*
   cu2          *nods--*
   cu2          ->•,,,,,,--->
05 CU1:    [ah
06 SEL:    [•an:d#
   cu2    ->•points->
   fig            #fig.3.9A/3.9B
```

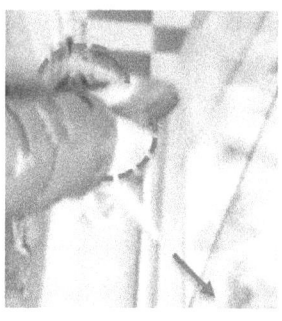

Figure 3.9

```
07         (0.4)+•(0.8)ø(0.2)
   sel         -->+bends down to look at products-->
   cu2         -->•
   cu1                  øpoints->
08 CU1:    here also #hein?
                     French PRT
   fig             #fig.3.10A/3.10B
```

Figure 3.10

```
09  SEL:      it's-   +yeah.ø
                    -->+at CU1->>
    cu1                 -->ø
```

While the seller packs customer 1's previous order in a bag, customer 2 poses a question, pointing at items and asking about the ingredients (line 1). The seller hesitates in responding, and customer 1 comes in to repair the identification of the object by also pointing at it (Figure 3.8; dotted lines for CU1). However, the problem of immediate identification appears rather to relate to producing the name in English. The seller responds with the name of a fruit (line 3).

The demonstrative and pronominal *these ones*, in plural form, draws the attention of the participants to two items: the seller continues with *and* (line 6), and customer 2 only partially withdraws her pointing before moving her hand to the next item (lines 4–5). Now the seller bends down to see the indicated pastries better, orienting to a problem of visible identification of the item asked about. Customer 1 again joins the pointing to facilitate the identification (lines 6–9, Figures 3.9 and 3.10). She asks *here also hein* (using a French tag), thereby tying the question to the earlier one.

In this lingua franca interaction, there are two instances (lines 6, 8) of a problem in identifying the object that is dealt with by collaborative pointings without using any specific names or descriptions. In answering, the seller names a recognizable ingredient, but does not mention the local language-specific product categories (in this case, they would be *possumunkki* 'piggy bun' and *minipossu* 'mini piggy'). Indeed, the names of the products are not treated as jointly accessible or recognizable by the seller or the foreign customers. In this case, the ingredient *apple* is treated as sufficient information.

3.5.2 WH Questions with Identifying and Descriptive Elements

In addition to deictic expressions, more elaborate identifying elements are used in generic questions (cf. Section 3.4.2), such as mentioning the color of the product. An emergent description based on color can work to secure the visible identification of the product, but it can also do more by implying its edible composition.

A case in point is the following, which is also from a lingua franca exchange with foreign customers, this time in Basel.

Excerpt 3.11 (English LF, BAK_CH_BS_260515_02.46.39_CLI100)

```
01 CUS:     hallo
02          (0.4)
03 SEL:     hallo
04          *(37.0)                 *    (3.0)     *
   cus      *inspects the showcase*looks at SEL*at item->
05 CUS:     •what is in• this one? this: *yellow one?
            •..........•points->
                                        ->*at SEL-->>
06          (0.7)
07 SEL:     äh:m it's ä:::• (0.7) lemon (1.2) [lemon] taste=
08 CUS:                                        [okay ]
                     -->•
09 CUS:  → =i'm gonna have one like this and a cappuccino ple[ase]
10 SEL:                                                     [ye ]s
```

After careful inspection of the content of the showcase (line 4), the customer asks a WH question (line 5) concerning the ingredient(s). She further specifies the demonstrative and pronominal expression (*this one*) by rephrasing it, adding the color of the product. The description is built on a visible quality – the yellow color – which hints at an ingredient of the same color. Indeed, the seller answers by mentioning *lemon* (line 7), and the customer buys the product. This case shows how the customer's orientation to a visible feature, color, promptly establishes the relevance of a constitutive ingredient.

The fact that in both cases the customers are not residents in the country where the shop is located shows the particularity of plain WH questions about ingredients, which occur in specific cases of not knowing. What is particular about them is that they show no naming of the kind of product as the basis for asking about more detailed properties. In the data, this is rare in comparison to using some way of naming the product when inquiring about its detailed characteristics. However, the two alternatives share the feature that the type of product is not oriented to as informative of the inquired properties.

3.5.3 Polar Questions about Ingredients

In comparison to asking about overall ingredients, customers' questions formatted as polar questions specifically address some characteristics of the product. Thereby they also display more knowledge or guesses about the product by the customer. These polar questions contain a reference to the product with a demonstrative only, or with a noun phrase containing a demonstrative determiner and a common or proper noun as the head. These elements variously work toward the identification of the objects and structuring the turns.

A case in point is provided in the next excerpt.

Excerpt 3.12 (French, BAK_F_STL_100415_ap29.38_CLI17_V)

```
01            (1.4)
02 CUS:    pis •j'vais• prendre eh une:  c'est aux amandes ça?
           then I will take eh a:        that's with almonds this
              •......•points----->
03         [là? ou::
            there? or::
04 SEL:    [oui c'est ça•
            yes that's it
                      ->•,,,,->
05 CUS: →  -fin• j'en prends un croissant aux amandes là
           well  I take      a croissant with almonds there
              ->•
```

The customer initiates a request. However, at the point where the name of the product is projected by the determiner (*une* 'a', line 2), he suspends the request and instead restarts with a question. The latter is a declaratively formatted polar question mentioning a candidate ingredient, ending with a demonstrative (*ça?* 'this?', line 2), continued at line 3 by a locative (*là?* 'there?'), and a conjunction (*ou::* 'or::') opening up for possible alternative description. The answer is immediate and merely confirms the assumption. The customer withdraws the pointing at the sequence completion and decides to buy the product: at this point, he integrates the ingredient in the turn naming the product (line 5), retrospectively displaying its relevance for the choice made.

In the next excerpt, the type and main ingredient of a product are known and mentioned, but the issue is to find out whether it contains a specific substance, lactose, which the customer treats as having to be avoided.

Excerpt 3.13 (Finnish, BAK_FIN_HEL 210415_1.40.45–CLI301 & CLI30.2/ SEL1)

```
01 CU1:    øtuo ov varmaa raikas tøuo  [•juustoøpiirasø
           that must be fresh    that   cheese pie
02 CU2:                               [ni tuo mä<
                                       yes that I
03 SEL:                               [( )
    cu1    ø.....................øpoints-----ø,,,,,,ø
    cu2                              •.........--->
04 CU2:    nii juusto< onks       se (.)•onks       se (.) tuota
           PRT cheese  be.3SG.Q.CLI DEM3  be.3SG.Q.CLI DEM3  PRT
           right cheese is it                is it           uhm
                                  --->•points------->
05         noi ni +laktoositon tai +vähälaktoosine ‡toi [piiras
           PRT PRT lactose.free or low.lactose        DEM2 pie
           like    lactose free or low lactose        that pie
06 SEL:                                               [öö (0.2)
                                                       uhm
             +at CU2----------+at prod, slightly bent down->
                                           ‡....->
07         niin tää +‡juustopi[iras;+
           (you mean) this cheese pie
```

```
08 CU2:                      [n•ii.
                              yes
                             -->•,,,-->
   sel         -->+at CU2---------+
   sel         -->‡points-->
09             (0.4)• ‡(0.4)‡
   cu2         -->•
   sel         -->‡,,,,,‡
10 SEL:    ↑mun tietääkseni [on
           as far as I know yes
11 CU2:                     [(hyvän näkönen)
                             good looking
12 SEL:    eiks se Eki< onks se (.) (  ) juustopiiras
           isn't it Eki, is it     (  ) cheese pie
           ((goes to the back room))
```

Customer 1 has asked the seller to recommend something for her and customer 2, and they are now discussing what could be a 'refreshing' (a term used by the seller earlier) choice instead of something sweet. In the assessment at line 1, customer 1 introduces the cheese pie as an option. Customer 2 joins in pointing at the pie to check whether it is lactose free/low lactose before deciding (lines 3–5). She ties her question to customer 1's turn with the resumptive particle *nii* (Vilkuna 1997) followed by *juusto* 'cheese' (line 4); the unfolding turn involves two subsequent co-indexical mentions, *se* (DEM3) and the right-dislocated 'that pie'. However, customer 2 never uses the name of the pie as one unit. The seller makes an understanding check, also pointing at the product and now, in the sequence expanding turn, using the full name (*niin tää juustopiiras* '(you mean) this cheese pie', line 7). Customer 2 withdraws the pointing only toward the end of the seller's turn, while confirming with *nii* 'yes' in overlap.

For the customer, there is no problem in recognizing the product as 'pie' or the ingredient as 'cheese'. The issue here is whether the pie contains lactose; it is likely raised by having cheese as the ingredient, and made relevant for determining whether the product is suitable for the customer. Lactose is a component that is not apparent from visual inspection: this is also evidenced by the seller's epistemic self-restriction ('as far as I know', line 10) and by her forwarding the question to a colleague. After receiving the information, the customers buy a slice of the pie (not shown in transcript). The excerpt shows how customers use polar questions about specific features to navigate within their own personal taste and constraints, which are not addressed by standard names.

In the instances examined so far, we have seen how one product is identified as an object with particular characteristics, relevant here and now, and thus singularized among a set of available products as the one to buy or not.

Customers' Inquiries about Products   99

Identifying single objects at the bakery always concerns distinctions among a variety of products on some level.

In the final excerpt, the customer makes these differentiations explicit by comparing a product to another, more desirable one. Moreover, it shows the interplay between defining what something is in terms of a type of product and its particular features, which the customer may adjust while searching for a suitable product.

Excerpt 3.14 (Finnish, BAK_FIN_HEL 210415_0.38.56–CLI12/SEL1)

```
01 CUS:     (voisin ottaa) jotaki sellasta (pikkusen)
            I could take something like a little bit
02          (1.1)‡
   sel         -->‡organizes boxes on top of showcase-->
03 CUS:     vieraallek:i    ku (.) tulee     iltapäivällä    mutta (ku)
            guest.ALL.CLI   PRT    come.3SG  afternoon.ADE   but       PRT
            for a guest also who comes in the afternoon but since
04          tota (1.6) ei    oo       ihan    sämpylää            mut•ta
            PRT        NEG   be.3SG   quite   bread.roll.PAR      but
            uhm              there isn't actual bread roll but
                                                                  •...-->
05          onks            tuom+mo•ne#  ‡rou+he ni
            be.3SG.Q.CLI    DEM2.ADJ     groat   PRT
            is that kind of groat
                                    -->•points-->
   sel                              +gaze at CUS+at breads-->>
                                       -->‡walks twd shelf->
   fig                              #fig.3.11
```

Figure 3.11

```
06          se   o     •v:ähä  vastaava•        vissiinki  ‡(ku  se).
            DEM3 be.3SG somewhat corresponding  presumably PRT   DEM3
            it is presumably somewhat corresponding to it
   cus         -->•,,,,,,,,,,,,,,,,,•
   sel                                                     -->‡stands->
```

```
07            +(0.8)                    +
   sel     +inspects product+steps back->
08 SEL:    joo-o [tai sitte+
           yes   or then
                              -->+
09 CUS:           [(vois leikata)
                   could cut
10         ‡(1.0)                                    ‡
   sel     ‡turns around, walks to other shelf‡
11 SEL:    on tääl on tämmösiä;
           there are these kind of
((7 lines omitted))
19 CUS:  → ↑joo. (.) (no) ↑mää voin ottaa sitte
           yes           well I can then take
20         niit sämpylöitä kaks.
           two of those bread rolls
```

The customer scrutinizes the shelves for quite some time. After she hesitantly begins her request (line 1), the seller engages in organizing some boxes on top of the showcase, thereby displaying an interpretation that the inspection of products will take some time. This is indicative of a serendipitous choice as opposed to a planned choice (as in Excerpt 3.11). However, the utterance announcing the absence of bread rolls (line 4) indicates that the customer has searched for a particular, desired product. When she begins the question (line 5), the seller quickly reorganizes her position so that she is now available to serve the customer, who is already pointing at the shelf (Figure 3.11).

The customer requests confirmation (line 6), with a declarative clause, for whether the 'groat' bread corresponds to the unavailable product. In an earlier case (Excerpt 3.5), the name *rouheleipä* 'groat bread' was given as a response to a customer's question and treated as sufficient information for the decision to buy. Here, the customer herself uses that characterization (*rouhe*) as a shorthand for the whole product. Using this label demonstrates some recognition, but at the same time shows that this knowledge about the product is not yet enough to facilitate the decision to buy.

In the question about the product, the customer does not explicate the form of bread that the 'groat' represents, and this is in line with how she continues. She supposes a certain flexibility regarding objects more or less similar to the desired product: the object is 'somewhat corresponding' (line 6) and even possible to 'cut' (slice) to be consumed like the rolls (line 9). After inspecting the products for a while, the seller confirms (line 8), but in the same turn tells that there are, in fact, some bread rolls available. In the end, the customer buys the rolls (lines 19–20).

The final excerpt demonstrates more explicitly the general point that not only are the characteristics of the objects asked about at the bakery mutable

Customers' Inquiries about Products   101

and negotiable, but the way in which they are seen is influenced by the set of other available, possible, and/or sought for products. Individual objects are thus not treated merely as pre-established entities ready to be picked up, but as possible buyable products inspected and assessed through their potential and relevance for the particular consumer, locally inquired and explored through their questions. The customer is the one less knowledgeable about the products but, at the same time, the one who controls the search for what is suitable to buy.

3.6   Conclusions

Confronted with a wide choice of products and subtypes of products, customers often do not request something right away, but engage in preliminary inquiries about the objects exposed in the shop. Asking questions serves to inform the decision of whether or not to buy certain products. This chapter has offered a discussion of the methods customers use in choosing a suitable product and the reasoning for their choice in diverse bakeries and languages. The analysis contributes to the study of questions and answers in institutional settings, to reference in interaction, and, more generally, to situated lay semantics.

The ways of asking questions highlight the relevant features of a product for the customer. In their different formats and scopes, they make it relevant for the seller to produce or confirm the lacking piece of information with an orientation to features that emerge as defining for the customer's final choice. The analysis has explored the mapping of question formats with the generic versus specific overall scope of the questions, as well as the linguistic, gestural, and spatial resources used to identify and characterize the objects in the questions.

The questions deal with two different, though intertwined, issues for the customers: on the one hand, they concern the identification of the type of product; on the other hand, they deal with the more detailed characterization of the product tailored for the customer. The main tendencies in this process are summarized below.

Firstly, in the questions with the generic type of the product as their scope, the customers either display no particular knowledge about the product, making a plain WH question (Section 3.4.1), or they display knowledge of the generic class (e.g., bread, bread roll, flan) or access to some visibly available properties (Section 3.4.2). The latter questions make it relevant for the seller to name the subclass that the particular item belongs to, which in the case of bakery products is typically based on ingredients (e.g., grain, filling). Achieving a sufficient answer to 'what' questions depends on the transparency of the name given. A name that is transparent enough to the customer allows them to immediately announce their decision to buy or not. However, names can be treated as opaque and necessitating further unpacking in terms of listing product ingredients. The seller can do this immediately after giving the name or as a response to a lack of indication of the customer's decision after an initial answer. Thus, names are overwhelmingly oriented to whether they reveal ingredients of the product. Even in the polar questions, in which the customer names the product and invites its confirmation ('is this x bread/ x pie?') (Section 3.4.3), the questions do not seem to concern recognition of the type as such. Instead, they again concern the subclass in terms of ingredients: the types to be confirmed include an ingredient (multigrain [bread roll], vegetable [pie]), and the pointed-at properties are treated as decisive for buying the product. All the questions in Section 3.4 thus show the customers' orientation to establishing the generic type of the product as a basis for discovering further locally relevant properties, while the format of the question (from plain WH questions to ones with more identifying elements, and to polar questions) shows a cline toward more straightforwardly targeting the assumed and locally relevant features of the product.

Secondly, in the set of specific questions (i.e., questions about particular edible properties, Section 3.5), the generic type of the product is not made relevant, and different motives for this come up in the section. As for the plain WH questions about ingredients, the customers are foreigners who orient to recognizable and desirable ingredients (Section 3.5.1) or features of ingredients (Section 3.5.2). In this case, a generic typification (or naming) of the product is not attempted by the customers, nor provided by the sellers. Thus, in these questions, both the type and specific properties of the products are treated as unknown. In contrast, in the polar questions concerning specific properties (Section 3.5.3), the speakers treat the recognition of the type as already established and unproblematic, and instead focus on the discovery of further, specific properties as critical for the decision to buy.

Regarding the sellers' responses, the analysis demonstrates that the relevance of certain types of answers is activity-specific and relates to design features beyond what is structurally projected by the question. Whether a minimal response by the seller – providing only a name for the product (to WH questions) or a polarity item (to polar questions) – is treated as sufficient depends on whether the reference forms used are enough to describe the relevant properties (e.g., ingredients) of the product to the customer. If not, they get expanded.

As shown, both formats (WH and polar) are used in all scopes of questions, the generic type, and specific properties of the products. Yet the formats and the referential practices used in them establish differently what the customers already know or recognize about the product and how they approach the unknown/uncertain aspects that come to be critical for the decision to buy. The generic WH questions deal with the establishment of a novel object and common focus of attention and do not disclose much about the customer's criteria for choice: when these questions involve a description, the descriptions concern visible features of the product ('longish breads', 'the one in the middle'), but not their significance or desirability. Thus, WH questions tend to be used for generic reference and identification, whereas polar questions treat the shared focus of attention as established (they also do not involve much use of description) and deal mainly with more specific characterizations. Although there are also polar questions about the generic type (see Section 3.4.3) and plain WH questions about ingredients (see Section 3.5.1), these appear less typical. Moreover, the generic polar questions were shown rather to invoke the relevance of desirable ingredients, and WH questions about ingredients occurred in cases where the speakers had limited overall access to the typology of the products.

The multimodal establishment of the reference is a practical task that all questions have to achieve in order to be adequately responded to, and this is what pointing serves to do. Pointing co-occurs with requests as well as with questions, and the pointing gestures can be expanded or held in a continuous way (without discontinuities or hitches) while a turn at talk is emergently transformed from a request into a question. The fact that pointing can be maintained until turn completion (also through transformation of the action), the establishment of shared reference, or sequence closing shows that it does more than locate a referent. It also secures the maintenance of intersubjectivity and a sense of responsibility, ownership, and authority over the sequence (Mondada 2007).

Visual descriptions accompanying pointing are sometimes used as reparatory devices for unsuccessful identification, but not necessarily so. As part of establishing a joint focus of attention, they spell out the spatial organization of the products in the bakery. Participants make sense of spatiality in terms of both semantic aspects and interactional space. For the former, the location of an item generates inferences about the types of products and their properties, given that products are spatially distributed according to their typology. For the latter, the location of the products can also be referred to relative to the positions of the interlocutors: the products are located next to, in front of, behind, close to, or further away from each other and from the participants. Moreover, visible features are helpful for both locating the product and evoking substantial features (such as the yellow color for lemon as an ingredient). In this case, too, the issue is not the mere formal identification of the object, but the identification of some of its features made locally relevant.

Through these analyses, the chapter has explored the possibility of conducting interactional semantic analysis through an examination of 'possible alternatives' (see Deppermann 2011) in the way of verbally identifying and specifying the bodily oriented-to, material objects in the customers' questions. The way of formulating the objects is situated, emergent, and contingent on the local activities. It reflects the participants' levels of knowledge about the products and their orientation to each other's relative knowledge. It also reveals their personal sets of relevancies and priorities, making specific and sometimes unique properties locally relevant within the local action. In this sense, more subjective aspects come to be articulated in relation to standard, conventional, shared ones. This situated interactional work of the participants shows how definitional and discriminatory features of an object or a (sub)class of objects can be practically negotiated by and with members for all practical purposes (Sacks 1989: 249).

The excerpts studied also reveal ambiguities between ways of referring to a product with ad hoc descriptions versus standard names. The same lexeme (e.g., 'groats') can be used as a shorthand for the whole product or to inform the interlocutor about some specific property of the product, according to the ongoing action and the level of detail at which the product is talked about. Interpreting the meaning of these items in their immediate context is thus an ongoing interactional task for the participants.

In this context, product names are used by sellers and customers as sources of information. The way names are used reveals an endogenous orientation toward the distinction between common versus proper noun, transparent versus opaque form. The participants orient to ingredients involved in the names (as in *Feigenbrot* or *rouheleipä*) as providing some transparency to the naming, making them sufficient and adequate to inform the customer's decision. In contrast, answers mentioning opaque names ('Hilde bread') can be immediately expanded by the seller. In this sense, turn and sequence organization (e.g., simple versus expanded answer) conveys the members' perspective on these semantic distinctions. Giving the name of the product in response to the customer's question or as part of an understanding check ('Maggia bread do you mean?') can also convey a professional stance, the viewpoint of the institution, an orientation to a standard, and to a label or a signature product. Names are thus more than ways of referring. They are more or less informative of the properties of the products, they feature in branding and in achieving the singularity of a product, and the difference in sellers' and customers' access to them marks their epistemic and social positions in the institutional encounter.

Thus, the 'what is x?' and 'is this x?' questions studied are formatted within complex multimodal Gestalts that achieve not only recognition of a referent but a variety of other interactional tasks. The more specific the questions, the more they reveal the identity, taste, preferences, and intolerances of the customer. These features do not just concern knowledge in general, but personal choices, showing that questions invite customization of the product and personalization of the service.

Acknowledgments

This chapter has been written within the FiDiPro project *Multimodality: Reconsidering language and action through embodiment*, in which Lorenza Mondada (P.I.), Katariina Harjunpää (postdoc), and Kimmo Svinhufvud (postdoc) worked together, hosted at the Centre for Excellence in Intersubjectivity of Helsinki from 2015 to 2017, thanks to the generous funding of the Academy of Finland and the University of Helsinki (project no 282931).

References

Ainiala, T., & Saarelma, M. (2012). *Names in Focus: An Introduction to Finnish Onomastics*. Helsinki: The Finnish Literature Society. https://doi.org/10.21435/sflin.17

Bilmes, J. (2015). *The Structure of Meaning in Talk: Explorations in Category Analysis, Volume 1: Co-categorization, Contrast, and Hierarchy*. Manoa: University of Hawaii. www2.hawaii.edu/~bilmes/. Accessed March 28, 2019.

Curl, T. S., & Drew, P. (2008). Contingency and action: A comparison of two forms of requesting. *Research on Language and Social Interaction*, 41(2), 129–153. https://doi.org/10.1080/08351810802028613

Deppermann, A. (2011). The study of formulations as a key to an interactional semantics. *Human Studies*, 34(2), 115–128. https://doi.org/10.1007/s10746-011-9187-8

(2019). Interaktionale Semantik [Interactional semantics]. In J. Hagemann & S. Staffeldt, eds., *Semantiktheorien. Band 2*. Tübingen: Stauffenburg, pp. 172–215.

de Ruiter, J. P., ed. (2012). *Questions: Formal, Functional and Interactional Perspectives*. Cambridge: Cambridge University Press. https://doi.org/10.1017/CBO9781139045414

De Stefani, E. (2011). *"Ah petta ecco, io prendo questi che mi piacciono". Agire come coppia al supermercato. Un approccio conversazionale e multimodale allo studio dei processi decisionali* ["Oh wait here, I'm getting these, cos I like them." *Acting as a couple at the supermarket. A conversational and multimodal approach to the analysis of decision-making*]. Rome: Aracne.

(2014). Establishing joint orientation towards commercial objects in a self-service store: How practices of categorisation matter. In M. Nevile, P. Haddington, T. Heinemann, & M. Rauniomaa, eds., *Interacting with Objects: Language, Materiality, and Social Activity*. Amsterdam: John Benjamins, pp. 271–294. https://doi.org/10.1075/z.186.12ste

Enfield, N. J., & Stivers, T., eds. (2007). *Person Reference in Interaction: Linguistic, Cultural and Social Perspectives*. Cambridge: Cambridge University Press. https://doi.org/10.1017/CBO9780511486746

Eriksson, M. (2009). Referring as interaction: On the interplay between linguistic and bodily practices. *Journal of Pragmatics*, 41(2), 240–262. https://doi.org/10.1016/j.pragma.2008.10.011

Etelämäki, M. (2009). The Finnish demonstrative pronouns in light of interaction. *Journal of Pragmatics*, 41(1), 25–46. https://doi.org/10.1016/j.pragma.2008.09.005

Fox, B., & Heinemann, T. (2015). The alignment of manual and verbal displays in requests for the repair of an object. *Research on Language and Social Interaction*, 48(3), 342–362. https://doi.org/10.1080/08351813.2015.1058608

(2016). Rethinking format: An examination of requests. *Language in Society*, 45(4), 499–531. https://doi.org/10.1017/S0047404516000385

Fox, B., & Thompson, S. A. (2010). Responses to wh-questions in English conversation. *Research on Language and Social Interaction*, 43(2), 133–156. https://doi.org/10.1080/08351811003751680

Garfinkel, H. (1991). Respecification: Evidence for locally produced, naturally accountable phenomena of order, logic, reason, meaning, method, etc. in and as of the essential haecceity of immortal ordinary society (I) – an announcement of studies. In G. Button, ed., *Ethnomethodology and the Human Sciences*. Cambridge: Cambridge University Press, pp. 10–19. https://doi.org/10.1017/CBO9780511611827.003

Goodwin, C. (2003). Pointing as situated practice. In S. Kita, ed., *Pointing: Where Language, Culture and Cognition Meet*. Mahwah: Lawrence Erlbaum, pp. 217–241. https://doi.org/10.4324/9781410607744

Hakulinen, A., & Selting, M., eds. (2005). *Syntax and Lexis in Conversation: Studies on the Use of Linguistic Resources in Talk-in-Interaction*. Amsterdam: John Benjamins. https://doi.org/10.1075/sidag.17

Harjunpää, K., Deppermann, A., & Sorjonen, M.-L. (2021). Constructing the Chekhovian inner body in instructions: An interactional history of factuality and agentivity. *Journal of Pragmatics* 171, 158–174. https://doi.org/10.1016/j.pragma.2020.09.034

Heinemann, T. (2006). 'Will you or can't you?' Displaying entitlement in interrogative requests. *Journal of Pragmatics*, 38(7), 1081–1104. https://doi.org/10.1016/j.pragma.2005.09.013

Heritage, J. (2012). Epistemics in action: Action formation and territories of knowledge. *Research on Language and Social Interaction*, 45(1), 1–29. https://doi.org/10.1080/08351813.2012.646684

Hindmarsh, J., & Heath, C. (2000). Embodied reference: A study of deixis in workplace interaction. *Journal of Pragmatics*, 32(12), 1855–1878. https://doi.org/10.1016/S0378-2166(99)00122-8

Kuroshima, S. (2010). Another look at the service encounter: Progressivity, intersubjectivity, and trust in a Japanese sushi restaurant. *Journal of Pragmatics*, 42(3), 856–869. https://doi.org/10.1016/j.pragma.2009.08.009

Lindström, A. (2005). Language as social action: A study of how senior citizens request assistance with practical tasks in the Swedish home help service. In A. Hakulinen

& M. Selting, eds., *Syntax and Lexis in Conversation: Studies on the Use of Linguistic Resources in Talk-in-Interaction*. Amsterdam: John Benjamins, pp. 209–230. https://doi.org/10.1075/sidag.17.11lin
Merritt, M. (1976). On questions following questions in service encounters. *Language in Society*, 5(3), 315–357. https://doi.org/10.1017/S0047404500007168
Mondada, L. (2007). Multimodal resources for turn-taking: Pointing and the emergence of possible next speakers. *Discourse Studies*, 9(2), 194–225. https://doi.org/10.1177/1461445607075346
   (2012). Deixis: An integrated interactional multimodal analysis. In P. Bergmann, J. Brenning, M. Pfeiffer, & E. Reber, eds., *Prosody and Embodiment in Interactional Grammar*. Berlin: De Gruyter, pp. 173–206. https://doi.org/10.1515/9783110295108
   (2014). Pointing, talk and the bodies: Reference and joint attention as embodied interactional achievements. In M. Seyfeddinipur & M. Gullberg, eds., *From Gesture in Conversation to Visible Utterance in Action*. Amsterdam: John Benjamins, pp. 95–124. https://doi.org/10.1075/z.188.06mon
   (2016). Challenges of multimodality: Language and the body in social interaction. *Journal of Sociolinguistics*, 20(3), 2–32. https://doi.org/10.1111/josl.1_12177
   (2019). Contemporary issues in conversation analysis: Embodiment and materiality, multimodality and multisensoriality in social interaction. *Journal of Pragmatics*, 145, 47–62. https://doi.org/10.1016/j.pragma.2019.01.016
   (2021). Sensing in Social Interaction. Cambridge: Cambridge University Press.
Mondada, L., & Sorjonen, M.-L. (2016). First and subsequent requests in French and Finnish kiosks. *Language in Society*, 45(5), 733–765. https://doi.org/10.1017/S0047404516000646
Moore, R. J. (2008). When names fail: Referential practice in face-to-face service encounters. *Language in Society*, 37(3), 385–413. https://doi.org/10.1017/S004740450808055X
Pomerantz, A. (1988). Offering a candidate answer: An information seeking strategy. *Communication Monographs*, 55(4), 360–373. https://doi.org/10.1080/03637758809376177
Raymond, G. (2000). *The Structure of Responding: Type-conforming and Nonconforming Responses to Yes/No Type Interrogatives*. Doctoral dissertation, University of California, Los Angeles.
   (2003). Grammar and social organization: Yes/no interrogatives and the structure of responding. *American Sociological Review*, 68(6), 939–967. https://doi.org/10.2307/1519752
Sacks, H. (1963). Sociological description. *Berkeley Journal of Sociology*, 8, 1–16.
   (1989). Lectures 1964–1965. Edited by G. Jefferson, Introduction/Memoir by E. A. Schegloff. *Human Studies*, 12(3–4), 1–408.
   (1992). *Lectures on Conversation, Vols 1 & 2*. Edited by G. Jefferson. Oxford: Basil Blackwell.
Sacks, H., & Schegloff, E. A. (1979). Two preferences in the organization of reference to persons in conversation and their interaction. In G. Psathas, ed., *Everyday Language: Studies in Ethnomethodology*. New York: Irvington, pp. 15–21. https://doi.org/10.1017/CBO9780511486746.003

Schegloff, E. A. (1972). Notes on a conversational practice: Formulating place. In D. Sudnow, ed., *Studies in Social Interaction*. New York: The Free Press, pp. 75–119.

(1996). Some practices for referring to persons in talk-in-interaction: A partial sketch of a systematics. In B. Fox, ed., *Studies in Anaphora*. Amsterdam: John Benjamins, pp. 437–485. https://doi.org/10.1075/tsl.33.14sch

Sorjonen, M.-L. (2001a). *Responding in Conversation: A Study of Response Particles in Finnish*. Amsterdam: John Benjamins. https://doi.org/10.1075/pbns.70

(2001b). Simple answers to polar questions: The case of Finnish. In M. Selting & E. Couper-Kuhlen, eds., *Studies in Interactional Linguistics*. Amsterdam: John Benjamins, pp. 405–431. https://doi.org/10.1075/sidag.10.18sor

Sorjonen, M.-L., & Raevaara, L. (2014). On the grammatical form of requests at the convenience store: Requesting as embodied action. In P. Drew & E. Couper-Kuhlen, eds., *Requesting in Social Interaction*. Amsterdam: John Benjamins, pp. 243–268. https://doi.org/10.1075/slsi.26.10sor

Stivers, T., Enfield N. J., & Levinson, S. C., eds. (2010). Question-response sequences in 10 languages. *Journal of Pragmatics*, 42(10), 2615–2860. https://doi.org/10.1016/j.pragma.2010.04.001

Svinhufvud, K. (2011). Varovasti edeten ja taas perääntyen: Opponentin palautevuoron rakentuminen [Gently forward, then back again: Constructing opponent feedback]. *Virittäjä*, 115(2), 156–192.

Thompson, S. A., Fox, B., & Couper-Kuhlen, E. (2015). *Grammar in Everyday Talk: Building Responsive Actions*. Cambridge: Cambridge University Press. https://doi.org/10.1017/CBO9781139381154

Vilkuna, M. (1997). Into and out of the standard language: The particle *ni* in Finnish. In J. Cheshire & D. Stein, eds., *Taming the Vernacular: From Dialect to Written Standard Language*. London: Longman, pp. 51–67.

ate # 4 Offering a Taste in Gourmet Food Shops
Small Gifts in an Economy of Sale

Lorenza Mondada

4.1 Introduction

Offering a taste is a common action in gourmet food shops and constitutes a typical commercial gesture. It represents a form of gift – the salesperson giving a complimentary object for free to the customer – although it is embedded in an economy of buying and selling. Both participants orient to this double nature of offering a taste. They do not primarily treat tasting as a form of culinary exploration, curiosity, and pleasure, or as a form of learning and socialization into food – although these aspects are not excluded. They orient to the gift as a delicate matter (Llewellyn 2011a), as something that, far from being 'free' (Douglas 2002), hints at a form of reciprocity (Mauss 1924/1967). Thus, they orient to the gift as part of the business encounter. The sequential environments in which these offers are proffered – which constitute the focus of this chapter – display these orientations and their consequentiality.

Providing a systematic analysis of the action of offering a taste, the chapter aims at contributing both to a better understanding of the *action of offering* and its situated and embodied contingencies, and of the *institutional shaping of offers* in specific settings, and more particularly to the economy of gifts in commercial encounters. Even if offers have been frequently mentioned in the literature, they are much less investigated than requests. Mostly studied in ordinary settings (Curl 2006; Schegloff 2007; Kärkkäinen & Keisanen 2012; Clayman & Heritage 2014; Couper-Kuhlen 2014; Kendrick & Drew 2014), offers in institutional settings have been generally neglected.

Offers of products in an economic encounter represent a perspicuous situated activity for understanding the institutional context in which offers emerge. I explore a variety of questions here, including: How do offers contribute to the ongoing activity? How do they shape the categories and rights and obligations of the participants? This concerns the issue of who is the beneficiary, what are participants entitled/expected to give/take, and how the 'felicific calculus' (Clayman & Heritage 2014) is achieved in an observable way. These dimensions all shape the trajectory of sequences of offers/acceptances or refusals.

Thus, this chapter contributes both to the study of offers in general and to the study of a type of offer constitutive of economic encounters. By focusing on offers in institutional settings, and more specifically offers to taste in gourmet food shops, I propose a systematic inquiry about the way they are tailored and embedded in the context of the ongoing commercial encounter.

4.2   Formats, Sequence Organization, and Context of Offers

In the conversation analytic literature, offers constitute an exemplary case of adjacency pair (Schegloff 2007: 14). They are often mentioned in studies of preference organization (Schegloff 2007: 59–60; Pomerantz & Heritage 2012): offers have been treated as preferred over requests (Schegloff 2007: 83–86). They also possibly anticipate and preempt requests, as shown by offers given as preferred responses to pre-requests. However, more recently, offers have been revisited as possibly being as delicate as requests, as engendering obligations – and even a sense of debt – and attributing and even imposing needs to Other (Kendrick & Drew 2014; Lindström & Fox, this volume). As a matter of fact, offers can sometimes be seen as not being 'genuine' (Clayman 2013: 298), and as disguising requests – as shown by possible transformations of one into the other (Couper-Kuhlen 2014). Offers are characterized by the fact that the participant making the offer is the agent of the offered action, and the participant accepting it is the benefactor (Couper-Kuhlen 2014). But these categories and relations are locally negotiated and established by the participants evaluating the balance between the service rendered, its overall cost, and the local definition of benefices (what Clayman & Heritage 2014 call the 'felicific calculus').

Several alternative formats of offers and their sequential distribution have been systematically described by Curl (2006) in English ordinary phone calls: speakers select a format for their offer depending on the sequential environment in which these offers are made. For instance, pre-planned offers initiating the conversation as reasons for calling, use the conditional form (*if X, Y*), whereas offers generated during the course of the interaction use the *Do you want* format to address a possible problem that has surfaced in the prior stretch of interaction, and the declarative format in contexts in which an explicit problem has just been mentioned. For Raymond et al. (2020), the variation between *do you want?/you want?/want?* in American English manifests the stance of the action's initiator. Beside verbal formats, offers can be made and accepted in embodied ways (Kärkkäinen & Keisanen 2012).

Offers in institutional settings remain under-studied. Offers of advice have been discussed (Jefferson & Lee 1981; Heritage & Sefi 1992; Kinnell & Maynard 1996; Hutchby 2006). In medical settings, Gill (2005) shows how patients may exert pressure in order to get doctors to offer the medication or service they would like, instead of requesting it. These institutional contexts and their actions differ quite importantly from the economic encounters studied in this chapter, at least because of very different definitions of the rights and obligations of the participants involved.

4.3 Focus and Data

This chapter studies offers addressed by salespersons to customers in gourmet shops. More specifically, the analysis focuses on offering a taste in cheese shops. Offering a taste is a common professional gesture in this kind of commercial interaction.

While requests in shop encounters have been thoroughly studied (Sorjonen & Raevaara 2014; Mondada & Sorjonen 2016; Fox & Heinemann 2015, 2016), offers have been neglected in this context (but see Raymond et al. 2020, who relativize the opposition between requests and offers on the basis of their syntactic format). Nonetheless, they are a pervasive action accomplished by sellers in shops, constituting one possible action corresponding with possible conceptions of the *service* encounter, in which is at stake is "the satisfaction of the customer's presumed desire for some service and the server's obligation to provide that service" (Merritt 1976: 321). This context also provides for an interesting contrastive case with respect to ordinary conversation: requests and offers in shops are category-bound actions that are locally interpreted relative to institutional rights and obligations, but also commercial interests as well as knowledge and expertise of the participants.

The present study is based on a larger corpus of shop encounters in cheese shops across Europe, the *int-counter corpus*, including hundreds of interactions in 12 European languages video-recorded in 15 cities, in 2015–2016, with the informed consent of all parties. For the analyses presented here, data in French, Spanish, German, Swiss German, Finnish, and English have been considered.

Offering a taste does not occur in all cheese shops; in some shops, especially the more traditional ones, they are rather rare; in others, especially fashionable shops, they can be very frequent. The peculiarity of these offers is constituted by the fact that they represent a complimentary free item that is given in a context in which buying and selling goods is the primary activity. They represent a gift in an economy of sales. As such, they present a possible paradox, and a source of inquiries about the real benefactors of the offer. Participants orient to this complexity: generally, they do not treat offering a taste as a pure gift or as an opportunity to satisfy their gastronomic curiosity and pleasure, but orient to offering a taste as providing an assistance and as basis for decision-making concerning their ongoing purchase. At the same time, offering a taste makes possible a particular social practice, tasting, that represents an original experiential and sensorial access to the product (Mondada 2018), and constitutes a unique basis for making choices and decisions (Mondada 2022).

The particular relevance of tasting shapes the sequential environments in which offering a taste is made and that condition either acceptance or refusal, as well as the formats in which these offers are packaged.

In this sense, offering a taste and their responses are a perspicuous phenomenon to investigate (a) the way in which offers might be tailored in specific contexts, depending on how the definitions of general benefices, commercial interests, rights and obligations are locally accomplished, and (b) sales encounters as a specific form of institutional activity, in which relevant and legitimate actions, adequate categories, category-bound activities and congruent epistemic and deontic stances are situatedly negotiated.

The following analysis proposes a systematic investigation of the sequential environments in which offering a taste is produced. First, it positions these offers in different sequential contexts (Section 4.4), in order to then focus on offers made during ongoing purchases and in service of their progressivity (Section 4.5). Finally, it contrasts the previous sequential environments, in which offers are generally accepted, with environments in which they are often rejected (Section 4.6).

4.4 Locating Offering a Taste within the Encounter: Some Options

Offering a taste in cheese shops can be made in a variety of sequential positions, with different stakes and outcomes. In order to locate our focal cases, which represent the most typical offers, I contrast here a few environments in which offering a taste is observable.

4.4.1 Requesting vs. Offering a Taste

The opportunity to taste a free sample of food – here, cheese – is implemented in two different actions by customers and salespersons. Either the customer requests a chance to taste the product, or the salesperson offers them the possibility to taste it.

Requests can be produced by customers in various sequential positions, asking to taste a product: they can open a new sequence targeting the next product to choose, or can emerge during the search, selection, and decision concerning a product to buy. Requests to taste a sample adopt various formats. In some cases, they are rather straightforward and display the right of the customer to have a taste (e.g., *can I try some munster with cumin.* FRO_UK_LDN_020415_49.09–CLI29.1-2/SEL2), treated as such in immediate positive responses by the salesperson. But in other cases they can display the delicacy of the action (e.g., *est-ce qu'on peut goûter le bleu d'bonneval ou::?* 'can we taste the bleu d'bonneval or::?' FRO_F_THO_180415_CLI48–15.36) and be treated as such, e.g., in teasing and delayed responses.

Offering a Taste in Gourmet Food Shops 113

By contrast, *offers* are produced by salespersons inviting the customer to taste, and are more frequent than requests. The sequential positions in which they occur, systematically described later on in this chapter, are consequential for their acceptance/refusal and for their broader sequential outcome. A typical case is represented by the following instance, recorded in a shop in France; we join the action as the customer (CUS) requests the seller (SEL) the first item (line 1), just after the greetings:

Excerpt 4.1 (FRO_F_LYO_sess1_cam2_CLI21_1-18-36)

```
01 CUS:    euh par hasard vous auriez pas du gouda:
           eh by any chance wouldn't you have any gouda
02         au: basilic: eh?
           with basil eh?
03         (0.6)
04 SEL:    pas^encore.
           not yet
05 CUS:    °d'accord°
           alright
06 SEL:    on: on l'a eu fait effectivement, mais on l'a pas
           we we have had it actually       but we don't have it°
07         °encore° .h on a: l'or- aux orties pour l'instant
           yet .h we have the nett- with nettle right now
08         (0.6)
09 CUS:    aux orties?
           with nettle?
10 SEL:    oui, v'voulez goû*ter?
           yes, do you want to taste?
                              *looks at cheese->
11         (0.4) *
     sel       ->*extends hand->
12 CUS:    (ça a quel *goût)? #
           (which taste has it)?
                      ->*takes cheese from shelf->
     fig                      #fig.4.1
```

Figure 4.1

```
13 SEL:    un p`tite note de cu:be ±beurre ±soupe
           a little note of bouillon cube butter soup
  cus                               ±leans ov cheese±smells-->
14         (0.6)± * (0.8)
  cus          ->±
  sel          ->*
15 CUS:    <d'accord.>
           <alright>
16 SEL:    v'voulez* qu`j`vous l- j`vais vous l`faire goûter?
           do you want that I you it- I will let you taste?
                  *walks behind the counter w cheese->
17         (2.9)
18 SEL:    (      *       )
                  ->*cuts cheese->
19         (3.6)
20 CUS:    c'est *mon [p`tit dej] ha±ha*
           that's my [breakfast] ha ha
21 SEL:               [tenez    ]
                      [take (it)]
  sel          ->*holds out abit of cheese*
  cus                                ±puts bit in mouth and chews->
22         (0.6)
23 SEL:    allez-y
           go ahead
24 CUS:    °merci°
           °thanks°
25         (5.0) +   (1.6) + (0.3)±
  cus            +rep nods+
  cus                            ->±
26 CUS:    bah j`vais en prendre deux cent grammes (.) °de c`lui là°
           well I'll take two hundred grams of it (.) from that one°
```

In formatting his request (lines 1–2), the customer orients to the particularity of the requested cheese and to its possible unavailability in the shop: he uses a preface with *by any chance* hinting at the difficulty of the query, and a negative interrogative format, with a verb in the conditional mood. The response (line 4) is negative, but lets transpire that the item could be available in the future. Furthermore, it is expanded by mentioning an alternative gouda (line 7), flavored with nettle instead of basil. After a delay, the customer responds by repeating the ingredient with an interrogative emphatic surprised intonation (line 9). The salesperson confirms and offers a taste (line 10).

Instead of accepting, the customer asks a question about its taste (line 12), answered by the salesperson with a description of the taste (line 13), while she grasps the cheese from the shelf and shows it (Figure 4.1). The customer not only listens and looks at the piece of cheese, but also bends over it and smells it (lines 13–14). Thus, the question delays the response to the offer, and favors other modes of sensorial access to the product, through verbal description, gaze, and especially olfactive perception. The delay, these alternative accesses, as well as a slowly pronounced particle in response (line 15) all display a careful, even reluctant, orientation to the alternative item proposed.

In this context, the salesperson produces a new version of the offer (line 16): it begins with the same verb used in the prior (*do you want*) now introducing an action that is not the customer's action (as in the prior version, *v'voulez goûter?*) but the seller's (*v'voulez qu'j'vous l-*), in which the verb is not realized, but all the entities involved are pronominally realized (*j'vous l-*first person singular, second person singular, object in the third person singular). This format is self-repaired into another one (*j'vais vous l'faire goûter?*), using the factitive, a construction in which the seller is the subject of the verb, and responsible for the action that is done by the customer. With this construction, the seller is presented as having full agency, without attributing any desire or need for the action to the customer (vs. the form *do you want to taste?*). This format is sequentially responsive to the reluctance of the customer.

The new offer is produced as the salesperson walks behind the counter with the cheese, projecting the next actions of cutting a slice (line 18) and giving it (line 21) to the customer (who comments about the odd time of the day to have cheese, line 20). The customer does not produce any verbal response, but accepts the offer by taking the offered bit (21), and engaging in tasting (line 25). Early on, while still chewing, he nods repeatedly in a positive manner, as a form of positive assessment; the outcome of the tasting is the decision to buy that cheese (line 26). Significantly, his *bah*-prefaced final turn registers the delicateness of a seller's proposal that did not correspond to the customer's initial request.

So, here we see that tasting (not our focus here, but see Mondada 2018) occurs in a situation in which the salesperson does not have the requested product and proposes an alternative one, which is met in a dispreferred way by the customer. Tasting occurs as an alternative to other forms of access to the object. Crucially, it occurs as a method for deciding whether to buy that cheese or not – and here the outcome is positive.

This shows a general feature of these offers to taste a sample of cheese, their embeddedness in the sales encounter and their crucial contribution to decision-making. Tasting grounds the assessment of the product – often positive – followed by the decision to buy. This is the case in all the instances I will analyze in Section 4.5. Furthermore, in order to demonstrate the crucial importance of the sequential position of these offers, I will show how, in alternative positions (Section 4.6), the offer is refused and/or does not lead to the decision to buy. But before moving on with the sequential organization of offers, a further distinction can be made, between two types of offered tastings in shops.

4.4.2 *Offering Customized vs. Pre-Cut Taste Samples*

In food shops, two types of tastings can be distinguished, which have not only different commercial implications, but are sequentially organized in different ways. On the one hand, the salesperson can invite the customer to taste a bit of a specific cheese, which has been progressively targeted during the exchange with the customer (see Excerpt 4.1). On the other hand, the salesperson can offer a taste of some pre-cut bits of cheese that are on display on a plate on the counter, which can also be taken by customers in a self-serviced manner. The latter differ in their sequential trajectory from the former, on which Section 4.5 will focus. Here I discuss an instance of these predefined and not-customized offers, in order to show the particular sequential environment in which they occur and their consequences: in this context, they are generally *not* followed by a decision to buy.

We join the action as the customer is asking for a piece of Brie (line 1) and chooses a Coulommiers (line 6). While the seller is fetching the requested cheese, she offers a taste of another one, Brousse, available on the counter:

Excerpt 4.2 (FRO_F_STL_2.06.12_CLI9)

```
01 CUS:    un morceau de: (.) brie
           a bit of (.) Brie
02         (2.1)
03 SEL:    brie de meaux? (.) brie de melun:? coulommiers?
           Brie de Meaux? (.) Brie de Melun? Coulommiers?
04 CUS:    lequel est l`plus crémeux?
           which one is the most creamy?
05 SEL:    alors le coulommiers là
           then the Coulommiers there
06 CUS:    ouais? bon +alors + allons-y.
           yeah? good then go ahead
                       +points+
07         (1.2)
08 SEL:    *si vous voul•ez dégu#st:•er
           if you want to taste
           *RH grasps Clm->
                          •LH pushes dish on counter twd CUS•
     fig                  #fig.4.2
```

Figure 4.2

Offering a Taste in Gourmet Food Shops 117

```
09              (0.7)*(0.4)•(0.4)•
                ->*places Clm on board->
                      •LH...•points at brousse->
10 SEL:         c'est de la brou•sse:• (.) au lait **•d` brebis
                it's Brousse          (.) with sheep milk
                            ->•,,,,•
                                          -->**unwraps Clm->
11              (1.7) + (0.3)
   cus                +...about to take a bit of younger cheese---->
12 SEL:         do•nc là+ vous en+ avez• eh des ( ) de deux s`maines,•
                so there you have       eh some ( ) two weeks old
                ->•..................•LH points at younger Brousse-•
   cus              --->+,,,,,,,,+
13              •(0.5)
                •points at older Brousse--->
14 SEL:         et du plus affiné de• un •mois•*
                and some more mature one month old
                                ->•,,,,•
                                        **continues to unwrap->
15              (0.3)
16 CUS:         +°(oké, j`vais goûter)°
                 °(okay I will taste)°
                +takes a bit of older Brousse and eats it->
17              (2)+ (1) ±     (6) **•(0.3) ± (1) ±
   cus          ->+
   cus                       ±looks at brousse±,,,,,±
   sel                            ->**puts knife on brie-->
18 SEL:         comme ceci pour le brie?
                like this for the Brie?
19              (1.5)
20 CUS:         euh:: un p`tit peu plus petit
                ehm    a little bit smaller
21              (0.5)
22 CUS:         voilà.*•
                there it is
   sel           ->*•cuts--->>
23              (13.2)
```

As the customer has decided to take the Coulommiers, the salesperson bends over the fridge, grasps a piece of it and puts it on the counter with her right hand (lines 8–9). Meanwhile, with the left hand, she points at a plate containing another cheese, Brousse (lines 8–9), and offers a taste of it (line 8, Figure 4.2). Made as a side sequence, the offer is in a conditional format, prefaced by 'if'. Moreover, the seller uses the verb *déguster*, whereas in the other context described in Excerpt 4.1 and Section 4.5, s/he always use *goûter*. The former verb is specialized for tasting sessions, whereas the latter can be used in a variety of contexts, e.g., when checking a sauce in the kitchen, which are consequential for making a decision. The offer is completed by an explanation (lines 10–14), pointing at two versions of the cheese offered, a younger and an older.

The customer responds to the offer in an embodied way, by bringing her hand to the cheese, suspending her gesture, and finally completing it when the salesperson's description is completed, while verbally accepting the offer (line 16). She eats a bit, as she looks at the corresponding cheese in the display counter (line 17). As the tasting is ongoing, in silence (line 17), the seller unwraps the Coulommiers and positions the knife on it, proposing a quantity to the customer (line 18). This reorients the customer's gaze from the tasted cheese to the cheese she is buying. After a specification of the requested quantity (lines 20–22), the customer does not gaze at the Brousse anymore, and no further mention of it is made during the encounter.

The offers of pre-cut samples on display are produced as a side sequence in the ongoing purchase of another cheese; they are not related to any detail made relevant during the encounter, and they are disconnected from the ongoing purchase (the very fact of being available on the counter makes them accessible at any time for the customer, independently of the local interactional circumstances: they constitute a kind of standing offer). These offers are generally accepted, but they are most often not followed by any assessment (vs. the personalized tastings) and in the corpus they are never followed by a decision to buy (vs. the personalized tastings, in which the decision to buy occurs after a positive assessment). Their *sided* character makes them peripheral; as soon as the main activity resumes, they are not considered anymore. Personalized tastings, by contrast, are *embedded* in the actual course of the purchase, in the sense that they respond to local, occasioned, interactionally emergent questions, relevancies, and features; they contribute to the ongoing choice-making by helping to confirm, support, and stabilize selections and decisions.

In this respect, offers of pre-cut samples and personalized offers not only occur in different sequential environments and trajectories, but also result in opposite commercial outcomes. The systematic analyses constituting the main object of this chapter will focus on personalized offers to taste some particular cheese that has been targeted during the exchange, occurring in environments similar to Excerpt 4.1.

4.5 Three Sequential Environments for Offering a Taste

Offering a taste occurs most frequently in the corpus – with a remarkable coherence across settings in different European cities – in specific environments that will be explored in this section. They happen in contexts in which the customer does not produce a straightforward request. They are positioned after the customer has requested advice and the seller has offered an array of options (Section 4.5.1), after a question about a specific product, and often the seller's verbal answer (Section 4.5.2), and after a claim or display of not knowing a particular cheese (Section 4.5.3).

These three environments are characterized by the emergent manifestation of the customer's lower epistemic stance (K−) (Heritage 2012), displaying

Offering a Taste in Gourmet Food Shops   119

partial or nonexistent knowledge of a product. In these environments, the salesperson offers a cheese to taste, which has been targeted as relevant during the previous turns. The offer is frequently formatted as a polar interrogative question – *do you want to taste?*, *voulez-vous goûter?*, *quieres probar?*, *wollen Sie ein bisseln probieren?* – although other formats can be used. This format corresponds to the one described by Curl (2006) for offers targeting a possible problem that has surfaced in the prior talk. Here, the problem might concern the customer's indecision, partial or absent knowledge and therefore insufficient grounds for decision-making. An alternative format is used in shops in which samples to taste are very frequently offered, and almost systematic for each product identified as a possible candidate to buy – like in a Spanish shop in Madrid: in this case, the offer is often formatted in the imperative (*pruebalo*, *mira prueba esto*). Importantly, offering a taste can also be achieved silently, by merely handling a slice of cheese out to the customer (cf. Kärkkäinen & Keisanen 2012).

The collection assembled in this chapter focuses on the environments leading to the offer. The tasting itself is not the focus here (but see Mondada 2018), nor the outcome of the tasting (see Mondada 2022); but in all the cases discussed in this section, the customer ends up buying the cheese s/he has tasted.

4.5.1 Requesting Advice

A first environment in which offering a taste occurs is after the customer has requested advice or recommendations. This initiating action establishes a standardized relational pair of categories (Sacks 1972) – advice seeker vs. advice giver – typical of service encounters (Jefferson & Lee 1981). Offering a taste is not made immediately after this request of advice, but after some choices and options have been mentioned in responses to questions.

We join the opening of an encounter in a small town in Germany, in which the customer asks for recommendations concerning a 'nice Brie' (line 6):

Excerpt 4.3 (FRO_D_FREI_CLI24_01.38.45)

```
01 CUS:    gut`n ta:g=
           good morning=
02 SEL:    =gut`n ta:g?
           =good morning
03         (0.5)
04 CUS:    .tsk
05         (1.4)
06 CUS:    ich wü[rd mir gern `nen schönen brie empfehlen lassen,
           I would be happy to be advised about a nice Brie
07 SEL:         [was darf's sein?
                [what might this be? (= what do you want?)
08         (0.2)
```

```
09 SEL:     ja::? (.) wollen sie was kräftiges oder eher was
            yes (.) do you want something strong or rather something
10          mil:des::?
            milder
11 CUS:     ruh:ig was kräft[iges. °so gern°
            cool something strong °like this please°
12 SEL:                    [schön kräftig.* `n schönen brie de meaux
                           [nicely strong    a nice Brie de Meaux
                                            *pts BdM w knife---->
13          (0.2) wär* [schön kräftig, *(0.3) `n coulommier*:,
            (0.2) would be [yet strong  (0.3) a Coulommier
14 CUS:                [ja.
                       [yes
   sel      -->*                       *pts C w knife------*
15 SEL:     *(0.2) fein `n würzig wär dieser* Fougerus,
            (0.2) fine and spicy would be this Fougerus
            *points F w knife---------------*
16          (1.1)
17 CUS:     °tzja°.
            °yes°
18          (0.8)
19 CUS:     empfehlen sie mir was?
            advise me about something?
20          (0.3) * (0.6)
   sel           *grasps the C---->>
21 SEL:     °le coulommier°. (0.2) wollen sie mal
            °the Coulommier° (0.2) do you want
22          ein bissel probieren?
            to taste a bit?
23          (0.4)
24 CUS:     °(ja) ( [   )°
            °(yes) ( [  )°
```

After the greetings, the customer hesitates, projecting the first request but delaying it (lines 4–5), before producing a request for advice about a Brie (line 6), while the salesperson addresses her (line 7). The salesperson does not give a recommendation straight away, but instead asks a question about the customer's preferences, offering two alternatives (lines 9–10), one of which is picked up by the customer (line 11). This generates a new series of options (lines 12–15), in which the salesperson names, points at, and briefly describes three possible cheeses corresponding to a relatively strong taste. The list projects a choice by the customer, but she remains silent (line 16), produces a particle (line 17) further delaying her response, and ends up asking again for advice (line 19). The salesperson grasps a piece of cheese (line 20), names it (line 21), and offers a taste of it (lines 21–22): this is accepted by the customer. After tasting it, she positively assesses it, and buys it (not shown).

The offer occurs *after a series of options has been provided*, with cheese names and descriptive categories, as well as visual access to pointed-at items. It occurs when these resources have been treated by the customer as insufficient grounds for making a decision. In this context, tasting constitutes a further way to access the specific features of the cheese and to ground its selection.

Offering a Taste in Gourmet Food Shops   121

Therefore, offering a taste is a practice that allows the participants to solve the difficulties of choice and thus, to secure the progressivity of the encounter.

A similar trajectory happens in the next excerpt, recorded in London:

Excerpt 4.4 (FRO_UK_LDN_0204_01.17.40_CLI36)

```
01 CUS:    uhm, (0.2) I like blue cheeses. so: [(what would) you
02 SEL:                                        [blue cheeses? yeah
03 CUS:    recommend °(   )°
04 SEL:    what about (0.5) a dozen of them?
05         (0.4)
06 CUS:    hahaha
((12 lines omitted))
19 SEL:    so we`ve go- we`ve got# italia:n, (.) we`ve got a lot
   fig                            #fig.4.3
```

Figure 4.3

```
20         from england, wales, french, (0.8) we`ve got creamy,
21         we`ve got hard, we`ve got (.) sharp, we`ve got
22 CUS:    cr- a creamy [blue cheese
23 SEL:                 [I would like to say mild, but a blue
24         cheese is [never really mild [so
25 CUS:              [no no no          [should not be. would be
26         wrong if it (was)
27         (0.7)
28 CUS:    allright then (0.4) I'd love a creamy: creamy blue cheese
29 SEL:    a creamy blue cheese? yeah of course
30         *(0.7)
    sel    *walks to the shelf-->
31 SEL:    let me give you a taste of the cashel* blue here
                                          ->*grasps 1 piece->
32         from irela*nd
                    ->*unwraps->>
```

The customer states his personal taste, targeting a type of cheese (blue), asking for recommendation (lines 1, 3). The salesperson responds by highlighting the wide range of options (line 4), and after some jokes, he proposes a list of cheeses available (lines 19–21) – while they both stand in front of the refrigerated shelf (Figure 4.3). The customer picks up on one of the qualities mentioned, *creamy* (lines 22 and 28). This is acknowledged by the salesperson (line 29), who walks toward the shelf where the blue cheeses are and grasps one, while offering a taste of Cashel blue (lines 31–32). Here the offer is formatted with the construction *let me give you a taste of* ... (line 31), which foregrounds the proposing action of the seller, rather than the needs or desires of the customer (cf. Hoey 2020).

In a nutshell, the customer's request for recommendations manifests their readiness to buy: the issue is less to decide *whether* to buy, than to decide *what* to buy. In response to requests for recommendations, sellers give a list of options to choose from. These options include some verbal information – like names of products and descriptions – but also sensorial features allowing the customer some visual, tactile, or olfactive access, albeit restricted. Even if the salesperson provides for grounds to select among these options, these work as methods for narrowing down the choice rather than for making the last decision about what to buy. When a candidate product is finally identified, and proposed, tasting provides for a method to make the final decision.

4.5.2 Asking Questions

Asking questions about products is a recurrent practice in cheese shops. With questions, customers identify a product – often by using a demonstrative reference and pointing gestures – but also display a K- stance, inviting the salesperson to give more information (Harjunpää et al., this volume) – typically the name of the cheese and some explanation – and therefore to expand the ongoing sequence (Heritage 2012). Questions both seek information and target some cheese as a possible object to be requested, thus functioning as possible pre-requests.

Sacks (1992 vol. I: 688–691) shows that questions can be designed as seeking information (incomplete-statement type questions) or as pre-requests. In the latter case, they provide for the opportunity for their recipient to do a 'pre-emptive offer' (Schegloff 2007: 90–91), which retrospectively displays an interpretation of the question as a pre-request. Sacks discusses, on the basis of an introspective example, the difference between these two actions in terms of format: he contrasts 'what is- what are those, cigars?' with 'what are those, cigars?' by showing that the first "exhibits that the speaker from the start did not know that those were cigars" and "perhaps in the course of his utterance he learned what they are, came to see better" – his not knowing providing the basis to ask a simple question – whereas the second displays that the speaker knows what is being targeted and thus makes the question interpretable as a pre-request (Sacks 1992 vol. I: 690–691).

In the following cases, both types of questions are used – both display either not knowing or knowing partially. They are not responded to immediately with an offer, but first with an answer, which gives information and explanations about the cheese pointed at. Only after that, an offer of a taste of that cheese might be made, which expands verbal information into an embodied and sensorial access to the referent targeted.

Questions displaying low knowledge of a product are typically formatted with a deictic reference, like in the two next examples, from Freiburg in Germany and from Helsinki:

Excerpt 4.5 (FRO_D_FREI_CLI13.2)

```
01 CUS:     und was ist das da vorne für eine[r?
            and what is the one in the fron[t?
02 SEL:                                    [d- das is äh der (.)
                                           [t- that is eh the (.)
03          coulommiers saint-jacques
04          (1.1)
05 SEL:     [wollen sie `n bisschen probieren?
            [do you want to taste a bit?
06 CUS:     [( )
07          (1.2)
08 CUS:     °j::a. h°
            °yes    h°
```

Excerpt 4.6 (FRO_FIN_1704_2.02.47_CLI34)

```
01 CUS:     +mikä tämä on nää näyttää ( )
            what this is these look ( )
            +points and leans over the window counter->
02          (0.5)* (0.5)
    sel          *looks towards pointing--->
03 CUS:     noi palat*
            those pieces
                   ->*moves towards the indicated item->
04          (0.9)
05 CUS:     ( ) #toi kelta+sempi *
            ( ) that more yellow
                              -->+
    sel                         ->*takes asmall piece out->
    fig         #fig.4.4
```

Figure 4.4

```
06         (0.7)
07 SEL:    tää o[n sittes sveitsi*läistä juust[oo
           this i[s then  Swiss             cheese
                         ->*shows--->>
08 CUS:        [( )                            [( )
09 SEL:    tää on (.) [bio velle
           this is (.) [bio Welle
10 CUS:               [se näyttää tosi (.) se näyttää tosi hyvältä
                     [it  looks       very (.) it looks    very good
11 SEL:    nii joo (.) haluutsä     maistaat [tätä piänen
           oh yeah (.) do want you to taste [this a little
12 CUS:                                      [joo
                                            [yeah
13         (0.3) * (0.7)
    sel       ->*unpacks->>
```

The German customer uses a demonstrative (*das*), and a spatial reference (*da vorne*) (line 1) in a very general WH question, that is answered with the name of the cheese (lines 2–3). Likewise, the Finnish customer uses demonstratives (*tämä*, *nää*, line 1, *noi* line 3, *toi* line 5) as well as a visual cue, the color (line 5), in order to refer to the cheese. In response, the salesperson does not only give the origin (line 7) and the name of the cheese (line 9), but immediately turns toward it (Figure 4.4) and takes it out of the fridge, showing it to the customer.

In the German case, the customer does not respond when the name is given (line 4) and this might occasion the offer (line 5); in the Finnish case, the customer makes a comment about the visual aspect of the cheese (line 10), which might occasion the offer. Moreover, *tosi hyvältä*, 'very good', also refers to taste, which might be a strong hint to build the relevance of tasting.

In other cases, the customer displays partial knowledge of the product, inviting the seller to expand – also projecting a possible request. In these cases, the question mentions the name or the general type of cheese, as information that is available upon visual inspection, namely by reading the products' labels.

In the following case, recorded in Savoie (France), a nonlocal customer (CUS) asks a question about Beaufort, a local cheese, mentioning the name as something she was able to read in the material environment. A local (CLI) contributes to advise her.

Excerpt 4.7 (FRO_F_THO18_cli64_65)

```
01 CUS:    du beaufort ce serait quoi?
           some Beaufort what would that be?
02 SEL:    le beaufort? (.) c'est c[elui-ci.
           the Beaufort? (.) it's t[his one
03 CLI:                            [c'est très très bon
                                   [it's very very good
04 CUS:    c'est très très bon, (.) [ah oui?
           it's very very good  (.) [oh yes?
05 CLI:                              [ah ouais.
                                     [oh yeah
06 SEL:                              [beaufort jeune (.) beaufort
                                     [Beaufort young (.) Beaufort
07         plus vieux (.) plus de goût celui-là
           older       (.) more taste that one
08         (0.9)
09 SEL:    vous voulez goûter?
           you want to taste?
10 CUS:    ouais peut-être (.) volontiers parce que là
           yeah maybe      (.) with pleasure because here
11         je connais pas du tout alors ((laughs))
           I don't know at all so ((laughs))
```

When the customer asks about Beaufort (line 1), the salesperson localizes it in the window counter (line 2), while another customer produces a very positive assessment about taste (line 3), which he then confirms (line 5). The seller points at two types of Beaufort (lines 6–7), also referring to different ways they taste. So, there are multiple verbal references to taste in these turns; in the absence of a response by the customer (line 8, cf. Excerpt 4.5, line 4), an offer to actually taste Beaufort is made. In this case, the customer does not only accept, but gives an account, claiming not to know (lines 10–11).

Finally, the customer can use both deictic references and the name – as here in a shop in Madrid, where the customer displays some knowledge about smoked cheese by asking about the difference between the proposed one and the quite popular Idiazábal:

Excerpt 4.8 (FRO_E_MDR_3012_cam2_1.45.51)

```
01 SEL:    qué más cositas:?
           what else?
02 CUS:    pue:s este ahumado que es pare- tipo:: idiazábal
           PRT this smoked what's li- sort of Idiazabal
03         [o: algo así?
           [or something similar?
```

```
04  SEL:    [.h (.) bueno, me- eh* quizás es un poquito más intenso
            [.h      well    me eh perhapsa bit more intense
                                  *grasps cheese--->
05          sabes, idiazábal es más elegante entre comillas
            you know Idiazabal is more elegant in quotation marks
06          es un poco si- tsk. esto es un ahumado
            this one is a bit si- tsk. this is a smoked
07          ahuma*do. sabes, .h: es un queso que se pasa
            smoked      you know .h it's a cheese that is left
                  ->*cuts a tiny slice--->
08          dos o tres días en una cabina de humo,
            two or three days in a smoking room
09          (0.3)*
                 ->*gives CUS slice to taste->
10  SEL:    co:+n: madera de haya entonces +eh:*
            with beech wood              so       eh
     sel                                          --->*
     cus         +.........................+grasps & puts to mouth->>
```

The customer's question draws a comparison between two smoked cheeses (lines 2–3). The seller engages in a comparative description (lines 4–8). Very early in his turn, he turns to the cheese, grasps it, and cuts a little slice. In his explanation he refers to sensorial features, like intensity (line 4), but also encounters some difficulties in completing the description (line 6), ending it with a tautology (lines 6–7). He continues with an explanation about smoking techniques – while he gives the slice to taste to the customer. In this case, offering a taste is embodied and silent, as is the acceptance (line 10).

In sum, when the customer asks a question about a cheese, s/he identifies a possible candidate product among many – through deictic elements, pointing, and gaze. These resources display the customer as an unknowing participant, relying on what s/he sees (location, visual appearance – even when the name is produced, like in Excerpt 4.7, this relies on the reading of the label and not on a previous knowledge of the product). Consequently, the answer given by the salesperson mentions the name of the product, and describes some features – some abstract and encyclopedic (like the origins), others more sensorial. Tasting is then offered, either verbally or gesturally. By offering a taste in this context, the seller treats these verbal descriptions as not constituting sufficient grounds for deciding whether to select that product. The progressivity of the selling activity is secured thanks to direct sensorial access to the products. In cases in which the customer has displayed an interest and even some excitement regarding the product (Excerpt 4.6), the acceptance is immediate. In cases in which the customer has not responded to the previous verbal description (Excerpt 4.5, line 4, Excerpt 4.7, line 8), the offer orients to the absence of response and overcomes it: it is accepted with some delay (Excerpt 4.5) or some hesitation (Excerpt 4.7). In other cases, the offer is made in an embodied

Offering a Taste in Gourmet Food Shops

way during the verbal description of the product (Excerpt 4.8), occasioning a gestural acceptance, without necessitating a verbal agreement. In all of the cases mentioned, the tasting is followed by a positive assessment and the decision to buy that cheese.

4.5.3 Claims of Not Knowing

Questions display the speaker as an unknowing recipient concerning the specificities of a product. Alternatively, the speaker can explicitly say that s/he *doesn't know*, either by initiating the claim or in response to a query by the salesperson. These two contexts – recurrent in the corpus – show that both parties orient to the relevance of knowing for buying. Here too, making not-knowing explicit invites the knowing participant (the seller) to expand the sequence and provide information (Heritage 2012).

In the next fragment, recorded in Paris, the customer looks for some time at the cheese, while the salesperson is packing his previous order. He reads the label and points at a cheese (Figure 4.5), saying that he does not know it (lines 1–2):

Excerpt 4.9 (PAR1007_2.11.47_cli20)

```
01 CUS:    (irish porter cheddar) °j'con+nais +pas°
           (Irish porter cheddar)  °I don't know°
           >>looks at porter cheddar on the shelf---->
                                          +points+
02         +j`connais+ pas# ça+ moi:?+
           I don't know this
           +.........+points--+,,,,,,+
    fig                #fig.4.5
```

Figure 4.5

128   L. Mondada

```
03 SEL:    alors ça c'est un cheddar jeune qui va être affiné
           so this is a young cheddar which will be curated
04         avec de la guinness. .h c'est beaucoup plus doux (0.3)
           with some Guinness    .h it's much sweeter (0.3)
05 SEL:    [que euh:] que c`qu'±on pourrait croire. (.) quand on
           [than ehm] than what you could imagine (.) when you
06 CUS:    [ouais]
           [yeah]
    cus                        ->±gazes at SAL-->
07         1` voi:t± ça fait un peu: euh impressionnant: euh
           see it it looks quite eh impressive eh
    cus        -->±looks at the cheese------>>
08         sombre, [et en fait en termes-]
           dark,   [and in terms-]
09 CUS:            [ça fait pain d'épices]
                   [looks like gingerbread]
10 SEL:    un p`tit peu ouais
           a little bit yeah
11         (0.2)
12 SEL:    j` peux vous faire goûter, si vous voulez.
           I can make you taste if you want.
13         (0.9)
14 CUS:    avec plaisir
           with pleasure
```

In response to the claim of not knowing, the salesperson engages in an explanation of the cheese production first, then in describing the taste (sweet), which he contrasts with the visual appearance (dark). The elaboration of this sensorial description is overlapped by a comparison with gingerbread that the customer (line 9) produces on the basis of the visual appearance (*ça fait* literally 'it makes' meaning 'it looks like'). The salesperson minimally acknowledges it (line 10) and at this point offers to taste it. The previous description and the response of the customer show the difficulty of verbally rendering the taste of the cheese. Tasting is offered in this context as a way to overcome the limitations of the verbal description of its sensorial features. The format of the offer (line 12) uses the factitive (cf. Excerpt 4.1), focusing on the salesperson as agent and showing his readiness to serve the curiosity of the customer, although with a modal verb ('I can') and a condition ('if you want'), displaying that tasting is optional (later, before tasting, the salesperson warns the customer that he might be disappointed). The offer orients to the cheese as a curious object contingently found in the shop: it is a case of 'discovered' product (vs. planned purchase) by the customer (vs. recommended by the salesperson).

Not knowing is responded to with an expansion of the sequence – here with descriptions and explanations. Offering a taste is a way of further expanding it. This is the case in another French shop, in Savoie, in which, after the first request, the customer looks at the counter, reads the label 'Bleu de Termignon' and claims not to know it (line 1):

Offering a Taste in Gourmet Food Shops   129

Excerpt 4.10 (FRO_F_THO_1804_CLI41_2.22)

```
01 CUS:    et l'bleu d'termignon? (.) jcon+nais pas.
           and the Bleu de Termignon (.) I don't know
    cus    >>looks at cheese--------------+looks at SEL->>
02 SEL:    bleu d'termignon? *vous connaissez pas?
           Bleu de Termignon? you don't know?
                                 *moves twd BdT->
03 CUS:    non.
           no
04         (0.6)
05 SEL:    c'est fait en haute-maurien*ne,
           it's made in Haute-Maurienne
                                      ->*grasps BdT->
06 CUS:    ±connais   ± pas.
           don't know
           ±shakes head±
07         (0.5) * (2.4)
               ->*places BdT on counter and cuts a tiny slice->
08 SEL:    c'est un bleu ru:sti*que,
           it's a rustic blue
                               ->*holds it out to CUS->
09         (1.6) *± (0.5)            ±
    sel          ->*
    cus            ±takes and puts in mouth±chews->
10 CUS:    merci
           thanks
```

The customer's reading of the name and claiming not to know are recycled in a request for confirmation by the salesperson while she moves toward the product (line 2). The customer confirms she does not know (line 3) and repeats that (line 6) after the seller has added a bit of information (the origins of the cheese, line 5). In response to this repeated claim, the seller not only adds an extra bit of information (line 8), but more importantly cuts a slice (line 7) and gives it to the customer, who takes it (line 9) and thanks the seller (line 10). Here offering a taste is silently embodied; it is responsive to the multiple negative epistemic claims of the customer.

Even when the customer has hinted that he is about to buy a specific type of cheese, if the request displays him as not knowing, the salesperson can check his knowledge and – in case of a negative answer – offer a taste of that cheese. This is the case of the next fragment, in Madrid:

Excerpt 4.11 (FRO_MDR_0104_SEL2_1.25.15_CLI3.1)

```
01 SEL:    algo más queríais?
           do you like something more?
02         (0.7)
03 CUS:    sí. e+h:: este+ de# aquí?+ que:+ tiene buen aspecto,
           yes eh   this from here? which is good looking
                    +........+points----+,,,,,+
    fig                       #fig.4.6
```

Figure 4.6

```
04            °pues me llevo un trozo°
              °then I take a piece°
05   SEL:     el a- el azul este lo conocéis? es un azul
              the b- the blue do you know this one? it's a blue
06            *+que elabora+mos nosotr[os,
              that we produce ourselv[es
              *...->
     cus      +head shake-+
07   CUS:                                 [no lo conozco
                                          [I don't know it
08            (0.3)*
     sel         ->*grasps azul->
09   SEL:     en valladolid en nuestra quesería,* (.) mira,
              en Valladolid in our cheese farm    (.) look
                                            -->*grasps knife->
10            probalo. a ver qué os parece*
              taste it to see what does it look like for you
                                            ->*slices->>
```

In response to the query of the salesperson, initiating a new sequence and moving to the next purchase (line 1), the customer responds positively (line 3), but displays – through the pointing (Figure 4.6), the use of the demonstrative and the spatial deictic, as well as the orientation to the visual aspect of the cheese – that his choice is contingent and relies on visual evidence. Even if the customer treats this evidence as enough to decide to buy the product (line 4), the salesperson responds with a description of the cheese and inserts a knowledge check (*este lo conocéis?* line 5) – orienting to the customer as not-knowing and to knowing as a basis for buying. The customer indeed confirms, by negatively shaking his head and saying that he does not know (line 7). The salesperson continues the verbal explanation, but ends up offering a taste of the cheese (line 10).

These excerpts show that both customers and salespersons orient to the relevance of knowing for deciding to buy – possibly orienting to the transparency of the deal but also to the socialization of the customer. Either the customer manifests not knowing – here I focused on explicit claims, but other displays are possible (Mondada 2022) – or the seller checks to see if s/he knows. Finding out that the customer does not know, the seller expands the sequence not only with a description, but also with an offer. Whereas in the first case (Excerpt 4.9) the sequence is initiated by the customer claiming not to know, in the following ones (Excerpts 4.10 and 4.11), the only response by the customer to the seller's description is a claim not to know (cf. the nonresponse in Excerpts 4.5 and 4.7), making the offer to taste the cheese the only way to remedy to it.

The relevance of epistemics in identifying, selecting, choosing, and deciding to buy is explicitly addressed in the last excerpts (Section 4.5.3). However, there is an orientation to the customer as not knowing in the previous cases too: the epistemic stance is displayed through the actions s/he does, such as asking for advice or asking questions. In all the cases, the salesperson responds with a verbal provision of information but also orients toward the opportunity of an offer (prepared by grasping the cheese and slicing it). Tasting represents a sensorial method for overcoming the limitations of a purely verbal or visual access to the product. Thereby, it is also a method for securing the progressivity of the activity in a context in which an unknowing participant has to make a decision. In this sequential environment, the offer to taste a sample of cheese benefits the customer and solves the problem s/he is facing at that point. But it also serves the interest of the salesperson, fostering the decision-making and the progression of the sequence into the sale. In all of the cases we analyzed in this section, tasting is followed by a decision to buy. Even in other cases, in which tasting results in a negative assessment, another product is proposed, possibly tasted, and bought.

Nonetheless, offers are not always accepted; their rejection is frequent in particular sequential environments – showing that participants treat offers as more relevant in some contexts, and less acceptable in others. In order to demonstrate the crucial importance that different sequential environments make for the way offering a taste is interpreted and responded to, I finally turn to some contexts in which offers are rejected.

4.6 Rejected Offers

Offering a taste is an action that is sometimes rejected. While some rejections are based on accounts (the customer does not eat any cheese, it is too early in the morning for that, etc.), showing the dispreference of rejecting the offer, other refusals rather treat the offer as not adequate or not relevant. I discuss two sequential environments in which this is the case. The first concerns offers made in the very opening of the encounter (Section 4.6.1), just after the greetings. The second concerns offers made after a decision to buy has been made (Section 4.6.2). These two contexts show the importance of a specific sequential environment – identified in Section 4.5 – for offering a taste to be considered as legitimate.

4.6.1 Offering a Taste in Openings

In some cases, salespersons offer a taste as soon as the customer has entered the shop. While this might be presented as a way of welcoming the customer, it is interesting that these offers might be turned down.

This is the case of an encounter recorded in London:

Excerpt 4.12 (FRO_UK_LDN0204_CLI46)

```
((CUS1 and CUS2 have entered the shop and looked around for a
while))
01 SEL:      do you need any help? or if you want to try something?
02 CUS1:     no thank [you
03 SEL:              [yeah alright
((SEL walks away and the couple leaves the shop without buying
anything))
```

The seller offers both help and tasting (line 1). The customer refuses (line 2) without any hesitation and without giving any account. The seller accepts the refusal very quickly too, in overlap (line 3), and walks away. Both turn-formats display that the refusal is unproblematic and expectable.

Interestingly, the format used by the seller (although a nonnative speaker of English) is an 'if'-format – convergent with Curl's (2006) identification of that format as used for 'pre-planned' offers occurring at the very beginning of the interaction. Moreover, the object of tasting, at this point, and contrary to the previous fragments examined, cannot be specified (*something*, line 1), since there have not been any other previous actions to infer what the customer may be after.

These refusals show that offering a taste is treated by the customer as something other than just a complimentary gift of something tasty. Customers orient to the offer as a preliminary for something else, projecting other actions expanding the commercial exchange and possibly implying some obligations to buy. It is thus significant that people not buying anything – just browsing the shop – refuse the offer. By so doing, the person also resists becoming a customer, being a 'just-looking' (a category that is recognized and used by the salespersons of that shop).

4.6.2 Offering a Taste after a Decision Has Already Been Made

While the previous offers were produced very *early* in the encounter, other offers are produced relatively *late* within a buying episode, that is, when the customer has already made a decision, and the seller is implementing it in asking about the quantity s/he wants or cutting the requested quantity.

We join the next excerpt in Helsinki, where the customer requests some Emmental (line 1), treating it as a straightforward order (e.g., she does not engage in a search, does not inspect the counter window, and does not look at the cheese she is requesting):

Excerpt 4.13 (FRO_FIN_1704_0.43.18_CLI10)

```
01 CUS:    oisko sulla sitä Emmentaalia.
           do you have that Emmental
02 SEL:    joo
           yes
03         (43) ((SEL searches and fetches the cheese))
04 SEL:    minkä verran haluat[te?
           how    much  do you want?
05 CUS:                       [jos siitä vaikka, puo*let.
                              [if from it (=let's say) half
     sel                                          *..->
06         (1)
07 SEL:    ha*luatteko maistaa?         *
           do you want   to taste?
           ->*puts knife in the middle*cuts->
08         (0.2) + (0.2)    +
     cus          +head shake+
09 CUS:    ( +  + )
             +refusal gesture+search for purse in bag->>
```

The seller responds positively to the request (line 2) and fetches the cheese (line 3), which takes some time to be found and brought to the counter. The next step in the purchase concerns the quantity requested (line 4). The customer looks at the piece of cheese – a typical cube piece of Emmental – and requests half of it (line 5). In response, the seller promptly places her knife in the middle of the piece, ready to cut it (lines 5–7). In the meanwhile, she offers the customer a taste of it (line 7).

This offer is produced after a straightforward request has been made, and the requested quantity has been decided; it is produced as the seller has already put her knife in a position that clearly projects the cut of the requested piece – and not the cut of a sample to taste. In this environment, tasting is not necessary and it is not projected by the actual embodied action of the seller.

The customer refuses, by shaking her head (line 8), a gesture that conveys refusal (line 9), and probably her (inaudible) turn (line 9): the refusal is clear and straightforward. Moreover, she projects the closure of the encounter, by reaching for her purse in her bag.

The way the refusal is formatted orients to the sequential position and multimodal format of the offer as unnecessary – which accounts for the unproblematic character of the refusal (which is *not* produced in a dispreferred format).

In the last two fragments, the sequential environment in which tasting is offered is similar to the previous one. Moreover, the customer explicitly displays that he knows the cheese, as an account for refusing to taste. The customer requests a piece of Abondance fermier (lines 1–2):

134   L. Mondada

Excerpt 4.14 (FRO_F_THO_1704_cli1_14.55)

```
01 CUS:    et pis eh un tout p'tit morceau euh: (0.5) °j'allais
           and then eh a very little bit ehm    (0.5) °I was about
02         l'oublier.° d'abondance fermi[er.
           to forget it° of Abondance from the farm
03 SEL:                                  [mais oui::
                                          of course
04         (5.0) * (4.0) * (1.9)
   sel          *walks--*brings back a piece from the shelf->
05 CUS:    le p'tit mor- à gauche c'est du fermier aussi?
           the little bi- on the left it's also a farmhouse cheese?
06         le p'tit bout qui* reste?
           the small remaining bit?
   sel                     -->*stops and looks back at CUS->
07         (0.2)
08 SEL:    le p'tit bout là?* (.) ou[i::
           the small bit there? (.) ye[s
09 CUS:                             [voilà, c'est parfait
                                    [that's it, it's perfect
   sel                      ->*shows a smaller bit--->
10         ça m'[ira *très bien
           this w[ill be perfect
11 SEL:         [c'est* bon. ça va aller?
                [is it okay  will be that fine?
                     ->*puts back the big piece and takes the small->
12         (0.4)
13 SEL:    d'a:ccord
           alright
14 CUS:    >voilà.< (.) comme ça y'a pas besoin [d'couper
           >right.< (.) so there is no need [to cut
15 SEL:                                          [v'voulez pas
                                                 [you don't want
16         l'goûter?*#
           to taste?
   sel             ->*holds the bit->
   fig              #fig.4.7
```

Figure 4.7

```
17         (0.4)
18 CUS:    non. >mais j'sais qu'c'est bon<
           no   >but I know it's good<
19 SEL:    oua*is? #
           yeah?
               ->*puts the bit on the balance and weights->>
    fig             #fig.4.8
```

Figure 4.8

```
20 CUS:    hé hé [hé
21 SEL:          [sûr hein?
                 [you are sure right?
22 CUS:    >oui oui<
           >yes yes<
23         (1.5)
```

The customer requests a specific type of cheese while the salesperson is weighing and wrapping the previous purchase. The salesperson finally walks toward the shelf where the Abondance is, and grasps a big piece of cheese (line 4). But the customer spots a smaller bit and asks to have that one instead (lines 5–6), occasioning the salesperson to replace the cheese she has brought back on the counter (line 11). This is accounted for by the customer, hinting at the simplification of the cutting (line 14). At this moment, in overlap, the salesperson offers a taste of the cheese (lines 15–16). The format used is a negative interrogative – which indeed orients to a possible negative response. The offer is produced while the seller is stopping the current trajectory of her right hand, bringing the cheese onto the counter, holding it above the balance and showing it (Figure 4.7). The changed trajectory of the gesture manages the offer as an alternative course of action to the one that is initiated and projected, suspending it until the response of the customer is completed. The customer rejects the offer (line 18), adding an account in which she claims her knowledge of the cheese. As soon as the rejection is clear, the salesperson puts the cheese on the balance and weighs it (Figure 4.8).

A very similar rejection characterizes the following offer, in Madrid:

Excerpt 4.15 (MDR_3012_cam2_cli8_1.19.41_2149)

```
01 SEL:    *quizás esto que es un queso que elaboramos
           perhaps this one that is a cheese that we make
           *grasps piece and puts it on the counter--->
02         nosotros en [valladolid.*
           ourselves in [Valladolid
                                 ->*
03 CUS:                [sí.
                       [yes
04         (0.4)
05 SEL:    s[í, el cuarenta de vaca.*
           y[es the forty of cow
06 CUS:    [vale pues ponme
           [alright then give me
    sel                            *approaches knife->
07         (0.3)
08 SEL:    quieres probarlo# un poquito? te apetece?
           do you want to taste a bit? do you fancy?
    fig                   #fig.4.9
```

Figure 4.9

```
09 CUS:    eh:: no. (.) [l:o conozco.
           eh   no (.)  [I know it.
10 SEL:                 [no?
                        [no?
11 SEL:    sí?*
           yes?
           ->*holds cheese and show a possible size->>
12         (0.3)
13 CUS:    sí.
           yes
14         (0.9)
15 CUS:    perfecto ponme un: [una#
           perfect give me    [one
16 SEL:                       [sí?#
                              [yes
    fig                         #fig.4.10
```

Offering a Taste in Gourmet Food Shops

Figure 4.10

```
17 CUS:   efectivamente la cuña esta:: perfecto
          right the corner is perfect
```

The seller proposes a cheese, which he shows and puts on the counter (lines 1–2). The customer accepts immediately (line 3), and begins to request a specific quantity (line 6), in overlap with the seller's explanation (line 5). At this point, the seller brings his knife to the side of the cheese (Figure 4.9), in a position that projects slicing rather than cutting: this prepares the sample to be tasted (line 8). The offer is formatted by focusing on the willingness and desire of the customer. But the customer refuses (line 9) and adds an account for that – claiming to know the cheese. When the rejection is clear, the seller moves the knife on the cheese and grasps it in such a way as to show a possible cut (Figure 4.10). This is understood as such by the customer (lines 15 and 17). By so doing, the seller moves from offering a taste to the satisfaction of the customer's request.

In the two last fragments, the offer, as in the previous cases discussed in this section, is positioned *after* the customer has already made a decision, and more specifically in a sequential environment where the expected next or the ongoing step is the decision of the size and quantity, and the corresponding cut. The offer is placed in an ongoing trajectory of action, and suspends it. Although the offer is inserted in this ongoing trajectory, it is not generated or motivated by it; it is not responsive to a customer's problem or difficulty – although it might anticipate a possible not-knowing of the customer (like in Excerpt 4.15, in which the customer has quickly accepted the proposed cheese without any other display). The rejection of the offer is expressed with a blunt negative particle, followed, in the last two cases, by an account that discloses the knowledge of the cheese by the customer. After the rejection, the seller resumes the course of the ongoing trajectory, and weighs or cuts the cheese.

4.7 Discussion and Conclusion

In Section 4.6, I have described some sequential environments characterizing offers that are rejected. Their examination deepens our understanding of the sequential environments characterizing offers that are accepted, analyzed in Section 4.5.

Offering a taste is made relevant in contexts in which the customer is already engaged in the process of buying – having asked for recommendations, formulated a generic request, or shown an interest in a buyable – and in which the progression and completion of this process is suspended by the presentation of various options and choices or conditioned by the provision of some extra information. These contexts are also characterized by an unknowing stance of the customer, and by knowledge as a condition for fair and transparent buying. Offering a taste does not only concern an object offered – a sample of a product – but also the possibility of engaging in an action – tasting – which gives an opportunity of direct sensorial access to the product, in a manner that overcomes the limitations of previous verbal descriptions and visual evidences (Mondada 2021). In this context, the offer is generally accepted.

By contrast, in sequential environments in which the customer is not yet engaged in buying something (as in the openings) or has already made a decision (as in the final phase of the purchase), offering a taste loses its relevance and is oriented to as such by the customer – and sometimes by the salesperson, as demonstrated by the format s/he chooses for the offer. Moreover, in these contexts, the customer often accounts for the rejection with a claim to know the cheese. Whereas claiming or displaying not knowing makes offering a taste relevant, claiming or displaying knowledge provides an account for rejecting the offer.

These contrasted environments show the interplay between (a) the sequential organization of the purchase and the slots in which opportunities for offering a taste become relevant, (b) the legitimacy of offers, (c) the epistemic positions exhibited by recipients of the offer, and (d) ultimately, the definition of the 'benefice' for the 'beneficiary' of the offer. Moreover, (e) the formats of the offer display an orientation to these contingencies too. The most frequent format of offers is the equivalent of 'do you want to taste?' (see Curl 2006), but significant variations are sensitive to the local circumstances, namely, offers in which a need or a desire is attributed to the recipient, vs. offers that are clearly initiated and under the responsibility of the seller, as well as offers in the factitive format putting the agency on the seller – when the object offered might not be the one the customer had originally requested (see Excerpts 4.1 and 4.9).

An offer is characterized by the fact that the participant offering something is doing the action and the recipient of the offer is the beneficiary (Couper-Kuhlen 2014; Clayman & Heritage 2014). In this chapter, I have discussed category-bound offers produced in a commercial setting, by participants acting as 'salespersons' to 'customers' and even 'buyers'. Although proposing a complimentary and free small sample, offering a taste is not oriented to by the participants as disengaged from the activities of buying and selling, but as bound to the engagement to buy. This is demonstrated by the crucial importance of sequential positions where offers are made and their differentiated outcomes. Offers are accepted when proposed at key moments in the process of buying, when the decision to buy something has been more or less clearly made and *before* the final decision about what to precisely buy occurs. Offers are rejected when proposed too early – when the encounter has not yet properly started and the person entering the shop has not yet become a 'customer' (but might be a 'just-looking') – or too late – when the decision to buy a particular product has already taken place. This means that offering a taste is understood by customers and salespersons alike as a crucial device for supporting the activity of buying and selling.

Offering a taste fosters the progressivity of the encounters, when there are indecisions, options, insufficient evidences for choosing, selecting, and deciding. In this context, tasting is a form of access to the product beyond the limits of language and vision, providing sensorial grounds for decision-making. In this sense, offering a taste reveals a hierarchized order of solutions to the problem of customers: first, the sellers give information, then they give access to the materiality and sensoriality of the product.

The activity studied highlights how complex the category of 'beneficiary' of an action – as a central feature defining offers (Couper-Kuhlen 2014; Clayman & Heritage 2014) – might be in specific settings. In offering a taste in gourmet shops, it is not so clear who the final beneficiary is (the customer obtaining a product that suits her, the salesperson selling the product). Other relevant features, such as responsibilities, rights, and obligations, bound to the institutional categories of the participants, are also central. Although the customer might be the beneficiary of the gift of a gratuitous sample, s/he is also the one who finally pays the seller for the product. The local logic of economics and the market cast some original light on the more general praxeology of actions such as offers.

The study of the action of offering a taste contributes to a better understanding of how economic exchanges work in subtle ways. Presented as a gratuitous small gift, these offers are oriented to as in fact contributing to the logic of the commercial transaction. Mauss's (1924) approach to gifts is based on the notion of 'counter-gift' (*contre-don*) – which has been extended to a general principle of reciprocity (Gouldner 1960). Mauss links the circulation of goods and the ritual and symbolic meanings attached to them – treating them as a 'total social phenomenon' – and insists on the fact that the gift creates attachment, social expectations, and obligations. The gift escapes calculative and utilitarian economic exchanges (cf. 'the taboo of calculus', Bourdieu 1980 – *pace* the 'felicific calculus' of Clayman & Heritage 2014), and rather is meant to build bonding and trust over indefinite time. However, despite different rationalities characterizing gift economy vs. market economy, the sense of indebtedness and repayment have been pointed to by ethnographers of gift economies commenting on the 'dark side of the gift' (Sherry et al. 1993; Marcoux 2009). Likewise, this has prompted authors to relativize or at least resymmetricize the relation between gift and exchange (Callon & Latour 1997) and to consider that objects undergo constant transformations, and can evolve from gifts to commodities and vice versa (Thomas 1991: 39).

An ethnomethodological and conversation analytic approach to gifts in interaction (Llewellyn 2011b) invites us to consider how participants actually recognize and manage the emergence of a gift in interaction, its recognition, and the response of the would-be donor. For instance, reciprocity is not a taken-for-granted constitutive feature of gifts, but something that is enacted in situ and made publicly accountable – if relevant, it announces and organizes further actions between the participants. A gift, a treat, a present are categories that are differentiated by the participants (Llewellyn 2011b: 733), and that imply different rights and obligations.

The systematic analysis in the present chapter shows that offering a taste is never treated as gratuitous, because it is embedded in the organization of the commercial exchange and it is seen as contributing to it. Whereas Llewellyn (2011b) shows that gifts between customers picking up the bill are resisted to in dispreferred and peculiarly mild ways, offering a taste is either unproblematically accepted – when sustaining the ongoing sequential progressivity of the exchange and its projected outcome – or clearly refused –when placed in a less relevant way within the encounter. Both responses to the offer orient to the accountability of obligations contracted by the gift, which can be seen either as aligned with the ongoing emergent decision to buy or as unnecessarily imposing and constraining the next actions of the customer. In this sense, offering a taste fully contributes to an economy of gift in the service of the commercial exchange.

Acknowledgments

This chapter was written as part of the FiDiPro project *Multimodality: Reconsidering language and action through embodiment*, funded by the Academy of Finland and the University of Helsinki (project no 282931)

(2015–2017) as well as the project *From multimodality to multisensoriality: Language, body, and sensoriality in social interaction* which followed it, funded by the Swiss National Science Foundation (project no 100012_175969) (2018–2022).

References

Bourdieu, P. (1980). *Le sens pratique*. Paris: Minuit. Published in English as *The Logic of Practice*, Stanford: Stanford University Press, 1990.

Callon, M., & Latour, B. (1997). Tu ne calculeras pas! Ou comment maîtriser le don et le capital [You will not calculate! Or how to master the gift and the capital]. *Revue du MAUSS*, 9, 45–70.

Clayman, S. (2013). Agency in response: The role of prefatory address terms. *Journal of Pragmatics*, 57, 290–302. https://doi.org/10.1016/j.pragma.2012.12.001

Clayman, S., & Heritage, J. (2014). Benefactors and beneficiaries: Benefactive status and stance in the management of offers and requests. In P. Drew & E. Couper-Kuhlen, eds., *Requesting in Social Interaction*. Amsterdam: John Benjamins, pp. 55–86. https://doi.org/10.1075/slsi.26.03cla

Couper-Kuhlen, E. (2014). What does grammar tell us about action? *Pragmatics*, 24(3), 623–647. https://doi.org/10.1075/prag.24.3.08cou

Curl, T. S. (2006) Offers of assistance: Constraints on syntactic design. *Journal of Pragmatics*, 38(8), 1257–1280. https://doi.org/10.1016/j.pragma.2005.09.004

Douglas, M. (2002). Foreword: No free gifts. In M. Mauss, *The Gift*. London: Routledge.

Fox, B., & T. Heinemann (2015). The alignment of manual and verbal displays in requests for the repair of an object. *Research on Language and Social Interaction*, 48(3), 342–362. https://doi.org/10.1080/08351813.2015.1058608

(2016). Rethinking format: An examination of requests. *Language in Society*, 45(4), 499–531. https://doi.org/10.1017/S0047404516000385

Gill, V. T. (2005). Patient "demand" for medical interventions: Exerting pressure for an offer in a primary care clinic visit. *Research on Language and Social Interaction*, 38(4), 451–479. https://doi.org/10.1207/s15327973rlsi3804_3

Gouldner, A. W. (1960). The norm of reciprocity: A preliminary statement. *American Sociological Review*, 25(2), 161–178. https://doi.org/10.2307/2092623

Heritage, J. (2012). The epistemic engine: Sequence organization and territories of knowledge. *Research on Language and Social Interaction*, 45(1), 30–52. https://doi.org/10.1080/08351813.2012.646685

Heritage, J., & Sefi, S. (1992). Dilemmas of advice: Aspects of delivery and reception of advice in interactions between health visitors and first time mothers. In P. Drew & J. Heritage, eds., *Talk at Work: Interactions in Institutional Settings*. Cambridge: Cambridge University Press, pp. 359–417.

Hoey, E. (2020). Self-authorizing action: On *let me X* in English social interaction. *Language in Society*, 51(1), 95–118. https://doi.org/10.1017/S0047404520000779

Hutchby, I. (2006). *Media Talk*. Glasgow: Open University Press.

Jefferson, G., & Lee, J. R. E. (1981). The rejection of advice: Managing the problematic convergence of a 'troubles-telling' and a 'service encounter'. *Journal of Pragmatics*, 5(5), 399–422. https://doi.org/10.1016/0378-2166(81)90026-6

Kärkkäinen, E., & Keisanen, T. (2012). Linguistic and embodied formats for making (concrete) offers. *Discourse Studies*, 14(5), 587–611. https://doi.org/10.1177/1461445612454069

Kendrick K., & Drew, P. (2014). The putative preference for offers over requests. In P. Drew & E. Couper-Kuhlen, eds., *Requesting in Social Interaction*. Amsterdam: John Benjamins, pp. 87–114. https://doi.org/10.1075/slsi.26.04ken

Kinnell, A. M. K., & Maynard, D. W. (1996). The delivery and receipt of safer sex advice in pretest counseling sessions for HIV and AIDS. *Journal of Contemporary Ethnography*, 24(4), 405–437. https://doi.org/10.1177/089124196024004002

Llewellyn, N. (2011a). The delicacy of the gift: Passing donations and leaving change. *Discourse & Society*, 22(2), 155–174. https://doi.org/10.1177/0957926510392126

(2011b). The gift in interaction: A study of 'picking up the bill'. *The British Journal of Sociology*, 62(4), 718–738. https://doi.org/10.1111/j.1468-4446.2011.01388.x

Marcoux, J.-S. (2009). Escaping the gift economy. *Journal of Consumer Research*, 36(4), 671–685. https://doi.org/10.1086/600485

Mauss, M. (1924). Essai sur le Don: Forme et raison de l'échange dans les sociétés archaïques. *L'Année Sociologique*, 1, 30–186. Published in English as *The Gift: Forms and Functions of Exchange in Archaic Societies*, New York: Norton, 1967.

Merritt, M. (1976). On questions following questions in service encounters. *Language in Society*, 5(3), 315–357. https://doi.org/10.1017/S0047404500007168

Mondada, L. (2018). The multimodal interactional organization of tasting: Practices of tasting cheese in gourmet shops. *Discourse Studies*, 20(6), 743–769. https://doi.org/10.1177/1461445618793439

(2021). *Sensoriality in Social Interaction*. Cambridge: Cambridge University Press.

(2022). Attributing the decision to buy: Action ascription, local ecology, and multimodality in shop encounters. In A. Deppermann & M. Haugh, eds., *Action Ascription in Interaction*. Cambridge: Cambridge University Press, pp. 105–133.

Mondada, L., & Sorjonen, M.-L. (2016). Making multiple requests in French and Finnish convenience stores. *Language in Society*, 45(5), 733–765. https://doi.org/10.1017/S0047404516000646

Pomerantz. A., & Heritage, J. (2012). Preference. In J. Sidnell & T. Stivers, eds., *The Handbook of Conversation Analysis*. Chichester: Wiley-Blackwell, pp. 210–228. https://doi.org/10.1002/9781118325001.ch11

Raymond, C., Robinson, J. D., Fox, B., & Thompson, S. A. (2020). Modulating action through minimization: Syntax in the service of offering and requesting. *Language in Society (First View)*. https://doi.org/10.1017/S004740452000069X

Sacks, H. (1992). *Lectures on Conversation, Vols 1 & 2*. Ed. by G. Jefferson. Oxford: Basil Blackwell.

Schegloff, E. A. (2007). *Sequence Organization in Interaction: A Primer in Conversation Analysis, Vol. 1*. Cambridge: Cambridge University Press. https://doi.org/10.1017/CBO9780511791208

Sherry, J. F., McGrath, M. A., & Levy, S. J. (1993). The dark side of the gift. *Journal of Business Research*, 28(3), 225–244. https://doi.org/10.1016/0148-2963(93)90049-U

Sorjonen, M.-L., & Raevaara, L. (2014). On the grammatical form of requests at the convenience store: Requesting as embodied action. In P. Drew & E. Couper-Kuhlen, eds., *Requesting in Social Interaction*. Amsterdam: John Benjamins, pp. 243–268. https://doi.org/10.1075/slsi.26.10sor

Thomas, N. (1991). *Entangled Objects: Exchange, Material Culture, and Colonialism in the Pacific*. Cambridge, MA: Harvard University Press.

5 Embodied Trajectories of Actions in Shop Encounters
Giving or Placing Products on or over the Counter

Lorenza Mondada and Marja-Leena Sorjonen

5.1 Introduction: Interactional Economies

Economic exchanges are characterized by the circulation of products between institutional partners. In that process, a product, such as a physical object, changes possession as a result of being transformed from a buyable product to a purchase, from a *possessable* to a possession, and from a *payable* to paid. These changes are not abstract economic processes: when achieved in face-to-face encounters (vs. buying on the internet), they are embodied situated activities of selling and buying, giving and taking. Transactions can be conceived as involving companies and more abstract financial and economic organizations, enabling the circulation of goods around the world. But they can be also viewed as activities in the everyday lives of people, involving persons moving objects around, transferring them from the shop shelves or the like to the counter, from the counter to the customer's bag, and from shops to homes. In this case, the economic 'exchange' can be considered literally – as exchanges of turns-at-talk and as embodied actions of transferring material objects from one hand to another – rather than as abstract invisible macroeconomic transactions. The aim of this chapter is to investigate embodied encounters happening at the counter in convenience stores and to focus on the transfer of objects that characterizes these situated transactions.

By tracking the ways in which customers and sellers at the counter use their hands and other embodied resources to organize the stepwise transformation of objects into bought products, this chapter aims at re-embodying and re-praxeologizing economic transactions. That is, we observe the transactions as they are achieved in situ by embodied social participants interacting face to face, in contrast to research treating economic transactions as abstract and generic transfers of money and goods between nonhuman agents, like companies. We will show how ways of handling products – picking them up, offering, giving, taking, and grasping them – embody and materialize economic transactions. Furthermore, we will show that these activities are organized in a systematic fashion in concert by the interacting participants. In this way, the chapter aims to contribute both to recent trends in the study of the interactional practices that constitute the market and the economy, as well as to current issues in conversation analysis about the organization of situated actions, action formation, and the interplay of language, the body, and material objects.

Verbal exchanges in commercial settings have been investigated for quite some time from different pragmatic-discursive and sociolinguistic perspectives (see, for example, Félix-Brasdefer 2015: 23–48 for an overview). These studies often focus on issues of rapport, politeness, and social relations, but the commercial stakes of the encounters fall outside the investigation. They are mostly based on audio-recordings, and consequently do not consider embodiment and materiality, both central in these transactions. In our chapter, embodied actions, objects, and the spatial arrangement of the store form a central aspect of the investigation.

More recently, there has been a growing interest in ethnomethodology and conversation analysis in the interactional dimension of commercial encounters, seen as an example of institutional interactions but also as activities specifically involved in the shape of economic values and rationalities. Among studies on everyday sales contexts, some analyses have focused on the physical arrangements of buyers and sellers (e.g., in street markets, Llewellyn & Burrow 2008), whereas others have analyzed talk about and handling of material products or services that the customer considers buying (e.g., choosing products in supermarkets, De Stefani 2011, 2014; manipulating products and their packaging during a commercial negotiation, Streeck 1996; filling in the order form in quick print shops, Moore et al. 2010; handing over shoes in repair shops, Fox & Heinemann 2015; and feeling and sensorially assessing possible products to buy, Mondada 2019), including issues of payment (Llewellyn 2011, 2015). This literature has shown the relevance of the specific manipulation of objects (either products or money) for the accomplishment of actions relevant for the progressivity of the commercial encounter (such as handing over the exact amount of money as recognizably doing a request for a particular service, Llewellyn 2015).

The manipulation of objects in social interaction has more generally been the focus of a number of recent studies in multimodal ethnomethodology and conversation analysis (EMCA) (Nevile et al. 2014). More specifically, interactions in which objects are constitutive and represent the central focus of attention have received increasing attention. These include the role of the hammer in auctions (Heath 2013), and the manipulation of products in supermarkets (De Stefani 2011) and surgical tools during an operation (Heath et al. 2018). These studies show the interest in looking more closely at the way in which transfers of objects are accomplished in their detailed embodied way – for instance, involving specific shapes and movements of the hand adapted both to the specific shape and materiality of the objects grasped and to the action of the co-participant engaged in the transfer (Heath et al. 2018; Mondada et al. 2020). In the economic transactions we examine here, we show how the detailed embodied trajectories of object transfers reveal specific relations between customers and sellers, necessitate the organization of specific modes of practical coordination, and display orientations to the normative and moral aspects of the ongoing economic encounter.

In this chapter, we investigate economic encounters brought about by customers and salespeople when they handle products over the counter in convenience stores, also called kiosks, video-recorded in a variety of European countries. Focusing on embodied actions through and during which products are transferred from the hands of the customer to the hands of the seller allows us to describe the concrete methodic ways that form the bedrock of the transaction and lead to the completion of the purchase. It is over the counter that participants accomplish the most decisive and performative transformations that constitute the transaction. We will show how the interactional organization, and the exchange of objects in interaction, is implemented multimodally to proceed through systematic basic forms of paired actions, such as giving and taking a product over the counter, or placing a product on the counter before it is retrieved.

5.2   Data and the Phenomenon

The data we use in this study come from video corpora recorded in three European countries – Finland, France, and Switzerland – and spoken in four languages: Finnish, French, Swiss German, and Italian. The Finnish corpus, which contains some 800 encounters (ca. 10 hours in total) at kiosks[1] belonging to the same chain and located in four different regions, was collected in 1999–2002.[2] The corpus *int-counters*,[3] comprising recordings in convenience stores (*tabac presse*) in France (80 encounters), and in kiosks in French-speaking (40 encounters), German-speaking (120 encounters), and Italian-speaking (60 encounters) Switzerland, was collected in 2015–2016 (ca. 8 hours in total). An earlier French corpus from 1986 in a *tabac presse* in Lyon[4] consists of more than 120 encounters (ca. 2 hours in total).

---

[1] 'Kiosk' is the corresponding term for the shops in Finland (Finnish *kioski*) and in Switzerland (German *Kiosk*, Swiss-Italian *chiosco*, French *kiosque*). In France, they are variously called *bureau de tabac/tabac/tabac presse/presse-tabac*, referring to tobacconists also selling newspapers and magazines, as well as some convenience goods. Here, we use the term *kiosk* for the former and *convenience store* for the latter.

[2] The data were collected in a research project on service encounters at the Institute for the Languages of Finland.

[3] The data of the corpus *int-counters* were video-recorded in 2015–2016, within Lorenza Mondada's Finland Distinguished Professorship project *Multimodality: Reconsidering language and action through embodiment*, funded by the Academy of Finland (grant no. 282931) and hosted by the Centre of Excellence on Intersubjectivity of the University of Helsinki.

[4] The corpus *tabac* has been bequeathed by Jacques Cosnier at the ICAR research lab (CNRS, University of Lyon, ENS Lyon) and is part of the CLAPI data bank (clapi.univ-lyon2.fr).

The commercial transactions recorded in these convenience stores are based on a variety of transfers of objects involving different types of product, uses of the counter, actions, and recipients. A basic difference in the organization of actions mobilizing the products concerns whether they have to be requested by the customer at the counter (what we call products *fetched* by the seller) or are available to the customer to pick up her/himself (products *picked up* by the customer). Whereas the former (typically, cigarettes) are brought to the counter by the seller after having been scanned by the barcode reader and thereby registered in the till, the latter (typically, drinks and candies) are brought to the counter by the customer and manipulated by the seller before coming back to the customer. The modes of object circulation and transfer are therefore associated with the type of product.

Likewise, money – whether in the form of bills, coins, or bank card payments – crosses from one side of the counter to the other (see Halonen & Koivisto, this volume). A specific type of product in kiosks is constituted by lottery tickets, which are handed over to the seller by the customer either for buying (after they have filled them in) or checking. In the former case, the customer has to pay for them, as for other products; in the latter, the customer is already the owner of the lottery ticket and receives some money back from the seller if they win. These different transfer types thus implement different actions (requesting to buy, requesting to check, paying, giving change, etc.) which happen at different sequential moments within the transaction. Through them, a change in the status of the product is achieved from a product that is sellable and buyable to one that is on its way to become possessable and possessed (see Garfinkel & Wieder 1992: 185 on *possessables* vs. *possessitives*), to be bought and possessed by the customer (see also De Stefani 2014 on *purchasable* vs. *non-purchasable*).

The following simple transaction, recorded in Lyon in the 1980s, provides examples of these different transfers, containing exchanges of words, products, and money. (The transcription conventions of verbal and embodied actions, as well as the key for the glossing symbols, are provided in the Appendix to this volume.)

Excerpt 5.1 (Tabac02_01_14/2.01.40; CUS = customer, SEL = seller)

```
01            +(0.7)            + * (0.2)
    cus    +places nwsps on c+
    sel                          *manipulates nwsps->
02 SEL:    alo:rs? dix:  (0.3) trei:ze?(0.2) trei:ze?
           so       ten   (0.3) thirteen (0.2) thirteen
03         vingt:-qua+tre:
           twenty-four
    cus                +...hands a 50F bill->
```

```
04          (0.2) + (0.5)#+ (0.2)
   cus            ->+holds it+,,,,,,,->
   fig                     #fig.5.1
```

Figure 5.1

```
05 CUS: → °mettez aussi+ une+ gauloise# ble*ue°*
           °add also a Gauloise blue°
                        -->+places bill on c+
   sel                                     -->*grasps bill*
   fig                                  #fig.5.2
```

Figure 5.2

```
06       *(1.5)
   sel   *turns w bill to shelf->
07 SEL:  vingt-quatre:,* (.)   tren*te-deux soixan*te.*#
         twenty four            thirty two sixty
                        ->*grasps cig*turns to CUS--*puts cig on c*
   fig                                                    #fig.5.3
```

Embodied Trajectories of Actions in Shop Encounters   149

Figure 5.3

```
08          +(0.4)      + *    (1.6)    * (0.6) + (0.4)
   sel                     *opens drawer*picks up coins->
   cus     +grasps cig+                   +grasps the nwsp->
09 SEL:   trente-trois trente-cinq (.) quarante+
          thirty three thirty five (.) forty
   cus                                            ->+
10          (0.2) * (0.8)
   sel           *places coins on the counter->
11 SEL:   et voi*là+
          and that's it
                ->*
   cus              +grasps coins->
12          (0.2)  # (2.3)  *    (0.3)   * (3.0)  +
   sel                     *closes drawer*
   cus                                            -->+
   fig           #fig.5.4
```

Figure 5.4

```
13 CUS:   °°allez au r'voir°°
          let's go    good bye
14 SEL:   °°r'voir°°
          good bye
```

The customer first places on the counter products (newspapers and magazines) that he has picked up himself; he does that without saying a word (line 1). The products are retrieved by the seller, who counts their amount and price, doing it aloud and calculating the cost progressively as she flips through the magazines (lines 2–3). This calculation is responded to by the customer with an offer of money. The money is first handed (lines 3–4), then held (as the seller is occupied with folding the magazines), and, finally, after a retraction, placed on the counter (line 5). The bill is picked up by the seller a moment afterward (line 5), after the customer has changed the trajectory of his gesture from handing the money directly to the seller to placing it on the counter.

As this happens, the customer makes a further request, now for a product (cigarettes) located on the shelf behind the seller's back. The seller now has two parallel actions to respond to: the payment and the new request. What she does is to grasp the bill and turn to the shelf with the bill in her hand to grab the requested cigarettes (lines 6–7), which she places on the counter and the customer immediately picks up. She simultaneously calculates aloud the final price (24 → 32.60 francs). She then opens the drawer where her coins and bills are and picks up coins, again counting aloud the change to be given to the customer (line 9). As soon as the seller begins to prepare the return coins, the customer picks up the newspapers. This not only projects the end of the transaction, but also orients to this precise moment as achieving the change of possession of the goods. When the seller puts the coins on the counter, the customer right away picks them up while the seller closes the money drawer.

This fragment shows a transaction that constitutes an exchange of several goods (first, second, etc., requests), and types of goods (picked up vs. fetched) over the counter, as well as the exchange of money, back and forth (the bill and the change). Talk provides an audible access to the incremental price calculation and therefore the transparency of the process of paying and giving the change. Thus, the handling of objects, including money, is not only a practical achievement but it is symbolically exhibited, made observable and witnessable for all of the parties. By verbalizing in an explicit manner the institutional and legal value of the products, the participants manifest their orientation toward issues of trust, normativity, and morality of action.

The sequential organization of talk and the manual handling of the objects in this excerpt raises questions such as (i) when is the transaction completed and (ii) when do the products change their status from buyable into bought, from possessable into possessed? An orientation toward these issues is displayed in ways of making use of the spatial affordances of the counter. The objects on the counter are located in a certain way. The newspapers occupy the center of the counter (Figure 5.1) when the customer hands over the bill. As soon as the newspapers manipulated by the seller are put a bit apart by her, making some space on the right corner toward the customer, the customer puts a 50-franc bill there (Figure 5.2). This corner is also the location where the seller places the requested cigarettes (Figure 5.3) and where she puts the return money (Figure 5.4). This corner, the one closer to the customer, appears to be devoted to the process of making objects into ones now 'belonging' to him, and he orients to that by picking them immediately. The newspapers are taken later. The counter is thus a variable space, with specialized locations which are locally and contingently defined, indexing the status of the objects. Both the time of the sequential unfolding of the exchange and the location of objects centrally feature in the legal-economic transformations of the objects from products of the shop into purchased items now privately owned.

In the sections to follow, we pay particular attention to the trajectory, projection, and accountability of the participants' embodied movements. Our analysis aims to show how the coordinated handling of products – sometimes silent, sometimes coordinated with talk – achieves the economic transaction in ways that reveal a variety of key issues of social interaction and sociability, such as formatting and recognizing actions, designing one's conduct for the current recipient, and normative expectations and trust.

The analyses focus on transfers of products that the customer has picked up herself or that s/he is bringing to the counter, as is the case for lottery tickets (for products that the seller needs to fetch, see Mondada & Sorjonen 2016; Sorjonen & Raevaara 2014). We will analyze two types of embodied paired actions through which products are transferred from the customer to the seller: in the first one, *placing and grasping*, the customer puts the product *on* the counter and the seller retrieves it from the counter; in the second, *giving and taking*, the customer hands over the product to the seller *over* the counter.

The study of these trajectories of hands handling products and the temporal coordination of sequences of action in which objects are given or placed, taken or grasped, contributes more generally to the study of embodied actions, their local intelligibility and interpretation. It also contributes to better understanding the sequential organization of the coordinated realization of these embodied actions. We will show that a product left on the counter is intelligible only relative to past and future actions. With our analyses, we will show the different kinds of inferences and displays of mutual understanding concerning physical objects in shop encounters.

5.3   *Placing and Grasping* vs. *Giving and Taking*

When the customer approaches the counter holding a product that they have picked up in the shop, or bringing a lottery ticket to the seller to check if it has won a prize, there are two possible next actions: the customer either *places* the product on the counter or *gives* it to the seller. In turn, the seller either *grasps* the product from the counter or *takes* it directly from the customer. These alternative actions and their responses are related to the next action, which is the barcode reading by the seller that registers the purchase and, in so doing, establishes an obligation to pay it – the process having become mandatory at some point in the history of technological infrastructures equipping the shop (vs. earlier times, like in Excerpt 5.1) – and the consequent transfer of the possession of the object to the customer. Clark (2003) speaks of the gesture of *placing* as moving the object into the field of attention of the co-participant, and contrasts it with *pointing*, which consists in directing attention toward the object. Here we rather contrast two ways of using the hand, *placing* vs. *giving* an object, and their responses. Placing is defined here in relation to the environment where the object is put and to issues of coordination of actions by the two parties to organize its transfer, rather than to the recipient's attention to it (as we will show, placing can be achieved when the recipient is *not* gazing at the object).

These two alternatives raise the question of whether placing the product on the counter vs. giving it to the seller are two distinct and systematic practices. What kinds of orientation to the ongoing encounter are these two ways of handling the transfer of the product used for? We will investigate the embodied movements of the hands, their temporal-sequential organization, their ecologies (e.g., types of spatial arrangements of furnishings, tools, and goods, and the spatial position of the interactants), as well as other contingencies that may motivate why and when customers perform the action of *placing* vs. *giving*. We start by exploring the simplest organization of these two practices (Section 5.3). In a next step (Section 5.4), we show some sequential environments that favor one over the other. Finally, we turn to more complex cases in which the choice between the alternatives (*placing* vs. *giving*) is more ambiguous (Sections 5.5 and 5.6).

5.3.1 *Placing* a Product to Be *Grasped*

One possibility for the customer who picked up a product is to place it on the counter and let the seller grasp it and retrieve it from there. Placing the product on the counter tacitly achieves an economic action, showing that the customer has selected that item, has removed it from the shop, and is now requesting to buy it.

In order to show how these actions are organized, we discuss a case recorded in Fribourg (Switzerland). The customer buys two products: a can of soft drink, held with his right hand (product 1, pr1 in the excerpt), and a package of bonbons in his left hand (product 2, pr2).

Excerpt 5.2 (KIO_CH_ FRI-1-06-36)

```
01            (0.8)        *(0.6)±(0.2)°(0.2)#(0.3)‡(0.1)
    cus   >>walks to counter--->
    sel   >>monitors CUS*looks at pr1--->
    cus                            ±LH places pr1 on counter---->
    sel                             °...->
    cus                                          ‡RH puts pr2 on c->
    fig                                  #fig.5.5
```

Figure 5.5

```
02 SEL:   m±er°:#ci±
          thanks
    cus   ->±,,,,,,±
    sel       ->°RH grasps pr1----->
    fig        #fig.5.6
```

Figure 5.6

```
03             (0.2)  °  (0.1)  *  (0.15) ‡ (0.15)  °Ω  (0.3)  Ω‡  (0.4)°
    sel              ->°reads b-c/pr1-----------°puts back on c--°
    sel                  ->*looks at pr2-------------------->>
    cus                           ->‡,,,,,,,,,,,,,,,,,,‡
    sel                                       Ω.......ΩLH grasps pr2->
04 SEL:        ça c'est Ωtout?
               that is all?
    sel              ->Ωreads b-c/pr2--->
05             (0.2) Ω
    sel             -->Ωputs pr2 back on the counter->>
```

As the customer walks to the counter, the seller is available and monitors him: she follows with her gaze the trajectory of the first product, which the customer brings toward the counter, stretching over his hand (line 1). The seller then moves her right hand (in Figure 5.5 she is beginning to move it): the precise timing and trajectory of this responding gesture is designed to indicate that she is *not taking* the product from the customer's hand, but rather *grasping* it from the counter.

Shortly after having put the drink on the counter with his right hand, the customer puts the bonbons on the counter with his left hand, while the seller is still extending her right hand to grasp the first product from the counter (Figure 5.6) and saying *mer:ci* (line 2). Having taken the first product (drink), she reads its barcode (line 3) and puts the reader back on the counter. She then grasps the second product (bonbons) with her left hand and does the same operation again (lines 3–4), while asking ça c'est tout? 'that is all' (line 4), thereby orienting to possible completion of the purchase.

Using both hands, a different hand for each product, allows both participants to manage the handling of the products successively and swiftly one after the other. This complementary use of his hands by the customer for *placing* is possibly aligned to by the seller when she organizes her *grasping* with the same distribution of the hands, mirroring and reciprocating what the customer does. In this way, the customer's gestures are immediately responded to by the symmetric gestures of the seller, leading to an immediate processing of the product with the barcode reader. The way in which the grasping is timed can thus exhibit the seller's readiness for service and close monitoring of the ongoing action.

5.3.2   Giving a Product to Be *Taken*

The other possible way of organizing the transfer of products between customer and seller consists of giving and taking the product *above* the counter, in the air. We detail the sequential organization of this practice with two excerpts. In the following excerpt, recorded in Helsinki, the customer is bringing the seller a lottery ticket to have it checked to see if he has won something.

Excerpt 5.3 (KIO_FIN_T796)

```
01          (0.3)
   cus   >>approaches counter, takes lottery ticket from wallet->
02 SEL:   *moi
          hello
          *gazes at CUS->
03 CUS:    m*o:i
          hello
   sel   ->*gazes at ticket->
04        (0.2)#(0.2) †± (0.35) ± (0.15)
   cus              ->†stops-->>
   cus                   ±........±hands ticket->
   fig             #fig.5.7
```

Figure 5.7

```
05 CUS:   °ka°toksä        onks°  #         tuol      mitää±
          look.2SG.Q.youSG be.3SG.Q.CLI     DEM2.ALL  any.PAR
          would you check if there is anything
   sel    °[..]°opens/closes----°takes----->
   cus                                                --->±
   fig                            #fig.5.8
```

Figure 5.8

```
06 SEL:   >joo.h<
          yes
07        (0.2)•°
   sel          •walks to the machine--->>
   sel          ->°
```

As the customer approaches the counter, greetings are exchanged (lines 2–3), and the seller immediately moves her gaze from the customer to the lottery ticket he is taking from his wallet (Figure 5.7). The customer begins to hand over his ticket as soon as he stops in front of the counter (line 4), and quite before he starts producing a request specifying the service he wants (line 5). During his turn, the seller takes the ticket. She quickly moves forward with her arm, as the customer is already handing the object across the counter (Figure 5.8), opens her hand and takes the ticket (line 5). She responds to the request with a claim of complying (*joo.h* 'yes', line 6), projecting a delayed fulfillment of the request (Mondada & Sorjonen 2016; see also Rauniomaa & Keisanen 2012), and she indeed walks toward the machine to process the lottery ticket (line 7).

Here, the transfer of the object indexes an action asked from the seller that differs from the one in the previous case, and that is formulated verbally (vs. tacitly implemented by the gesture in the former case; see Llewellyn 2015). The action of *giving* is initiated by the customer, who then adjusts the timing of extending his hand to the progression of the responsive arm of the seller. Throughout, the seller monitors the progression of the encounter, the actions by the customer, showing her availability. She responds promptly to his way of formatting the *giving* of the lottery ticket by extending her arm to *take* the object from his hand.

Whereas in the previous excerpt the action of *giving* the object was initiated by the customer, in the next excerpt it is initiated by the seller. In this encounter in Basel (Switzerland), the customer is buying a candy bar.

Excerpt 5.4 (KIO_CH_BS2_33.50_cli16)

```
01         (2.2)  °     (0.3) #       *(0.2)± (0.3)
    cus    >>approaches the counter->
    sel    >>monitors CUS approaching*looks at candy->
    sel           °extends RH--->
    cus                                   ±...-->
    fig                  #fig.5.9
```

Figure 5.9

Embodied Trajectories of Actions in Shop Encounters 157

```
02  SEL:       s°±o#::°:,        °±
                so
     sel       ->|°|opens|°|closes|°|takes----->|
     cus       ->±gives candy--±,,,,,->|
     fig              #fig.5.10
```

Figure 5.10

```
03            (0.4)±(0.2)†(0.5) °   (0.2)    °
     cus        ->±
     cus               ->†stops--->>
     sel                       ->°reads b-c°puts back on c->>
```

As shown in Figure 5.10, the paired actions of *giving* and *taking* are tightly coordinated. The sequence is initiated by the seller: he extends his arm when the customer is still approaching (line 1, Figure 5.9). He is not only ready to take, but also displays his readiness to take as an invitation to the customer to *give* him the product. As the customer comes closer with the candy bar, the seller opens his hand, closing it around the product, while he is producing *so:::* (line 2, Figure 5.10). Notice that the customer has not yet stopped in front of the counter when the seller has already taken the product and is bringing it toward the barcode reader (line 3). The readiness to take secures a smooth and quick service, as the customer is still on her way to the counter.

These excerpts show how the coordination between the seller and the customer can be timed in a fine-grained way. This is made possible by the fact that the seller monitors the trajectory of the approaching customer, as well as the product she is holding in her hands. The trajectories of walking and stepping, as well as the trajectory of the product held by the customer, provide for the seller hints as to the kinds of action that the customer is preparing for. This enables him to anticipate those actions and their timing, and even, reflexively, to preempt and invite them. In turn, the customer adjusts her extending hand to the inviting hand of the seller.

In this section, we have detailed the basic organization of two paired actions that constitute alternative formats used by participants to transfer products from one side of the counter to the other – either *giving* and *taking* it *over* the counter, or *placing* it *on* and *grasping* it *from* the counter. Although there appears to be a general division of labor between the two categories of participants, the customer initiating the sequence while handing over, in one way or another, the product, and the seller receiving it, a closer look at the details of these actions shows that the sequence can be equally initiated by either participant. For instance, instead of merely responding to the customer's handing over of the object, the seller can initiate the action with an anticipatory movement inviting the customer to perform either a giving or a placing action. In this sense, the receiver is not restricted to adjusting to the action of the giver, but can also initiate it. In all the cases there is a reflexive mutual shaping of each other's arm trajectory and prehensile hand within a form of micro-sequentiality constituted by continuous mutual adjustments (Mondada 2021). This is enabled by the fact that the execution of both paired actions relies on close monitoring, coordination, and mutual adjustment of the participants (for troubles and misalignments in passing an object, see Excerpt 5.12).

Whereas the paired actions of *giving* and *taking* require a perfect synchronized timing of the participants' hands moving toward each other and meeting on the product, the paired actions of *placing* the object on the counter and *grasping* it enable the participants to time their actions in a more or less asynchronous way. Even in this latter case, however, the actions might be finely coordinated, as shown in Excerpt 5.2. As we shall see, the trajectories of the body and the hands, the shape of the receiving hand, the type and form of the product, and the timing of both hands and bodies coming closer to each other are central in the finely tuned organization of both *giving/taking* and *placing/grasping*.

5.4 Praxeological Contexts Favoring Either *Placing* or *Giving*

Given the features of *placing/grasping* vs. *giving/taking* that we have begun to sketch in the previous section, the question arises as to whether there are circumstances and contingencies that make one methodic practice expectable rather than the other. In this section, we explore two contrastive praxeological contexts in which the ongoing activity clearly favors one practice over the other. As discussed earlier, placing the product on the counter by the customer is an action that does not require simultaneous coordination of the receiving hand. *Placing* something can be done unilaterally by the customer and independently by the seller. We explore this situation in Section 5.4.1. On the other hand, *giving* supposes a tight synchronization between the participants so that they produce well timed complementary movements of their hands; this might be initiated by one or the other participant, but it requires close mutual attention and adjustments. In Section 5.4.2 we explore conditions that make this possible.

5.4.1   *Placing* as a Unilateral Action

In our data, a situation that favors *placing* over *giving* is the unavailability of the seller – that is, when the customer approaches the counter, the seller is either absent or busy. Consequently, the customer might place the product picked up in the shop or the lottery ticket brought to the shop on the counter, waiting for the seller. In this case, *placing* is performed independently without the possibility of a responsive grasping by the seller.

This happens in the next excerpt from a kiosk encounter in northern Finland. When the customer approaches the counter, the seller is busy in another part of the shop and there is nobody behind the cash register. The customer places the lottery ticket on the counter.

Excerpt 5.5 (KIO_FIN_T222)

```
01            (0.7) ± (0.6) ±   (0.4) # (0.2)    ± (0.35) † (0.2)±
   cus        >>walks to the counter---------------------†
   cus                   ±.......±places ticket on c±,,,,,,,,,,,,,,,±
   fig                              #fig.5.11
```

Figure 5.11

```
02             ±      (0.4)    ± (1.2)•+    (1.0)
     cus     ±opens wallet    ±takes coins in his hand-------->
     sel                              •walks from back twd counter->
     cus                              +gazes at SEL--->
03 SEL:      h#ei+
             hello
     cus        ->+
     fig     #fig.5.12
```

Figure 5.12

```
04           (0.5)
05 CUS:      terve;±
             hi
     cus        ->±puts wallet on counter->
06           (0.3) ± (3.0) •(0.25) °(0.3)±(0.35)#±(0.2)± °
     cus        ->±counts coins--------±points-±,,,,±
     sel                ->•stops behind the counter->
     sel                          °.....................°
     fig                                        #fig.5.13
```

Figure 5.13

```
07  CUS:     ±°kaks rivi:ä.
             two rows
    cus      ±continues counting money->
    sel       °grasps lottery ticket-->
08           (0.4)°•      (1.1)       •°+±
    sel       ->°                    °types-->>
    sel        ->•walks to machine•
    cus                              +gazes at SEL-->>
    cus                               ->±
```

The customer enters the shop and walks toward the counter, extending his arm and putting the lottery ticket on the counter (Figure 5.11) in the absence of the seller. Next, he opens his wallet and looks in it, then taking out and counting some coins (line 2). This activity projects a possible payment, but also fills the waiting time. When the seller approaches the counter from the back of the shop, the customer turns to her and seller-initiated greetings are exchanged (lines 3–5, Figure 5.12). The customer then puts his purse on the counter and continues to count his coins (lines 5–6). Already, before the seller has fully reached her position at the counter, she begins to grasp the ticket (extending her arm, line 6, Figure 5.13). The customer, who is still counting coins, orients to that by pointing at the ticket (line 6, Figure 5.13) and explaining what he wants (line 7). While the seller grasps the ticket and walks toward the machine to process it, the customer continues to look at his coins: he glances at her only when he can hear her typing the numbers on the machine (line 8).

In this case, the customer placed the lottery ticket on the counter in the absence of the seller, and the seller grasped it some nine seconds later, when she arrived. During this time, the customer engaged in actions that projected the next activity, paying. He minimally engaged with the seller, although he highlighted the relevant purchase by pointing and explaining his request (line 7). So, this case shows not only a unilaterally initiated action and a clear asynchrony between the actions by the customer and the seller, but also the customer waiting and the seller hurrying.

Another case of absence and unavailability of the seller is observable in the next excerpt, which was recorded in Italian-speaking Switzerland. The customer approaches the counter with a lottery ticket and, in the absence of the seller, puts it on the counter. The seller comes and makes herself available 16 seconds later.

Excerpt 5.6 (KIO_CH_LUG_42.25)

```
01         (3.7)          †± (0.8) #    (0.2)   ±(0.5)±
    cus    >>walks to the c†stands-->>
    cus                             ±places ticket on c±,,,,,±
    fig                                     #fig.5.14
```

Figure 5.14

```
02         +(5.6)• (0.3)+    (1.0)    +
   cus     +looks at bag+looks at SEL+
   sel            •walks in and approaches the c->
03 SEL:    +guardo se ho lasciato qual+cos+a
           I look whether I left something
   cus     +looks at purse------------+SEL+purse->
04         (0.5)
05 CUS:    °b+uongio+r[no°
           good morning
   cus     ->+gz SEL+
06 SEL:               [no, sono qua     Bea
                       no they are here Bea
07         (0.2)+   (0.9)• (0.4)
   cus         +gz purse--->
   sel                  ->•turns to CUS->
08 SEL:    buongiorno signor[a
           good morning m'am
09 CUS:                     [°buongiorno°
                             good morning
10         (0.2)+(0.3)+ (0.35)± (0.3)±+
   cus         ->+.....+gz up at SEL---+
   cus                            ±points w purse±
11 CUS:    +°quell+o° Ω
           that one
           +gz dwn purse+
   sel                  Ω.....->
12         (0.5)
13 SEL:    quesΩto qua?Ω
           this one here
              ->Ωgrasps-Ω
14         (0.2)
```

```
15 SEL:     [lo fac•cio una volta?    ((this refers to how many times
            do I make one time?        the coupon goes in the machine))
16 CUS:     [si
            yes
    sel              ->•walks away w coupon--->>
17          (0.4)
18 CUS:     sì
            yes
```

As in the previous excerpt, the customer reaches the counter when the seller is away. As she stops at the counter, she places on the counter the lottery ticket she was holding in her right hand when she arrived (line 1, Figure 5.14). Next, like in the previous excerpt, she engages in waiting by focusing on her belongings and looking at the contents of her bag (line 2). After a while (almost 6 seconds), the seller approaches the counter from one side (line 2). The customer glances at her, but the seller continues a conversation she was engaged in with a colleague (talking to Bea, lines 3, 6). The customer displays her awareness of the continuing unavailability of the seller by looking back at her purse; at the same time, she monitors the seller by looking up and down again (line 3). When lifting her gaze to the seller again, the customer greets her (line 5) but receives no response, as the seller continues to talk with her colleague (line 6). She addresses the customer only later on, turning to her (line 7) and greeting her (line 8). The customer now returns the greeting in a very soft voice; during the greeting sequence, she does not look back at the seller. So, while she was regularly monitoring the seller in the environment of her first greeting, the customer does not glance at her when they finally greet later on, displaying she is rather busy with her purse, projecting the next action, the payment.

After the greetings, there is a lapse of a second: the customer looks up at the seller, who does not initiate any further action. The customer addresses this by pointing at the lottery ticket with her purse and referring to it with a demonstrative (°*quello*°, line 11), these actions working as a request. Thereafter she immediately looks down again. The seller now grasps the ticket (lines 11–13) while securing the correct referent of the demonstrative (*questo qua?*, line 13), confirmed by the customer (line 16). The seller then asks another question about the exact treatment of the ticket the customer expects (line 15).

As in the previous excerpt, the lottery ticket lying on the counter was pointed at by the customer, thus orienting to the fact that the gesture of placing had not been visible to the seller. Moreover, her use of the distal demonstrative (*quello*, line 11) indicates that, from her perspective, the ticket has been on the counter for a long time. However, from the perspective of the seller, it can be understood as a just-discovered item, as shown by the demonstrative used (*questo qua?*, line 13). The customer's pointing gesture and the verbal reference also orient to the absence of a next action of the seller and accelerate the progressivity of the encounter: the repair by the seller can be seen as securing the relevant referent and action, but also resisting the implication of a delay in fulfilling the request. Furthermore, the sustained gaze by the customer at her purse, her quick brief glances at the seller, and her withdrawal from a mutual gaze indicate her distancing from the interaction – similar to and even clearer than in the previous excerpt – and can be seen as addressing the nonavailability and delay of the seller as annoying and even as normatively reprehensible.

These two excerpts present similarities in that they not only show material and temporal conditions in which placing a product on the counter can be favored by the customer, but also its normative dimension. In both cases, in the absence of the seller, the customer first places the product on the counter and then engages in an action that is understandable as preparing and projecting the next relevant action they will make after the seller has handled the product. Furthermore, while the seller grasps the product and begins to process it at the till, the customer works to sustain their orientation to the current situation: they provide the information required for processing the product, but simultaneously display an orientation to the progressivity of the encounter (and what has hindered it, the nonavailability of the seller upon the customer's arrival). The paired actions of placing and grasping not only enable the next steps of the encounter in the absence of the other participant (the seller) to be organized, but also the projection and progression of the encounter while withdrawing from mutual contact (manifesting, for example, some irritation about the nonavailability of the seller). Therefore, the choice of this embodied format might orient not only to the practical organization of the exchange, but also to the moral and normative expectations related to the rights and obligations of customers vs. sellers.

5.4.2 *Giving* as a Visibly Projectable Action

While *placing* is a typical solution for situations characterized by the asymmetric accessibility of the other person (the seller), *giving* depends on the timed organization of reciprocity between the two participants. Two multimodal configurations make possible and even favor *giving*. Firstly, the trajectory of the customer's walk toward the counter works as a strong projective resource for the seller, who monitors the approach and can anticipate the way of making the imminent request. Secondly, the possible extension of the arm and hand of the seller toward the product, and her adoption of a particular hand shape, make it possible for the customer to identify and understand the action that the seller is inviting her or him to do.[5] Of these two circumstances

---

[5] If the customer has already initiated the sequence by extending their arm and hand, the seller displays their understanding of the action initiated by the customer and their preparedness to respond and align accordingly.

Embodied Trajectories of Actions in Shop Encounters   165

favoring *giving*, the first characterizes the customer's and the second the seller's initiative. Moreover, both require and are sensitive to mutual visibility and monitoring.

We explore these two possible initiating moves here within a Finnish excerpt where the customer initiates giving, and a French excerpt where the seller anticipates it.

Excerpt 5.7 (KIO_FIN_T 873)

```
01            (0.9)
   cus      >>walks to the counter, holding a ticket in the RH->
   sel      >>looks at CUS->
02 SEL:     >moi<
            hi
03          ±(0.6)*
   cus      ±hands the ticket--->
   sel           ->*looks at coupon->
04 CUS:     °he#°i:.    #tä°mmö°nen.
            hello        this kind
   sel      °[...]°RH opens°closes°takes--->
   fig          #fig.5.15#fig.5.16
```

Figure 5.15

Figure 5.16

```
05            (0.2) ± (0.1)
   cus             ->±,,,,,->
```

```
06 SEL:      >jo*ło< °•
             yes
   cus        ->ł
   sel             ->°
   sel       ->*looks away-->>
   sel                •walks twd the machine->>
```

When walking to the counter, the customer in the excerpt above visibly holds out a lottery ticket in his right hand, the arm extended (line 1, Figure 5.15). The seller's subsequent opening of her hand (Figure 5.16) indicates how she responds to and aligns with the customer. The customer uses the demonstrative *tämmönen* (line 4) to refer to the ticket, while the seller grasps it. The seller responds with the compliance-claiming particle >*joo*< (line 6), whereupon she moves away with the ticket toward the machine where it will be processed. Here, the projection of the action by the customer, monitored by the seller at the counter, enables their finely tuned coordination and smooth transfer of the object.

In other cases, it is the seller rather than the customer who initiates the kind of transfer of the object, indicating that the customer will *give* the product. This is the case in the next excerpt from a convenience store in France.

Excerpt 5.8 (KIO_F_VIL_1.25.23)

```
01         (1.8)  °  (0.3) *  (0.2)  °*  (0.3)      °#
   cus     >>walks with a magazine in RH->
   sel             °...............°extends LH°
   sel                         *........*looks at CUS--->
   fig                                             #fig.5.17
```

Figure 5.17

```
02 CUS:    °±°ce±lui (.) c#°i°         °
           this one
    sel    °opens LH------°closes°takes->
    cus    ±...±gives-->
    fig                    #fig.5.18
```

Figure 5.18

```
03 SEL:    mer±ci
           thanks
    cus    ->±
04         (0.2)
05 SEL:    ça c'est le hors °série hein c'est cui-là
           this is the special issue right it's that one
    sel                     -->°shows w both H-->
06         q'v' [voulez°
           that you want
07 CUS:         [oui
                yes
    sel                    -->°
```

When the customer comes from the back of the shop, walking toward the seller, the seller extends her arm even before she looks at him (she can clearly hear his steps), subsequently gazing at him while he is still holding the magazine in his hands, close to his body, without yet extending them (Figure 5.17). Moreover, when the customer uses a demonstrative pronoun (*celui-ci* 'this one') to indicate the magazine he chose (line 2), the seller opens her hand ready to grasp it (Figure 5.18). The transfer of the magazine is done during the customer's turn containing the demonstrative. As the seller takes the magazine, she thanks the customer, pointing to the gesture as a commitment to buy (line 3). Moreover, once she has the magazine, she shows it to the customer and requests confirmation of his selection of that specific issue of the magazine (lines 5–6).

Thus in both Excerpts 5.7 and 5.8, the encounter progresses smoothly with *giving* and *taking* coordinated in a synchronized way. This is made possible by an early and visible projection, done with an extended arm either by the customer preparing to give the product to the seller (Excerpt 5.7) or by the seller ready to take the product (Excerpt 5.8). In both cases, a demonstrative is used, co-occurring with the mutual actions of *giving/taking*.

In sum, *giving* and *taking* are characterized by systematic features that secure their recognizability. These features also make the projection of the action visible and enhance the smoothness of the product's transfer. The first and most visible feature is the initiation of an embodied movement – that is, the sequential and temporal way in which the arm and hand are extended either by the customer or by the seller. When the customer approaches the counter with an extended arm and holds the product in their hand, that can be understood as displaying preparedness to give the product to the seller. The second key element is the shape of the seller's hand. There is a distinctive *taking* form of the hand, which contrasts with the *grasping* hand responding to placing. A *taking* hand is open, with the fingers organized to pre-adjust to the object to be taken: the position of the hand fits the form of the object. Thirdly, the *taking* hand is located in a distinctive way *above* the counter: it is recognizably in the air (vs. at the level of the counter, as the *grasping* hand). These features form the distinctive Gestalt of a taking gesture, recognizable and accountable as such for both participants.

5.5 Adjustments

In the previous two sections, we have specified environments, temporal dimensions, and formats that distinguish sequences of *placing/grasping* from sequences of *giving/taking*. We have also explored contingencies that might favor one practice over the other, which has further revealed their systematic character. Nonetheless, the environments in which these actions are performed are not always so clear-cut, and the participants can perform *giving* even in environments in which *placing* would be easier, and vice versa. This section explores how participants achieve this by actively delaying their action, waiting for better conditions to be able to *give* instead of *place* (Section 5.5.1). Furthermore, similar waiting phenomena are observable for *placing*, showing that customers prefer to minimize the time span between *placing* and *grasping* (Section 5.5.2). This demonstrates a general preference for a quick transition between the two actions, not only when *giving* but also when *placing* is performed. Both paired actions can thus be seen to be organized in a timely, coordinated way between the participants, orienting to the progressivity of the encounter but also to normative and moral issues that the temporal disjunction between the paired actions might generate.

5.5.1 Waiting to Give

Customers confronted with the unavailability of the seller, either busy or absent, may choose to wait in order to give rather than just place the product on the counter (as in Section 5.4.1). In the following excerpt, the customer in a Finnish kiosk approaches the counter when the seller is busy in the backroom behind the counter.

Excerpt 5.9 (KIO_FIN_T869)

```
01          (2.3)    †± (2.7)#(0.2)+     (1.0)      +(0.2)•(1.2)±
    cus     >>appr c†stands-->>
    cus              ±flips and counts his 1. tickets-------±
    cus                        +gz SEL(noise)+
    sel                                            •walks twd c->
    fig                        #fig.5.19
```

Figure 5.19

```
02          ± (0.7)   #    ±(0.5)#(0.3)+(0.3) ± (1.8)    ±     +
    cus     ±lends ticket±places ticket on c±lifts up±
            ±until middle±holding one-------±the tckt±
            ±of counter--±extremity---------±
    cus                                     +monitors SEL coming+
    fig                  #fig.5.20 #fig.5.21
```

Figure 5.20

170 L. Mondada & M.-L. Sorjonen

Figure 5.21

```
03 CUS:     +±m[oi:.
             hi
04 SEL:        [>moi<
                hi
    cus    +looks at lottery tickets-->
    cus    ±lifts tckt further up-->
05         °(0.2)°(0.2)#° +±(0.2)±°(0.5)°
    sel    °.....°opens-°closes---°takes°
    cus                 ->+
    cus                 -->±,,,,,±
    fig                 #fig.5.22
```

Figure 5.22

Standing at the counter, the customer waits, flipping and counting his lottery tickets (line 1, Figure 5.19). He also gazes toward the backroom, possibly in response to a noise that is coming from there. When the seller comes out of the backroom, the customer monitors her approach to the counter (line 2). As soon as she appears and approaches, he holds out the tickets. Reaching the middle of the counter, he holds them (Figure 5.20). He continues to hold them in such a way that one part of the ticket falls onto the surface of the counter: the ticket is almost placed while still being partially held

(Figure 5.21). When the seller arrives, the customer lifts the tickets into the air, ready to give them. He returns a greeting to the seller in overlap (line 3), and at that point, looking at the tickets, he lifts them up further (Figure 5.22). In response, the seller takes them.

This excerpt shows how in a situation in which the object could well be, and often is, *placed* on the counter in absence of the seller, the customer works instead to *give* it to the seller, when the latter is available again. The customer uses the lapse between his arrival and the seller's arrival (about ten seconds) to position the tickets on/over the counter, testing different positions. Having partially placed them on the counter, he finally decides to lift them up in order to *give* them as soon as the seller comes closer. His orientation to the timing of their possible coordination is visible in his gaze and monitoring of the seller. In so doing, the customer actively manages the temporal character of the encounter, the unavailability of the seller, and her arrival at the counter, transforming a situation in which it would be easy to *place* into a situation in which he is able to smoothly *give*. By choosing this embodied action formation, the customer displays his local preference for *giving* over *placing*. In this way, both participants orient to the ratification of their co-presence and common engagement in the interaction, after a lapse in which this was not the case.

5.5.2 Minimizing the Time between *Placing* and *Grasping*

Customers orient to the temporality of the transfer of objects both when giving the product to the seller and when placing it on the counter. While the timing of *giving* is constitutive for the reciprocal symmetric coordination of actions between the co-participants, it appears that the customers orient toward the relevance of timing for *placing* too. This is revealed by the fact that even when they place a product on the counter to be grasped later by the seller, they *wait to place* it until the seller comes to the counter or can see them putting the product down. In this way, they orient toward minimization of the gap between *placing* and *grasping*, and, maybe more importantly, to the visibility of the action of *placing* (vs. *placing* unilaterally in the absence of the co-participant).

The following two excerpts show the same orientation toward waiting. The first is recorded in a kiosk in Basel in the German-speaking Switzerland.

Excerpt 5.10 (KIO_CH_BS2_49.53)

```
01          (1.2)     † (0.4)#(0.2)*(0.1)± (0.3)
     cus    >>walks to c†stands--->>
     sel    >>busy at cash register--*turns to CUS---->>
     cus                                    ±places bottle on c->
     fig                       #fig.5.23
```

Figure 5.23

```
02 SEL:    schö#nen guten tag
           a splendid good morning
    fig         #fig.5.24
```

Figure 5.24

```
03  CUS:      guten tag±
              good morning
                       ->±,,,,->
04            (0.3)±  °(0.4)°    (0.9)        °
     cus       ->±
     sel              °.....°grasps bottle°
```

The customer approaches the counter with a can in his hands, while the seller is present but busy with his cash register (Figure 5.23). The customer stands at the counter and waits (line 1). When the seller turns to him, he immediately places the drink on the counter while they exchange greetings (lines 2–3, Figure 5.24). The seller grasps the bottle as soon as the customer has retracted his arm (line 4).

The second excerpt comes from a French convenience store and presents a very similar trajectory.

Excerpt 5.11 (KIO_F_VIL_50.41)

```
01            (3.0)              † (0.4)•+ (0.9)
     cus     >>arrives at the counter†stands-------->>
     cus     >>holds docs with RH in a wallet------->>
     sel                                  •walks in from backroom->
     cus                                  +gazes at SEL->
02  CUS:      bon[jou:+r,#
              good morning
03  SEL:         ['jou+r
                  morning
     cus                 ->+looks at docs------>>
     fig                      #fig.5.25
```

Figure 5.25

```
04            (0.2) ± (1.9)
     cus            ±LH grabs a doc---->
05  SEL:      s'il vous plait#
              please
     fig                      #fig.5.26
```

Figure 5.26

```
06         (0.4)
07 CUS:    ±c'est un (  °  #  ) (à jour),#  ± mer°credi prochain.
           It's a   (  °    ) (updated)       next Wednesday
   cus     ±takes out doc, places on counter±
   sel                  °extends RH------------°grasps doc-->
   fig                       #fig.5.27     #fig.5.28
```

Figure 5.27

Figure 5.28

```
08          (0.3)  °(0.2)• (0.2)
   sel             ->°
   sel                    ->•stops and stands--->>
```

The customer enters and approaches the counter, standing for a short moment with his wallet in his right hand (line 1). The exchange of greetings happens when the seller is still far away from the counter. While the customer looks down at some documents in the wallet (Figure 5.25) and begins to grab one of them out of the wallet, the approaching seller utters *s'il vous plait* 'please' (line 5, Figure 5.26), an invitation to progress within the encounter often used in service encounters when the seller is not yet fully available (Harjunpää et al. 2018). The customer now takes out the document and places it on the counter (line 7). At the same time, although she has not yet reached her position in front of him, the seller extends her hand (Figure 5.27) in such a way that it allows her to grasp the document less than 0.2 seconds after he has placed it on the counter (Figure 5.28). Here the lapse between *placing* and *grasping* is minimized to the extent that the practice almost merges with the practice of *giving* and *taking*.

In sum, arriving at the counter while the seller is away and/or occupied with something else poses a possible dilemma for customers as to how and when to initiate the transfer of the product. As we saw in Section 5.4.1, the customer may opt to place the product on the counter and, in doing so, perform the action necessary for transfer on her or his part. In Section 5.4.2, we have discussed opposite cases, where the customer opts for the contiguity of the actions of *placing* and *grasping*, and minimizes the time between their own and the seller's necessary and complementary actions. In doing so, the customer can be seen to orient toward initiation of the business as soon as the seller is available.

The presence of the product either in the customer's hand or on the counter while the seller is unavailable provides for different forms of accountability of the object, either as a possession of the customer (e.g., when the customer has come to check the lottery ticket) or as an object yet to be purchased. By waiting to put the object on the counter and minimizing the gap between *placing* and *grasping*, customers seem to orient toward maximal visibility and accountability of the status of the object of transaction, as well as to the transparency of the process, enabling the seller to trace the relationship between the object and the customer. This not only makes the transaction more efficient and smooth, but also establishes its normative framework, visibly displaying that the lottery ticket has not been forgotten by another customer, the object relates to an action of the present customer, the product is being correctly bought and not stolen, etc. Thus, minimizing the time between the two paired actions not only orients toward practical matters, such as the progressivity of the encounter, but also toward normative, legal, and moral issues characterizing the buying and selling process.

5.6 Transformations: From *Placing* to *Giving* and from *Grasping* to *Taking*

The previous section has demonstrated how customers orient toward minimizing the lapse between the actions of the two parties during the transfer of the object, either for issues of progressivity or for issues of security and morality. As a consequence, when the seller grasps immediately the object that the customer has just placed or is still placing on the counter, this paired action may become very close to its alternative, *giving* and *taking*. The less time elapses between the two actions, the more the difference between the alternatives decreases and might even be blurred. This is observable in cases in which (a) the lapse is very minimal (see Excerpt 5.11, Figures 5.21–5.22); (b) one practice is transformed/reversed into another at the last moment (see Excerpt 5.11); or (c) one practice is misunderstood as being another (see Excerpt 5.12).

The analysis below reflects on these possibilities. It shows how the alternative actions of *placing/grasping* and *giving/taking* can possibly be misunderstood and how participants orient to that. A customer (CUS) in a French convenience store approaches the counter while another customer (CUP) is being served. The seller closes the encounter with CUP and then turns to CUS.

Excerpt 5.12 (KIO_F_VIL_1.13.07)

```
01         (1.0) ± (0.5)↑ (0.3) ± (0.7) # (0.2)     ±
    cus    >>walks in---↑stops and stands---->>
    cus           ±.............±plc magazines on c±busy w her bag->
    fig                                #fig.5.29
```

Figure 5.29

Embodied Trajectories of Actions in Shop Encounters   177

```
02           (6.8)
03 SEL:      si±x six sept. mer:c±i::
             six six seven thanks
   cus       ->±opens her purse--±takes out a lott. ticket->
04 CUP:      me:rci bien,
             thanks a lot
05           (0.6)
06 CUP:      bo[nne journée
             have a good day
07 SEL:         ['journée au °r'voir±
                  day and good bye
   sel                        °closes cash register->
   cus                        --->±
08           (0.3) ± ° ( 0.5)# (0.2) ± # (0.2) ° (0.4)     ±
   cus               ±hands ticket-----±retracts H w ticket±
   sel               ->°extends LH and grasps mag°reads b-cd--->
   fig                         #fig.5.30 #fig.5.31
```

Figure 5.30

Figure 5.31

```
09           (13.2)° (0.5) ±    (0.8) #°(0.7)°±
   sel            °puts back mag on c°takes°brings tckt to machine->>
   cus                      ±gives ticket-----±
   fig                              #fig.32
```

Figure 5.32

While another customer (CUP) is being served, a new customer (CUS) reaches the counter from the back of the shop where she has picked up a series of magazines. She places them on the counter (line 1, Figure 5.29). She then waits for a while (line 2), looking at her belongings and the contents of her bag. She orients to the imminent closing of the other encounter: as the seller is counting the money given by the previous customer, she grasps her purse, opens it, and takes out a lottery ticket (line 3). The previous encounter moves further toward closing (lines 4–7) and on the last goodbye the seller closes the cash register (line 7).

The closing is oriented to by the waiting customer, who promptly hands her lottery ticket to the seller (line 8). The seller also turns immediately to her, extending her left hand toward the counter and the customer. When they both progress in their movements, extending their arms and hands (Figure 5.30), they move from possibly undetermined or open trajectories of their actions into more definite ones. The trajectories, however, turn out to be divergent (Figure 5.31): the customer was *giving* her lottery ticket, but instead of *taking* the ticket, the seller *grasps* the magazines that were put on the counter. One reason for this mismatch can be the direction of their respective gazes: the seller looks at the magazines, while the customer looks at her ticket – neither monitors the gaze of the other. The customer, noticing that the seller is not taking her ticket, retracts her giving. She then waits until the seller has scanned the barcodes of all the magazines (line 9). Thereafter she reissues the giving of the lottery ticket: this time, the ticket is taken by the seller (Figure 5.32).

This excerpt shows how *giving* can be ignored when it competes with another trajectory of action, *grasping* products from the counter. This misunderstanding seems to be enhanced by the absence of participants' monitoring of each other's gaze and by the multiplicity of products handed by the customer, creating possible problems of order in which they have to be processed. This also shows how a *giving* trajectory can be momentarily suspended and even abandoned (and retracted) and reissued in more favorable conditions: here the customer chooses to initiate a new giving movement rather than simply placing her lottery ticket on the counter.

5.7 Conclusion

This chapter has described two alternative embodied paired actions for the transfer of objects within a commercial encounter: *giving/taking* and *placing/ grasping*. That has been done by systematically exploring their sequential and temporal organization, their embodied trajectories, the contexts and contingencies that might favor one over the other, the conditions of their local intelligibility, and their projection and/or misunderstanding by the participants.

The analysis has sketched the systematic and methodic sequential, temporal, and embodied features that characterize the distinctive organization of these paired actions. Placing an object on the counter is an action that can be achieved in a unilateral and asymmetric way by the two participants, one putting the product on the counter and the other grasping it from there. Contrary to *placing/grasping*, the *giving/taking* pair requires another type of coordination in which the two participants synchronize their hand movements to manage the transfer of the product from one to the other (Section 5.3). Indeed, some contextual and temporal contingencies might favor placing over giving, especially when the recipient of the object is absent or unavailable (Section 5.4.1), whereas giving requires mutual orientation, co-presence, and synchronous movements, favored by their visibility and projectability (Section 5.4.2). However, within similar contexts of unavailability, customers might also wait in order to give instead of placing the product on the counter (Section 5.5.1); conversely, they might place the product on the counter while still minimizing the time that it will take to the seller to grasp it, securing the visibility of their gesture (Section 5.5.2). These adjustments to the timing and the embodied actions show that the distinction between these alternative pairs of actions can be blurred – for instance, when the object is grasped as soon as it is placed, resulting in a form of giving and taking.

The temporal and sequential organization of these actions crucially relies on their detailed embodied trajectories. Giving and placing are accountably achieved by the way in which the doer hands the object, moves his or her arm, and generally mobilizes his or her entire body, walking, stepping, coming closer to the counter, turning toward it, and looking at the recipient. These embodied movements design both the overall projectability and visibility of the customer's approach, as does the specific detailed trajectory of the arm giving or placing the object. Reciprocally, the specific trajectory and shape of the hand receiving the object, either taking it in the air or grasping it from the counter, projects and makes intelligible the kind of action the seller is anticipating, expecting, and reflexively inviting the customer to do. The relationship between the approaching arm of the customer and the stretching hand of the seller shows the intricate multiple mutual adjustments the participants locally do moment by moment – also revealed by cases in which the actions are misunderstood (Section 5.6).

These mutual multiple adjustments not only characterize the completion of the hands' movements, but also their initial trajectories. When one of the participants clearly launches the course of action – both temporally, by moving before the other, and visibly, within an early design of the shape of the arm or the hand – it is clear who is initiating the sequence and who is responding to it; but when both of the participants begin to move at almost the same time, the issue of who initiates and who responds is less clear: in these cases, the sequential organization of action rather takes the form of micro-sequentiality, characterized by minimal mutual adjustments in which an incipient movement reflexively shapes the other's embodied action as they both emerge.

These trajectories of embodied action are sensitive to their material ecology – the materiality of the objects handed over and the materiality of the counter's space. Giving is an embodied action done over and across the counter, whereas placing is done on the counter. The former minimizes the relevance of the counter as a structuring transitional space and can be done in other positions and places – for example, above magazines or candies. The latter can exploit the specific geography of the counter, such as when the customer places a product in the exact center of the counter, or when s/he lifts an object toward the edge of the counter closer to the seller. The demarcation of parts of the area of the counter and occupying them with objects might index specific rights and obligations, and a territorialization of possessions and possessables, bought and buyable. The counter is both a reference point for action and a polymorphous and changeable space that can be shaped for specific trajectories of action.

The way objects are transferred on or over the counter might also be sensitive to their quality, size, and number. Bigger products, such as drinks, tend to be placed on the counter. Smaller products, like candies, tend to be given directly to the seller. Lottery tickets constitute a specific case, since they can be either a product still to be paid for or a product already paid for and just to be checked for the result of the game. They tend to be given rather than placed, especially when they have already been paid for. This might show an orientation toward rights and possession. Moreover, when the customer hands over more than one product, a problem of sequencing is raised: this might be solved by using different hands for different products (Excerpt 5.2), or it might produce misunderstandings relative to the object that will be grasped first (Excerpt 5.12).

These embodied actions, their trajectories, and their sequential and temporal orders manifest participants' orientations that address different types of relevance. Firstly, participants orient to practical issues of coordination and organization: these concern the intelligibility of the emerging action, and thus the problem of action formation as it is made recognizable from its visible dynamic features, its temporal organization, and its progressivity, minimizing gaps and delays. Secondly, participants orient to temporality and progressivity as also having a professional aspect – for instance, relating to the quality of service, as shown in the way the customers deal with the (un)availability of the seller, and to their entitlement to request a service/to be served. Thirdly, participants orient to the organization of the action and its accountability as hinting at normative and moral issues: giving or placing a product over or on the counter displays a decision to buy it, and thus a transformation of an object from sellable to buyable, and further to an item in the process of being bought – that is, in the process of changing possession. The minimization of the gap between placing and grasping, observable when the customer waits until the seller approaches and sees what they are doing before either giving or placing the object, shows an orientation toward the visible accountability of the status of the object relative to the customer and the buying transaction. This accountability does not just concern the type of action currently being done, but other possible alternative actions or contingencies that are clearly discarded (such as doubts about who possesses the object, legal or illegal action concerning the object, etc.). In this sense, the accountability of giving vs. placing movements centrally touches upon the moral-legal status of the product, the stage of the buying and selling procedure, and the identity of the customer. In this sense, the apparently simple embodied practices of *giving/taking* and *placing/grasping* are situated at the core of the commercial encounter as an economic phenomenon.

Acknowledgments

This chapter has been written during Mondada's stay in Helsinki as Finland Distinguished Professor, hosted by Sorjonen at the Centre for Excellence in Intersubjectivity (2015–2017). It has been supported by the FiDiPro project *Multimodality: Reconsidering language and action through embodiment*, funded by the Academy of Finland and the University of Helsinki (project no 282931) (2015–2017).

References

Clark, H. (2003). Pointing and placing. In S. Kita, ed., *Pointing: Where Language, Culture, and Cognition Meet*. Hillsdale: Erlbaum, pp. 243–268.

De Stefani, E. (2011). *"Ah petta ecco, io prendo questi che mi piacciono." Agire come coppia al supermercato. Un approccio conversazionale e multimodale allo studio dei processi decisionali* [*"Oh wait here, I'm getting these, cos I like them."*

Acting as a couple at the supermarket. A conversational and multimodal approach to the analysis of decision-making]. Rome: Aracne.

(2014). Establishing joint orientation towards commercial objects in a self-service store: How practices of categorisation matter. In M. Nevile, P. Haddington, T. Heinemann, & M. Rauniomaa, eds., *Interacting with Objects: Language, Materiality and Social Activity*. Amsterdam: John Benjamins, pp. 271–294. https://doi.org/10.1075/z.186.12ste

Félix-Brasdefer, J. C. (2015). *The Language of Service Encounters: A Pragmatic-Discursive Approach*. Cambridge: Cambridge University Press. https://doi.org/10.1017/CBO9781139565431

Fox, B., & Heinemann, T. (2015). The alignment of manual and verbal displays in requests for the repair of an object. *Research on Language and Social Interaction*, 48(3), 342–362. https://doi.org/10.1080/08351813.2015.1058608

Garfinkel, H., & Wieder, L. (1992). Two incommensurable, asymmetrically alternate technologies of social analysis. In G. Watson & R. M. Seiler, eds., *Text in Context: Studies in Ethnomethodology*. Newbury Park: Sage, pp. 175–206.

Harjunpää, K., Mondada, L., & Svinhufvud, K. (2018). The coordinated entry into service encounters in food shops: Managing interactional space, availability, and service during openings. *Research on Language and Social Interaction*, 51(3), 271–291. https://doi.org/10.1080/08351813.2018.1485231

Heath, C. (2013). *The Dynamics of Auction: Social Interaction and the Sale of Fine Art and Antiques*. Cambridge: Cambridge University Press. https://doi.org/10.1017/CBO9781139024020

Heath, C., Luff, P., Sanchez-Svensson, M., & Nicholls, M. (2018). Exchanging implements: The micro-materialities of multidisciplinary work in the operating theatre. *Sociology of Health & Illness*, 40(2), 297–313. https://doi.org/10.1111/1467-9566.12594

Llewellyn, N. (2011). The gift in interaction: The practice of 'picking up the bill'. *The British Journal of Sociology*, 62(4), 718–738. https://doi.org/10.1111/j.1468-4446.2011.01388.x

(2015). 'Money talks': Communicative and symbolic functions of cash money. *Sociology*, 50(4), 796–812. https://doi.org/10.1177/0038038515585475

Llewellyn, N., & Burrow, R. (2008). Streetwise sales and the social order of city streets. *The British Journal of Sociology*, 59(3), 561–583. https://doi.org/10.1111/j.1468-4446.2008.00208.x

Mondada, L. (2019). Participants' orientations to material and sensorial features of objects: Looking, touching, smelling and tasting while requesting products in shops. *Gesprächsforschung*, 20, 461–494. www.gespraechsforschung-online.de/fileadmin/dateien/heft2019/si-mondada.pdf

(2021). How early can embodied responses be? Issues in time and sequentiality. *Discourse Processes*, 58(4), 397–418.

Mondada, L. Bänninger, J., Bouaouina, S.A., Gauthier, G., Hänggi, P., Svensson, H., & Tekin, B. (2020). Doing paying during the Covid-19 pandemic. *Discourse Studies*, 22(6): 720–752. https://doi.org/10.1177/1461445620950860

Mondada, L., & Sorjonen, M.-L. (2016). Making multiple requests in French and Finnish convenience stores. *Language in Society*, 45(5), 733–765. https://doi.org/10.1017/S0047404516000646

Moore, R., Whalen, J., & Gathman, C. (2010). The work of the work order: Document practice in face-to-face service encounters. In N. Llewellyn & J. Hindmarsh, eds.,

Organization, Interaction, and Practice: Studies in Ethnomethodology and Conversation Analysis. Cambridge: Cambridge University Press, pp. 172–197. https://doi.org/10.1017/CBO9780511676512.009

Nevile, M., Haddington, P., Heinemann, T., & Rauniomaa, M., eds. (2014). *Interacting with Objects: Language, Materiality, and Social Activity*. Amsterdam: John Benjamins. https://doi.org/10.1075/z.186

Rauniomaa, M., & Keisanen, T. (2012). Two multimodal formats for responding to requests. *Journal of Pragmatics*, 44(6–7), 829–842. https://doi.org/10.1016/j.pragma.2012.03.003

Sorjonen, M.-L., & Raevaara, L. (2014). On the grammatical form of requests at the convenience store: Requesting as embodied action. In P. Drew & E. Couper-Kuhlen, eds., *Requesting in Social Interaction*. Amsterdam: John Benjamins, pp. 243–268. https://doi.org/10.1075/slsi.26.10sor

Streeck, J. (1996). How to do things with things: Objects trouvés and symbolization. *Human Studies*, 19(4), 365–384. https://doi.org/10.1007/BF00188849

6 Unpacking Packing

Anna Lindström and Barbara Fox

6.1 Introduction

In most shops, merchandise is not brought home by customers 'in the nude' but is rather packaged in bags or boxes.[1] Emballage is especially salient in food shops, as it is both unsanitary and impractical to transport a wedge of soft cheese or a bunch of tender asparagus without protective wrapping. In this chapter we examine packing at a fresh produce stall at a farmer's market. With the exception of small berries and chanterelles, goods at this market stall are typically not pre-packaged. Our analysis focuses on how different kinds of vegetables such as parsley, lettuce, and potatoes are packed after being requested by the customer and before the farmer adds up the merchandise and the customer pays and puts them in the basket or bag that they have brought to the market. In contrast with other phases of sales encounters such as assessing, recommending, and requesting, packing is not necessarily implemented through talk. It can be accomplished while seller and customer engage in small talk or during silence. Due to its seen but unnoticed feature, packing can be dismissed as trivial. However, we will show that although packing may appear to be done *en passant*, it is an integral part of the unfolding commercial transaction at the farmer's market.

The farmer's market offers a fruitful ecological niche for students of social interaction. Due to a lack of permanent physical structures such as store fronts, doors, and cash registers, the market is literally constructed and deconstructed through the organization of people and artifacts. Previous ethnographic research of farmer's markets has explored consumption at the market as cultural engagement and identity construction (La Pradelle 2006). The present study complements this work by documenting interactions between seller and customer through sequential multimodal analysis of video-recordings. Unlike some of the other settings analyzed in this volume, there was neither a cash register nor a proper sales counter at the market stall that provides the focus for our study. The farmer only accepts cash payment, and the flowers and produce are presented on a rectangular table within reach of both seller and customer.

---

[1] We would like to thank Trine Heinemann for encouragement and comments on earlier drafts.

Although the farmer typically stands alone behind the table, customers occasionally walk behind the table to inspect a product. In other words, there is not a clear-cut separation between a front and a back stage (Goffman 1959: 106–140). Furthermore, and in line with other food shops such as supermarkets, goods are readily accessible to customers. In supermarkets, customers are typically offered baskets or trolleys where they can place the items that they would like to buy. Placing an item in a trolley or basket is not just a practical matter; it also serves as a moral contract by signaling promise to pay. If you put unpaid merchandise in a pocket or purse you may thus be charged with shoplifting. Neither baskets nor trolleys were available at the farmer's market that provides the focus for this chapter. We will show that customers' readiness to buy is communicated through talk, gaze, body orientation, and manipulation of artifacts, and we will argue that packing is a resource whereby the farmer makes this readiness public and thereby ratifies it. Furthermore, our analysis of packing reveals a division of labor between customer and farmer as well as collaboration between the two.

The main goal of the chapter is thus to present a description and analysis of the details of the collaboration between customer and farmer as they work to pack the produce purchased by the customer. In addition, we explore a theoretical issue in the nature of collaborative action at the farmer's market. The collaborative facet of human interaction has been a long-standing research theme in Conversation Analysis. Drawing on previous research, Kendrick and Drew discuss "the linguistic and embodied ways in which assistance may be sought – requested or solicited – or in which we come to perceive another's need and offer or volunteer assistance" (Kendrick & Drew 2016: 1). They propose that these are organized along a continuum ranging from verbal methods such as requests for assistance to anticipations of trouble that prompt a co-participant to act in ways that enable the other to complete a projected action trajectory. An example they provide of the latter is when a person moves her chair to enable a co-participant to pass behind the chair to answer a ringing telephone (Kendrick & Drew 2016: 10). The authors do not provide detailed descriptions of the two corpora from which their collection of 300 cases of recruitment were drawn. The eight excerpts that they present appear to be drawn from multiparty English-language conversations between peers in noninstitutional everyday settings. Kendrick and Drew argue that there has been an undue emphasis on linguistic form in prior research on the organization of assistance. They attempt to remedy this by proposing an umbrella term – recruitment – that encompasses other aspects of the interaction and situation than the purely verbal and by devoting analysis to subsidiary actions that precede recruitments (cf. Drew & Couper-Kuhlen 2014). An example that they provide of the latter is a person twirling an empty glass so that the ice rattles. The outcome of this action, they argue, is that another person is recruited to fill the glass. The novelty in Kendrick and Drew's study lies not in the explication of new phenomena – that situational factors shape whether and how assistance is launched has been examined in earlier research (e.g., Goodwin 1995; Lindström 2005; Mondada 2014b; Wootton 1997) – but rather in refining terminology for capturing the broader scope of linguistic and situational factors that can precede and prompt assistance. This was also something that was emphasized in one of the two commentaries in the same journal issue where the author praised Kendrick and Drew for systematizing the understanding of "forms of local, here-and-now-assistance" (Heritage 2016: 27). The data examined in this study provide a new kind of environment in which to examine Kendrick and Drew's proposals; we return to the implications of our findings for their proposals in our discussion section.

6.2 Data

Our data are drawn from 10 hours of video-recordings of a weekly farmer's market in a mid-sized Swedish town (hereafter referred to as the *Uppsala University Interaction Corpus: Farmer's Market*, abbreviated as UUICFM).[2] The video-recordings were made over the course of two months during the height of the market season. The camera focused on a stall where an 80-year-old farmer and his adult daughter sold fresh produce and flowers.[3] The farmer had been trading at the market during the last 30 years. His seniority was evident in that his stall was set up at the privileged outer corner of the market square. The recordings capture the farmer's interactions with a stable clientele who show up around the same time each week as well as a range of individuals who appear to frequent the stall more intermittently or for the very first time. The data were collected in accordance with Swedish ethical research guidelines. The corpus used in this chapter consists of packing episodes drawn from 16 discrete commercial transactions. Some of these transactions involved several episodes of packing. The data were transcribed according to conventions developed for Conversation Analysis (CA) and multimodal analysis (Jefferson 2004; Mondada 2014a).[4] Faces have been blurred in images to preserve the anonymity of the participants.

6.3 Analysis

The analysis is organized in three parts. First, we situate packing within the trajectory of the commercial transaction. This involves teasing apart selecting

---

[2] Clara Iversen assisted during data collection.
[3] This study was launched within Uppsala University's research initiative on language and ageing where one aim was to document talk and interaction in work settings where individuals remain professionally active after retirement age.
[4] Hanna Liljeqvist, Daniel Lindbom, and Simon Magnusson assisted with transcription.

Unpacking Packing 187

merchandise from packing it. We will also show that different kinds of produce create distinct affordances and constraints for the organization of picking out and packing. For individual items such as lettuce, bunches of dill, or onions, items are typically picked out (and up) by the customer and packed by the farmer. Bulk items, by contrast, are both picked out and packed by the farmer. Deviant case analysis will show that the latter organization is normative. The second part of the analysis will focus on a subset of cases where the farmer has difficulties packing. The cases are presented on a continuum from one where the customer merely comments on the difficulties to ones where the customer assists. The third and final part of the analysis shows how offers of assistance are also used by customers as means to control the quality of the bulk produce (potatoes) that the farmer is packing.

6.3.1 Picking Out vs. Packing: Discrete Processes or Part and Parcel of the Same Thing

For products sold individually (rather than in bulk) there is a preference for customers to pick out a specific item and the farmer to pack it. In this selection process, customers primarily orient to the quality of a particular specimen rather than a variety or 'brand name'. The farmer typically refrains from persuading/engaging with the customer during the selection. Excerpt 6.1 is a case in point. The customer is looking at the display of lettuce and has picked up one head of lettuce that he is comparing with the ones that are left on the table. The interaction continues as follows.

Excerpt 6.1 (UUICFM:4:A; CUS = customer, FAR = farmer)

```
((Customer is holding a head of lettuce while the farmer is
retrieving and opening a plastic bag))
01 CUS:    Va    heter'om       hä:r
           What  called these here
           What are these called
   fig          #fig.6.1
```

Figure 6.1

```
02           (.)
03 FAR:      Plocksallad
             Leaf salad
04           (1.8)
05 CUS:      Har   du   nån  uppfattning vicka      som  e
             Have  you  any  idea        which ones that are
             Do you have any idea which ones that are
06           godast¿
             the tastiest
             the tastiest
07           (0.5)
08 FAR:      Aej, Smaken    å  baken    e    ju
             Aej  The taste n' the butt are  PRT
             Well To each his
09           del[ad,  (De- De-)
             split   (It- It-)
             own (It- It-)
10 CUS:         [Å:kej, Åkej,
                 Okay   Okay
11 CUS:      Ja ger  mej, Ing[a #fler  dumma=
             I  give me   No   more   stupid
             I  give in   No       more stupid
   cus                        #looks at customer to the right -->
12 FAR:                         [A,
                                 Yeah
13 CUS:      =[frågor,#
               questions
   cus            -->#
14 FAR:      [Hehehe, #*Ä:ej de- J-*ja kan äta (.)
              Hehehe    Äej it- I- I  can eat (.)
              Hehehe Well it- I-I can (.) eat
   far                #*takes lettuce from CUS hand*
   fig                #fig.6.2
```

Figure 6.2

```
15           *bägge två,
              both  two
              them both
   far       *begins to pack lettuce in plastic bag-->>
```

The customer asks for the name of the variety of lettuce in line 1. The indexical expression requires the farmer to orient to the head of lettuce that the customer is holding (Figure 6.1). The farmer replies by naming the variety.

Instead of receipting the name with a change-of-state token or appreciation, the customer asks a new question in lines 5–6. The new question highlights a different selection criterion, namely taste. This suggests that the customer is not oriented to variety as salient for selecting the lettuce. The question in lines 5–6 is marked as potentially unanswerable through the polarity construction *nån uppfattning* 'any idea' (Koshik 2002). The design and content of the farmer's response align with the expectation that the question is unanswerable. The turn-initial particle *aej* marks the response as misfitted to the question (Heritage 2015). The Swedish proverb <u>smaken och baken e ju delad</u> 'the taste and the butt are split' is a cheeky play on words that rhymes. Semantically, it is akin to the English expressions 'to each his own' or 'beauty is in the eye of the beholder', conveying that taste is an individual matter. The farmer thus implies that the question is unanswerable. The epistemic particle *ju* marks this as something the customer ought to already know (Heinemann et al. 2009).

The customer concedes by promising not to ask any more 'stupid questions' (lines 11 and 13) while glancing at a bystander who is waiting for his turn. By orienting to the bystander the customer shows that he understands that he may have breached a generally held norm. The farmer treats the selection as a done deal by grasping the lettuce from the customer (Figure 6.2) and beginning to pack it in the plastic bag (line 15). He assesses the difference between the heads of lettuce as equivocal ('I can eat them both'). That the assessment is proffered during the packing rather than the selection phase of the encounter supports the argument that it does not represent an attempt to persuade the customer to buy. In sum, the analysis shows that the farmer is reluctant to participate in selection even when invited to do so. The use of indexical expressions as well as reaching, pointing, and grasping require both parties to monitor one another and the artifacts at hand.

The analysis of the next excerpt shows the farmer playing a more active part in the selection process. On the face of it, this may seem to counter our point that the customer typically selects and the farmer packs individual items. However, we will argue that the contextual embedding as well as the implementation of the selection shows both parties orienting to the customer's final right to select. At the beginning of the excerpt the customer is looking in a pre-packaged plastic bag with spinach leaves that she apparently has mistaken for lettuce.

Excerpt 6.2 (UUICFM.2.L.4)

```
01 CUS:    €Nej e're spenat€ /ne men ja ska    ha     sall/ad
           No   is't spinach no but I     shall have lettuce
           Oh no is it spinach no 1 want lettuce
    cus    €looks in bag€   /closes and puts down bag-/
02 FAR:    Ja  de   har'u      #där
           Yes that have you.SG there
           Yes you have it over there
    far                        #points at lettuce down on counter
```

```
03              $(2.0)$
    cus         $walks over to lettuce$
    far         $walks over to lettuce$
04 FAR:         %Hä|#r
                Here
    far         %reaches hand to a head of lettuce
    cus          |reaches hand to a head of lettuce
    fig          #fig.6.3
```

Figure 6.3

```
05 CUS:         *Va   e  de    här* +de e: sån här-
                What is this here   it is such-
                What is this    it is one of these-
    cus         *touches back of FAR:s hand*
    far                               +displays lettuce-->
06              %Jamen ja+*tar    en* +såndär%,
                PRT    I   take one   such.there
                Well I'll take one like that
    cus                   *points at lettuce in FAR:s hand*
    far         --->+              +reorients torso twd plastic bags->>
    far         %places lettuce on table--%
07 FAR:         M¿ +#(.)+
                Yeah
    far            +#wets finger+
    fig             #fig.6.4
```

Figure 6.4

```
08 CUS:     Å,  Nu  +har'u         dill också,
            Oh  Now have you.SG dill too
            Oh Now you have dill as well
   far                +pulls out plastic bag->>
```

The customer notices the spinach with a change-of-state prefaced discovery and states that she wants lettuce (line 1). The farmer responds by indicating where the lettuce is with the deictic 'there' while pointing further down the table (line 2). The wording, idiomatically translated as 'yes you have it over there', displays the farmer's expectation that the customer will participate in the selection. This analysis is supported by the customer walking over toward the lettuce (line 3). The heads of lettuce are not accessible for visual inspection as they are placed 'face down' on the table. The customer is scanning different items even as she is still approaching the table; she arrives and leans in, still scanning. Meanwhile, the farmer begins to move his hand toward one of the heads of lettuce while uttering 'here' (line 4). The deictic reference contextualizes his reach as part of the ongoing action of guiding the customer toward the lettuce. The customer reacts by moving her hand toward the same head of lettuce that the farmer is reaching for. The customer and farmer are so closely coordinated in time and motion that their hands reach the lettuce simultaneously (Figure 6.3).

The customer asks 'what is this' (line 5) and goes on by stating 'it is one of these' (Harjunpää et al., this volume). That the customer answers her own question by replacing one indexical reference with another suggests that she is not in pursuit of the correct name of the vegetable. The farmer interprets the customer's actions as a request to look more closely by lifting and turning the lettuce to make it available for inspection (Fox & Heinemann, this volume). After scrutinizing the lettuce, the customer states that she will 'take one like that' while pointing at the head of lettuce that the farmer is displaying for her. As soon as her turn has reached recognizable completion, the farmer starts to reorient toward the plastic bags that are placed at the opposite end of the produce stand (line 6) and he displays commitment to comply with the customer's request with a minimal response and by preparing to tear off the plastic bag from the roll by wetting his finger (Figure 6.4.) and pulling out the bag (cf. Heinemann 2006; Sorjonen & Raevaara 2014). The customer's reorientation to a new vegetable (line 8) confirms that the selection sequence has been brought to a close (the completion of packing entails collaboration and will be analyzed in Section 6.3.2).

The analysis so far has shown that for certain types of produce such as lettuce, parsley, and dill, the customer's selection is based on inspection of the quality of individual specimens. Selection is the first part of an action sequence that is completed by the farmer preparing to pack the selected item in a bag, thus ratifying the customer's selection of a particular item. This ratification requires close coordination between the parties and can be accomplished in an embodied way without any talk. For bulk items such as potatoes or apples, by contrast, the farmer both picks out and packs. This difference between packing individual and bulk items is illustrated in Excerpt 6.3, which involves both types of produce: a bunch of onions that are tied together as one individual item and loose potatoes in a bin, a bulk item. The customer and farmer have exchanged greetings and the customer has grabbed a bunch of onions from the table when the transcript begins.

Excerpt 6.3 (UUICFM:2.M.4)

```
01 CUS:     #Dedär tar  ja,
             Those take I
             I'll take those
   cus      #hands over a bunch of onions
02 FAR:     &Den  tog  du¿
             That took you.SG
             You took that one
   far      &receives onions
03 CUS:     €En såndär liten,
             One such   small
             One of those small ones
   far      €looks down and walks toward paper bags
04          (3.5)
   far      reaches for paper bag
05 FAR:     §Ä're bra så,§
             Is it good so
             Will that be all
   far      §opens bag----§
06          $(1.0)
   far      $puts onions in paper bag
07 CUS:     &Hördudu  @dehär@    e färskpotatis¿
             Hey you.SG thishere is new potatoes&
             Listen are these new potatoes
   cus      &points at potatoes
   cus               @vertical movement index finger@
08 FAR:     A:¿
             Yeah
09 CUS:     Ja /tar  e:: +(.) ett kilo utav dom
             I   take er       one kilo of  them
             I'll have er (.) a kilo of those
   far         /places bag with onions on table
   far              +retrieves bags with onions from table
10          också dårå,
             also  then then
             as well then
11 FAR:     De-  dehär f-  dehär får ja handgräva
             The- this  g- this  get I  hand dig
             The- these I- I have to dig these up by hand
12          dehär, Maskin går ju inte serru,
             this   Machine goes PRT not you see
             these  A machine is no good you know
13 CUS:     Ne:j,
             No
```

```
14 FAR:     Ja å man- De e    ju  så torrt du     vet så
            Yes n' one- It is PRT so dry    you.SG know so
            Yes and you- It's so dry you know so
15          han växer inge     heller den jäveln,
            he  grows nothing either it  the bastard
            he doesn't grow either the darn thing
16          =Så ja tänkte   ja skulle inte ta    opp
             So I  thought I  should not  take  up
             So I wasn't planning to dig them up
     far    =removes onions from bag
17          (den) asså men (.) för nu  har
             it    PRT  but     for now have
             you know but (.) because now
18          [ju folk-
             PRT people-
             [people-
19 CUS:     $[Men men men men sånadär små    e$    ju
             But but but but such     small are   PRT
             But but but but those    small ones are
     far    $begins putting potatoes in bag$
20          e    ju fin[a,
            are PRT nice
            are nice aren't they
21 FAR:                [Ja.h,
                        PRT
                        Yeah.h
```

The customer picks up an individual item (a bunch of onions) and hands it to the farmer who reaches for a paper bag to pack the onions (lines 1–4) (Mondada & Sorjonen, this volume). The farmer treats the purchase as possibly complete by asking the closing implicative 'will that be all' (line 5). Meanwhile the customer walks over to the bin with potatoes (a bulk item). He points at the potatoes and asks whether they are 'new potatoes' (line 7).[5] The farmer confirms and the customer requests a kilo (lines 9–10). In contrast with Excerpts 6.1–6.2, the customer does not touch the produce. The farmer initiates small talk about the dry weather while beginning to comply with the verbal request, instead of inviting or providing a space for the customer to pick out which potatoes he would like. Here we see at work the differential organization provided by the affordances of individual and bulk items, which reveals packing as a seen but unnoticed feature of the interaction. In the next example, by contrast, this normative organization – normally not attended to overtly – is brought to the forefront.

Excerpt 6.4, a deviant case, shows a customer requesting to both pick and pack potatoes. The farmer treats the request as impertinent.

---

[5] 'New potatoes' are potatoes that are harvested in the early part of summer.

194 A. Lindström & B. Fox

Excerpt 6.4 (UUICFM.X.A.5.a)

```
01 FAR:    +T§a*ck+ &du,
           Thank    you.SG
           Thank You
   pcu     §turns and walks away from produce stand
   far     +hands over change to previous customer+
   cus        *looks at FAR-->
   far          &looks at new customer--->
02 CUS:    (Du,)*   Po&tatis,
           You.SG Potatoes
           (Listen) Potatoes
   cus     -->*looks down at bin of potatoes-->
   far     --------->&looks down at bin of potatoes-->
03 FAR:    M:¿
           Yeah
04         +(0.6)+
   far     +reaches for bag+
05 FAR:    +*[Hur-
             How-
06 CUS:    +*[Får& ja plocka &själv¿+*
             May I  pick   myself
             [May I pick them myself
   far     +grabs bag---------------+
   far     --->&looks at CUS&
   cus        *clutches pocketbook under arm*
07         +(0,2)+
   far     +shakes head+
08 FAR:    Ja, +I  #värsta+ [fall,
           Yes In  worst    case
           Yes If worst comes to worst
09 CUS:                    [HeheΔ*he,*Δ
   far     +throws bag in front of CUS+
   cus                     *picks up bag*
   cu2                      Δreaches for bag of potatoesΔ
   fig            #fig.6.5
```

Figure 6.5

```
10         Δ&(.)Δ& *(.)*
   cu2     Δgrabs bag of potatoesΔ
   far       &looks at CU2 grabbing the bag of potatoes&
   cus     -->*looks at FAR*
11 FAR:    &Δ(.)&Δ He*(hh), (.)*
   far     &looks at CU2 and smiles&
   cu2      Δlooks at FAR and smilesΔ
   cus              *smile stiffens*
```

The singular pronoun *du* at the end of the farmer's turn in line 1 is a pivot that is both backward and forward looking. Retrospectively, *du* can be heard as an integral component of the expression of gratitude ('thank you') directed at the previous customer.[6] Prospectively, *du* functions as a turn allocation device whereby the farmer selects the next person in line. The interactants' movement and body orientation favor the idea that *du* is used to select the next customer. The previous customer moves away from the table as soon as he has received his change, and the farmer has moved his gaze toward the approaching new customer simultaneously with the production of *tack* ('thanks'). The new customer responds to the farmer's summons (*du* in line 1) with a reciprocal identical summons and then gazes intently at the potatoes in the bin in front of the farmer while naming the produce (line 2).

The farmer receipts the customer's turn with a minimal acknowledgment (line 3) and shows that he understands it as a request to buy potatoes by reaching for a bag to pack them. His abandoned turn in line 5 can be heard as going for an inquiry about how many kilos of potatoes the customer would like to buy. In overlap, the customer asks whether she can pick the potatoes on her own (line 6). The act of requesting marks self-picking as out of the ordinary, as does the language of permission (the use of 'may' rather than 'can'). By immediately clutching her pocketbook under her arm to free up her hands for packing, she conveys her expectation that her request will be granted. This hurried pace is also in line with the task orientation that she has exhibited from the beginning of the exchange. The farmer treats the customer's request as problematic by first shaking his head and then responding with the disaffiliative 'yes if worst comes to worst' and throwing the bag in front of her (Figure 6.5). The problematic character of the customer's insistence on packing is also registered by a bystander (identified as customer two) who is gathering up her paper bags after having concluded a purchase that was handled by the farmer's daughter. Customer two leans over the vegetable stand to grab her bag and smiles at the farmer, who reciprocates her smile. This collusive interchange is registered by the first customer who tries to seek eye contact with the farmer in line 10. Her attempt is unsuccessful as the farmer is fully engaged (maintaining eye contact, smiling, and laughing) with the second customer. Having been unsuccessful at securing eye contact with the farmer, the customer reorients to the potatoes with a frozen expression on her face (line 11). In this excerpt, we thus see evidence of the normative orientation for the farmer to pack bulk items. Through his display of grudgingly complying with the customer's request to pack the bulk item herself and

---

[6] Unlike English, the Swedish word 'thank' (*tack*) is idiomatic as an expression of gratitude both as a single word and with the pronoun (*tack du*).

through the collusive eye contact and smiling between himself and customer two, the farmer enacts the problematic nature of the customer's request.

In the preceding, we have described how customer and seller transition to packing. For individual items, selecting and packing are discrete processes that involve a division of labor between customer and farmer. Customers typically touch, grasp, and pick up individual items for the farmer to pack. By beginning to pack an item, the farmer displays his understanding that a selection has been made. For bulk produce, by contrast, the division of labor is quite different as the farmer both picks out and packs. Selecting and packing are thus part and parcel of the same thing when it comes to bulk items. Participants in the exchange as well as bystanders orient to this as a normative structure by sanctioning or attending to departures from the norm.

6.3.2 Collaboration by Lending a Helping Hand

Having described the systematic organization of selecting and packing merchandise sold individually and in bulk, we will now consider a subset of cases where the customer assists the farmer with packing. On the face of it, this kind of collaboration might appear to contradict the neat division of labor between farmer and customer that we have argued characterizes packing. However, as Michael Moerman has eloquently observed, structure can provide a schema for breaking out of institutional roles:

> The metric of conversational sequencing provides co-ordinates – a sort of background graph paper – for tracking the motile shiftings of roles and relationships that characterize interaction. We can use it to tune into the rustlings and alarms of talk with which we are summoned to and released from our occasioned duty as policemen, daddies, neighbors, and friends. (Moerman 1988: 24)

In our corpus, we have noted two different categories of collaboration. The first category encompasses cases where the farmer is experiencing difficulties in opening a flimsy plastic bag, fitting vegetables in a bag, or filling a paper bag with two hands. In these cases, which provide the focus for the current section, customers may lend a helping hand, an interactional move that can be characterized as altruistic. The cases in the second category also emerge from contexts where the farmer is visibly displaying trouble packing. However, here the customers prolong the cooperative move longer than needed to inspect the merchandise that is placed in the bag. These cases will be analyzed in the last analytic section of the chapter.

Collaborative moves can be responsive to some visible difficulty (Kendrick & Drew 2016: 2) and close monitoring can be a precondition for collaboration. In the next excerpt, the customer notices the farmer's visible difficulties in fitting a head of lettuce in a plastic bag by assuming responsibility for selecting

Unpacking Packing 197

a specimen that is particularly difficult to pack. The excerpt is contiguous with Excerpt 6.1 where the customer was trying to engage the farmer in the selection of a head of lettuce.

Excerpt 6.5 (UUICFM:4:A)

```
15            *bägge två,
               both  two
                 them both
     far    *begins to pack lettuce in plastic bag-->
16         €(3.0)@(9.0)+(1.0)%(1.0)
     cus   €scans produce on tabler
     cus          @transfers cucumber from left to right hand
     cus             +looks at FAR packing bag-->
     cus                     %points cucumber at lettuce
17 CUS:    #(De var) dumt    att   ja tog  dendär
             (It was) stupid that  I  took that one there
                It was stupid that I took that
     fig   #fig.6.6
```

Figure 6.6

```
18         see I(hh)      [Ahahaha
             one I see that Ahahaha
     cus                -->+
19 FAR:                 [He(hh), Ne ja skulle
                         He(hh)  No I  should
                         He(hh) No I should
20         tagi     en  annan påse, Kom  ja på nu
            have taken one other bag  Came I  on now
            have taken another bag I realised that just now
21         men de (.) *(va,) [(Men nu-)
            but it (.)  (was)  (But now-)
            but that (.) (was) (But now-)
     far                --->*
22 CUS:                    [(Du    klara de,) Du
                             (You.SG made  it) You.SG
                               You did it You
23         klara't,
            made it
             did it
24 FAR:    Vi fixar't serru,
            We fix it you see
             We fix it see
25         (0.2)
```

198   A. Lindström & B. Fox

The farmer painstakingly tries to fit the lettuce in a plastic bag during the long silence in line 16. The customer disattends the farmer's efforts and 'does waiting' by scanning the other vegetables on the table and shifting the cucumber from his left to right hand. Toward the end of the silence the customer looks at the farmer and points with the cucumber toward the lettuce that the farmer is trying to put in the bag while stating that it was 'stupid' that he took 'that one there' (line 17–18, Figure 6.6); the customer thus takes responsibility for the farmer's trouble with packing. The verb of perception *ser* 'to see' (line 18) makes this come off as inferred from observing the farmer struggling to fit the lettuce in the bag. The laughter toward the end of the turn may orient to the dispreferred nature of creating trouble for another person and may also orient to the self-deprecation of the customer's turn. The farmer disagrees with the self-deprecating treatment of the trouble on the part of the customer and states that he is the one at fault for picking the wrong kind of bag (lines 19–21). After this first round of assuming responsibility for the difficulties (lines 17–21), a sequence of celebration follows. It is tied to the previous sequence by the customer who counters the farmer's self-blame in lines 19–21 by treating the result as an achievement by the farmer, who in turn treats the fixing of the problem as a joint achievement through use of the first person plural pronoun *vi* 'we' in line 24. The analysis of Excerpt 6.5 shows that customers are attentive to how packing unfolds moment by moment. The next examples show how this close monitoring can evolve into collaboration.

The sales transaction in Excerpt 6.6 involves a couple (identified as customer A and customer B) buying potatoes. As in the last excerpt, the farmer encounters problems during the packing process, but in this case the customer does not merely comment on the difficulties but also reaches out a 'helping hand'. There is a short interlude with a previous customer who is picking up her wallet from the vegetable stand (line 1) before the farmer reorients to customers A and B.

Excerpt 6.6 (UUICFM.3.G.3)

```
01 FAR:    #Då  +kan du     ta'en    som sagt var,#+
           Then can you.SG take it as   said was
           In that case you can take it as I said
    far    #sifts through potatoes--------------#
    cuA                   +moves closer to the potato bin---+
02         *(0.4)*((opening of bag collapses))
    far    *digs in bin of potatoes*
03 FAR:    +#(0,2) Jodå,
                   PRT
                   Well
    cuA    +reaches for bag, taps the bag and retracts-->
    fig    #fig.6.7, fig.6.8, fig.6.9
```

Figure 6.7

Figure 6.8

Figure 6.9

```
04 CUA:     (Ska    ja)+ hålla opp (den själva-
            Shall I      hold  up   it  itself-
            (Shall I) hold it up (the
     cuA             --->+
05          Sådär    du    har *näven    ändå,)#*+(.)+
            So there you.SG have the fist still
            There you can use your hands anyway)
     far                       *scoops potatoes with hands*
     cuA                                    +reaches for bag
                                            then retracts+
     fig                                    #fig.6.10
```

Figure 6.10

```
06 FAR:    Äh  de e  ba   å   gör sådär under vattkran,
           PRT it is just n'  do  like  that  under tap
           Yeah you just do like that under the tap
07 CUA:    A:  va   bra,
           PRT what good
           Oh good
08 CUB:    *A,*+(.)+
           PRT
           Yeah
    far    *packs bag*
    cuA         +reaches for bag then retracts+
09 FAR:    +Ska'ru         ha    ett #+kilo, Hur mycke
           Shall you.SG have a      kilo    How much
           Do you want a kilo              How much
    cuA    +reaches for bag--------+
    fig                                   #fig.6.11
```

Figure 6.11

```
10         [ska'ru         ha,
            shall you.SG have
           [do you want
11 CUA:    [Ja tar   ett kilo nu,
            I take a   kilo now
12         (1.2)
```

The farmer is sifting through the potatoes with both hands when the opening of the bag collapses (line 2). Customer A reaches out for the bag as if to grab it, but retracts his hand once the farmer has a managed to get a firm hold on the bag (Figures 6.7–6.9). The customer begins to make an offer in line 4 '(Shall I) hold it up (the)'. By offering to just hold the bag rather than packing it, the customer shows an orientation to the norm that customers should not pick out bulk items. Line 5 is not fully idiomatic, but the upshot of the utterance seems to be that the customer is noticing that the farmer is now able to 'scoop' the potatoes with two hands (Figure 6.10). The noticing evidences customer A's attention to the packing and implies that he assumes that the farmer can manage on his own. Customer A continues to closely monitor the packing and reaches out his hand toward the bag again in lines 5, 8, and 9 (Figure 6.11). The customer's embodied conduct in this sequence underscores the idea that the initiation of collaborative moves emerges from close observation of an unfolding scene (Kendrick & Drew 2016: 8–9). That the customer reaches out his hand without actually intervening displays both readiness to assist as well as subsequent confidence in the other party's ability to manage without any help.

The way the customer calibrates his helping gestures with the farmer's moves and mishaps in Excerpt 6.6 is reminiscent of the way an adult can scaffold the movement of a toddler who is in the process of taking some first, wobbly, steps. Customers' orientation toward assisting rather than taking over the packing is also evident in the verbal construction of the offer of help in the next excerpt.

Excerpt 6.7 (UUICFM.3.A.3.a)

```
((Princess (mentioned in line 1) is a variety of potatoes.))
01 CUS:    Ja tar  lite   princess då,
           I  take little princess then
           I'll have some princess then
02 FAR:    +Gör: så du(hh), Gör så du,
           Do   so you.SG  Do  so you
           Go ahea(hh)d Go ahead
    far    +bends down to get paper bag-->
03         (6.0)+
    far    --->+
04 FAR:    €Hu-hur mycke€ ska[  ('re va),
           Ho-how much  shall  it be
           Ho-how much       [(do you want)
    cus    €opening bag-€
05 CUS:                       [Ja.h,
                               PRT
                              [Yes.h
06 CUS:    Ja håller [i  ja så kan du    ha   i,
           I  hold   in I  so can you.SG have in
           I'll hold [it so you can put them in
07 FAR:                   [Hörrudu,
                          [Listen
08 FAR:    J-ja, (      )
           I-I   (      )
```

The farmer responds to the customer's request (line 1) by bending down to retrieve a paper bag from underneath the table (line 2). The customer proffers assistance by using the division of labor construction 'I'll hold it so you can put them in' (line 6) (Couper-Kuhlen & Etelämäki 2014). In contrast to Excerpt 6.4, this customer is offering assistance rather than taking over the packing, thereby upholding the normative preference to abstain from self-packing. This spate of interaction is partially blocked by another sales person–customer dyad, and so it is not possible to see whether the offer is preceded by visible trouble. Excerpt 6.8 (taken from the same transaction as Excerpt 6.2) shows a similar case.

Excerpt 6.8 (UUICFM.2.L.4)

```
01 CUS:     kan *frysa  ner   va  +el+ler,
            can freeze  down  what or
            can freeze  right or
   cus            *hand over mouth-->
   far                               +tears off plastic bag+
02 FAR:     •Ja: de   går   väl        bra,*•
            Yes that  goes  probably  good
            Well that should be fine
   cus                                    --->*
   far      •shifts torso twd lettuce w bag in hand•
03          #§(0.5)
   far      §tries to open plastic bag-->
   fig      #fig.6.12
```

Figure 6.12

```
04 CUS:     Ja tänkte *prismässigt,*
            I  thought pricewise
            I was thinking pricewise
   cus               *lifts chin--*
05          *(0.6)&(0,2)&
   cus      *Gaze at plastic bag in farmer's hands-->
   cus            &moves hands towards plastic bag&
06 CUS:     Ska  ja [hålla upp,*
            Shall I  hold  up
            Shall I [hold (it) up
   cus                          --->*
07 FAR:             [De-§
                    [It-
   far                   -->§
08 FAR:     +A  du+     kan #&hålla opp'en, De e  så
            Yeah you.SG can  hold  up it   It is so
            Yeah you can hold it up It is so
   far      +motions bag to CUS+
   cus                          &grabs bag and starts opening it-->
   fig                          #fig.6.13
```

Unpacking Packing

Figure 6.13

```
09          e're bra,
            is it good
            that's good
10          (1.0)&#*(3.0)
    cus     --->&
    cus         *collaborates with FAR in packing bag-->
    fig         #fig.6.14
```

Figure 6.14

```
11 FAR:     Ja¿*
            Yeah
    cus     -->*
12 CUS:     *Så,*
            So
            There
    cus     *lets go of bag*
```

The farmer prepares to pack the lettuce by tearing off the bag (line 1). He struggles to open up the bag during the silence in line 3 (Figure 6.12). The customer shifts her gaze to the plastic bag in the farmer's hand and starts to move her hands toward the bag in line 5 and offers to hold it up in line 6. The offer is indexical as the customer does not even use a demonstrative reference to the plastic bag. The farmer accepts the offer and motions the bag toward the customer (line 8, Figure 6.13). By stressing the second person pronoun in line 8 the farmer shows an orientation to the collaborative character of the offer, i.e., that the customer will not do the packing for him but rather assist with one aspect – holding the bag open – so that the farmer can pack the lettuce (Figure 6.14). The language of permission *du kan hålla opp'en* 'yeah you can hold it up' also reveals an orientation to collaboration that does not transcend the division of labor between the provider and the recipient of service. The collaboration comes to a close in line 12 where the customer produces the closing implicative *så* (Lindström & Heinemann 2009) while letting go of the bag.[7]

The analysis so far has shown that collaborative moves are typically occasioned by observable difficulties by the farmer during packing, such as when a paper bag falls over. Efforts to assist are tentative and may be withdrawn if it turns out that assistance is not needed, and customers appear to orient to not helping if help is not needed. In other words, helping, as we'll discuss more in Section 6.4, is not a universally desirable action, inasmuch as it may treat the other as not 'competent' in carrying out their professional tasks, which in this context entails the farmer being of service to the customer rather than the other way around. Verbal offers provide one resource whereby customers can make sure that help is welcomed; if the verbal offer is declined by the farmer, then physical help is not given. Furthermore, the visible nature of the difficulty (e.g., struggling to open a bag or trying to fit a big head of lettuce in the bag) legitimizes the farmer's problem and the possibility of helping him and makes the difficulties come off as contingencies rather than signs of incompetence (e.g., because of his age and possible health conditions, such as arthritis).

We have also seen that the lexical design of offers can highlight collaboration as joint action rather than as something done for the other. For example, the use of the pronoun *du* 'you, singular' can highlight the division of labor that 'I' and 'you' will engage in, which creates a mutual and shared responsibility for the action, rather than a unilateral responsibility. In addition, the absence of language of gratitude contributes to the portrayal of assistance as collaborative rather than as done as a kindness for one of the parties. This further highlights the interactants' visible orientation toward the rights and obligations associated with the categories of service provider and service recipient. Having examined instances of mutually beneficial collaboration, we now examine how collaborative moves can be sustained to contribute to more egotistic ends.

---

[7] This excerpt also involves subtle efforts to negotiate price. The customer's question in line 1 whether the dill is suitable for freezing implies that the dill may be of inferior quality. The farmer responds to the request at face value (line 2), whereupon the customer clarifies with a third turn repair (line 4) that her question concerned the price of the item.

6.3.3 Collaboration as a Means for Quality Control

In the final two examples, apparent collaboration emerges in environments where discerning customers have expressed concern regarding the quality or size of the produce (potatoes). In both examples the customers provide assistance with packing, but in these cases assistance comes off as a method to monitor the quality of the produce that is being packed. The customer in Excerpt 6.9 has just identified herself as the next person in line and requested potatoes when the transcribed excerpt begins.

Excerpt 6.9 (UUICFM.X.A.4)

```
01 FAR:    De e  princess,
           It is princess
           It's princess
02 CUS:    Ja  de  later   ju  +väldigt+
           Yes it sounds PRT very
           Well it sounds very
   far                     +grabs paper bag+
03         tre[vligt,
           ni [ce
04 FAR:       [Ja  de  later  väldigt bra
              [Yes it sounds very    good
05         [#(gissar ja,)
              guess   I
           [ (I suppose)
   far     #reaches toward bin
06 CUS:    [*A:  de  gör  de,*
            Yeah it  does that
           [Yeah it does indeed
   cus      *reaches beyond farmer's hand into bin of potatoes*
07 CUS:    *#Dendär vill ja inte* ha   i
             That   want I  not  have in
           I don't want that one at
   cus     *grabs a potato and removes it from bin*
   fig     #fig.6.15
```

Figure 6.15

```
08              alla fall,
                any case
                any rate
09 FAR:         +A   *dendär- Dendär kan ja ta    bort,+
                Yeah that-    That    can I  take away
                Yeah that one- I'll put that one away
      far       +throws rejected potato behind table--+
      cus            *smiles--->
10 CUS:         De(n) §skrämmer   folk,*
                It        frightens people
      cus             §looks at other customers-->
      cus                             --->*
11 FAR:         A,
                Yeah
12 CUS:         +(Räcker) §ett å't halvt      kilo
                  Suffice  one and one half kilo
                  (Is) about one and a half kilos
      far       +starts to open bag
      cus              ->§looks at potatoes in bin--->
13              ungef[är,
                approximately
                enou[gh
14 FAR:           +∆[E:tt å't∆  halvt¿
                   [One  and a half
      far       +both hands in bin
      bag            ∆bag collapses∆
15 CUS:         M:,(.)
                Yeah
16              #*(2.0)+(3.0)§*
      cus       *grabs and opens bag with left hand*
      far               +packs potatoes-->>
      cus               --->§looks toward other produce->>
                           and lets go of bag-->>
      fig       #fig.6.16
```

Figure 6.16

The customer assesses the variety of potatoes positively while the farmer prepares for packing by grabbing a bag (line 2). The customer then reaches into the bin to remove a potato that she places on the table beside the bin (Figure 6.15). This action is presented as warranted by self-interest: 'I don't want that one at any rate' (lines 7–8). The farmer aligns with the customer by throwing the rejected potato on the ground behind the table (line 9). This prompts the customer to back down from her self-serving stance by first smiling and then giving the more altruistic account that 'it frightens people', while looking at the other customers around the stand. The farmer starts to open the bag during the customer's specification of how much she wants in lines 12–13. He grabs the potatoes with both hands and the bag collapses, whereupon the customer grabs and opens the bag with her left hand. She holds the bag with her wrist raised so that she is able to scrutinize the produce the farmer is packing (Figure 6.16) . Having apparently been satisfied that the remaining potatoes in the bin are of good enough quality, she looks up and spots the red beets at the other side of the table. She lets go of the bag and walks over to inspect the red beets while the farmer continues to pack the potatoes.

In the talk leading up to Excerpt 6.10, the farmer has just informed the customer that the tomatoes are sold out. The customer then turns his attention to the potatoes with a positive assessment (line 1). The farmer disagrees with the positive assessment (line 2), which prompts a follow-up question from the customer (line 3).

Excerpt 6.10 (UUICFM.2.L.8)

```
((Ingrid (mentioned in line 25) is a female name as well as the
brand name of a machine for peeling potatoes.))

01 CUS:    Men potatisen ser    härlig ut,
           But the potato looks lovely out
           But the potato looks lovely
02 FAR:    Ne:j de gör  han inte,
           No   it does he   not
           No he doesn't
03 CUS:    Jaså¿  [E'ren inte god   eller vad¿
           Really  Is it not  good or   what
           Really [Does it not taste good or what
04 FAR:           [Nä.h,
                   PRT
                  [No.h
05 FAR:    Jo: men han jä-  De e   så jä:vla- Ja
           Yes but he  blo- It is  so bloody- I
           Yes but he  blo- It's so bloody- I
06         får ju  inga kilo,
           get PRT no   kilos
           don't get any kilos
07 FAR:    [Huh heh heh heh
08 CUS:    [Nä: men, Sånahär   go-  små,   Dom  e
            No   but  Such here goo- small They are
           [No but  These tast- small ones They're
09         godast,
           the tastiest
           the best
10 FAR:    Ja:, De ve-   Ja:, .hh
           Yes  It know- Yes
           Yes I know- Yes .hh
```

```
11            [Ä.h, N-
               PRT N-
              [Well.h N-
12  CUS:      [Ja tar   gärna   två kilo,
               I  take gladly two kilos
              [I would like two kilos
13  CUS:      Så små     som möjligt,
              As small as    possible
14  FAR:      Ja:, Du-du         (        )
              Yes  You.SG-you.SG
              Yes  Listen-listen (        )
15            (.)
16  FAR:      Ja ska    bara knyta opp denhär säcken
              I  shall only tie  up   this   the sack
              I just need to open this sack
17            [ska'ru-
               shall you.SG-
              [and then you'll-
18  CUS:      [De e    samma: (.) sort dedär,
               It is   same        kind that
              [They're the same (.) kind those
19  FAR:      Ja:, De e  samma sort.h,
              Yes  It is same  kind
              Yes They're the same kind.h
20  CUS:      Du    har'e minsta       kvar här  i  botten,
              You.SG have the smallest left here in bottom
              You got the smallest ones left here at the bottom
21            de skulle ja gärna   ta,
              it should I  gladly take
              I'd love to have those
22  FAR:      Ja du    tar   dom först då,  Innan vi
              Yes you.SG take them first then Before we
              Yes you'll take them first then Before we
23            slår ur¿
              hit  out
              empty the sack
24  CUS:      #Ja har   en potatisskalare hemma som
               I  have a  potato peeler   home  that
              I have a potato peeler at home
       far    #grabs bag to start packing
25            heter     ingrid [(            )
              is called ingrid
              called ingrid    [(            )
26  FAR:                       [A.h,
                                PRT
                               [Yeah.h
27  FAR:      Jä- De ti' bara å  göra schådär,
              Jä- It to  just n' go   like that
              You just do like that
28            ((15.33-15.34 inaudible))
29  FAR:      De e  ba  å  sätta under vattkran'
              It is just n' put   under tap
              You just put it under the tap
30            egentligen, [Så du      behöver inte=
              really       So you.SG need    not
              really      [So you don't need
```

```
31 CUS:              [A,
                      PRT
                     [Yeah
32 FAR:    =ha    nån ingrid heller,
            have any ingrid either
            any ingrid
33 CUS:    *Dom där    riktiga bamsingarna    låter* du      gärna
            Those there real    the big ones let    you.SG gladly
            You can leave out those really big
     cus   *points in potato bin----------------*
34         bli,
           become
           ones
```

A short discussion ensues in lines 4–11 where the farmer portrays the potatoes as commercially undesirable (they are too small to generate profit), whereas the customer portrays them as desirable from the point of view of consumption (smaller potatoes taste better than big ones). The customer requests two kilos of potatoes in line 12 and specifies with an increment in line 13 that he would like them 'as small as possible'. The farmer unties a new big string bag of potatoes, as the bin is almost empty (lines 16–17). The customer highlights once more his preference for small potatoes by stating that he would love to have the remaining smallest ones in the bottom of the bin (lines 20–21). The farmer acquiesces and grabs a paper bag to pack the last potatoes in the bin. The customer monitors the packing and requests that the farmer leave out the 'really big ones' in lines 33–34. The packing continues as follows.

Excerpt 6.11 (UUICFM.2.L.8)

```
35 FAR:    +Nä dom-  dom   +får'u      ha   kva:r &(.)&
            PRT they-  they  get you.SG have left
            Yeah you- you can keep those
     far   +opens paper bag+collects potatoes with hands-->
     bag                                          &bag collapses&
36 FAR:    Ä.h, *D-du   vet  de e   så torrt i  landet
            PRT  Y-you.SG know it is so dry   in the land
            Well.h Y-you know the ground is so dry
     cus        *takes hold of bag and supports it-->
37         vettu       så de dammar,
            know you.SG so  it makes dust
            it's all dusty you know
38 CUS:    Gör'e     de,
            Does it it
            It is is it
39 FAR:    A:   visst, Asså de- Ja titta  förra
            Yeah sure   PRT   it- I looked previous
            Oh yeah Like it- I checked last
40         veckan    vettu     å  dom  va  precis  lika
            the week know you.SG n' they were exactly like
            week you know and they were exactly the same
41         stora men nu  vinar dom  du     vet,
            big   but now vinar they you.SG know
            size but now they vinar you know
```

((14 lines of transcript where Farmer explains the expression
vinar))
```
55 CUS:    De  har   jag aldrig [hört,
           It  have  I   never   heard
           I've never          [heard that before
56 FAR:                        [(Jo.hh,)
                                PRT
                               [(Yeah.hh)
57 FAR:    De- Har-  Jo: de e  klart,  *Ä're  torrt*
           It- Have- PRT it is clear    Is it  dry
           It- Have- Yeah of course If it gets dry
     cus                               *lifts up bag*
58         asså- Finns  inge vatt'n asså, Då-då
           like- Exists no   water  PRT   Then-then
           like- There's no water like Then-then
59         då   ramlar ju  blasten,
           then falls  PRT the tops
           then the tops fall over
60 CUS:    Jaha,
           PRT
           Oh
61 FAR:    Ha, +(.)+*
           PRT
           Yep
     far        +grabs bag of potatoes+
     cus                             -->*
62         ((16.15-16.17 inaudible))
63 FAR:    Å  sen  när  vattnet  kommer, Va   t-  Va
           N' then when the water comes  What th- What
           And then when the water comes What d- What
64         tror   du    händer   då¿
           think you.SG happens  then
           do you think happens then
65         (0.8)
```

The farmer is holding a handful of potatoes with both hands when the paper bag collapses to the side (line 35). This prompts the customer to grab the bag and he keeps holding the bag open during the 30 seconds of packing. The collaborative move makes him a captive audience for a storytelling that is initiated with a place formulation in the same line where assistance is first proffered (lines 36–37). Holding the bag also allows the customer to closely monitor the potatoes that the farmer is packing during the course of storytelling.

Excerpts 6.9–6.11 involve discerning customers who reject items (Excerpt 6.9) or coax the farmer to pack particular specimens (Excerpt 6.10). In Excerpts 6.9 and 6.11 the customer provides more assistance than required by holding on to the bag even though the packing is proceeding smoothly. The suspended helping hand allows the customers to control (and if necessary reject) what is being put in the bag without breaching the normative preference that the farmer is the one with the right to pack.

6.4 Concluding Discussion

We introduced this chapter by reviewing the findings from Kendrick and Drew's (2016) study. One of their aims was to systematize the understanding of "the methods participants use to resolve troubles in the realization of practical courses of action" (Kendrick & Drew 2016: 1).

The present chapter has highlighted another aspect of assistance, namely how it both shapes and is shaped by social categories. Assistance can compromise independence and integrity. Seemingly innocuous moves such as giving up a seat for a fellow passenger on the bus are subtle but powerful devices for possibly categorizing the other as 'pregnant', 'old', or 'disabled'. This observation is salient for the data discussed in this chapter where the professional representative is well beyond retirement age, and where the offer of assistance impinges on the imperatives of professional service, and the rights and obligations related to them. We have shown that customers are careful to embed their collaborative moves for giving help in the details of the unfolding situation. By refraining from intervening unless help is obviously needed, customers pay respect to the farmer's capacity to carry out his work. We also showed examples where the way assistance is provided is shaped by the institutional categories of seller and customer. For example, when the customer lends a helping hand longer than actually required for implementing the task at hand, they are able to inspect and control the merchandise as it is being packed.

That social identities are interwoven with requests for or proffers of assistance is also evident in one of the examples from Kendrick and Drew's study. Their written transcript is reproduced below. The person who will make the request, Graham, has just rolled a cigarette to smoke but has no light.

Excerpt 6.12 (Extract 1 RCE06 07:00 [Kendrick & Drew 2016: 5])

```
1   GRA:    does anybody have a ligh[ter
2   DAN:                           [Kit can you do a partyboy
3           move [please.
4   JES:         [no::
5   SAT:    I have a lighter in my r+oom.=
6   gra                             +.....-->
7   JES:    =[Daniel do you have a lighter.
8   GRA:    =[Daniel can you pass me +those match+es.
9           .....................-->+points,,,,,+
10          (.)
11  DAN:    *yeah.
12          *picks up matches, tosses them to Graham-->>
```

Kendrick and Drew's discussion of this extract focuses on how a difficulty in the realization of a course of action (smoking a cigarette) can engender requests for assistance, and they discuss how Graham's embodied request in line 1 results in him obtaining matches. A facet of this spate of interaction that is not discussed by Kendrick and Drew is that it also involves negotiation of social categories. At the point when Graham's request is recognizably complete, Dan self-selects to comment on the social category that Graham is making relevant in the very doing of the request (lines 2–3). Over half a century ago, Sacks (1992 [1964]: 50) made the point that "asking for a light is so much a 'move' that if what you want is just a light, you just pretty much can't do it. It also seems that between males and females, asking for a light is a tremendously sexual thing to do." Applying Sacks's argument to this extract suggests that Graham is not just hearable as doing a request for an object but also initiating a social move that transforms his co-participants (or Others in Drew and Kendrick's terminology) into potential partners (or 'partyboys'). What we hope to have shown in this study is that social categories, including institutional ones, are also an important – and under-studied – force in shaping the proffering of assistance and in accepting/refusing it.

Our analysis of packing has focused on encounters and sequences of action within them which may at first be treated as utterly mundane and uninteresting, even bypassed. However, we hope to have shown that packing entails mutual attention and interaction, and thus contributes to the rich social life of the farmers' market. The commercial context that we have examined contrasts sharply with contemporary stores with self-scanners and self-service checkout counters. These technical developments transform the act of buying food from an interaction characterized by extreme sociality (as shown in our chapter) to an autonomous activity done in solitude. One of the attractions of the farmers' market may indeed be that it offers, and indeed requires, close social collaboration between seller and customer.

References

Couper-Kuhlen, E., & Etelämäki, M. (2014). On divisions of labor in request and offer environments. In P. Drew & E. Couper-Kuhlen, eds., *Requesting in Social Interaction*. Amsterdam: John Benjamins, pp. 115–144. https://doi.org/10.1075/slsi.26.05cou

Drew, P., & Couper-Kuhlen, E. (2014). Requesting: From speech act to recruitment. In P. Drew & E. Couper-Kuhlen, eds., *Requesting in Social Interaction*. Amsterdam: John Benjamins, pp. 1–34. https://doi.org/10.1075/slsi.26.01dre

Goffman, E. (1959). *The Presentation of Self in Everyday Life*. Garden City: Doubleday.

Goodwin, C. (1995). Co-constructing meaning in conversations with an aphasic man. *Research on Language and Social Interaction*, 28(3), 233–360. https://doi.org/10.1207/s15327973rlsi2803_4

Heinemann, T. (2006). 'Will you or can't you?' Displaying entitlement in interrogative requests. *Journal of Pragmatics*, 38(7), 1081–1104. https://doi.org/10.1016/j.pragma.2005.09.013

Heinemann, T., Lindström, A., & Steensig, J. (2009). Addressing epistemic incongruence in question-answer sequences through the use of epistemic adverbs. In T. Stivers, L. Mondada, & J. Steensig, eds., *The Morality of Knowledge in Conversation*. Cambridge: Cambridge University Press, pp. 107–130. https://doi.org/10.1017/CBO9780511921674.006

Heritage, J. (2015). *Well*-prefaced turns in English conversation: A conversation analytic perspective. *Journal of Pragmatics*, 88, 88–104. https://doi.org/10.1016/j.pragma.2015.08.008

  (2016). The recruitment matrix. *Research on Language and Social Interaction*, 49(1), 27–31. https://doi.org/10.1080/08351813.2016.1126440

Jefferson, G. (2004). Glossary of transcript symbols with an introduction. In G. H. Lerner, ed., *Conversation Analysis: Studies from the First Generation*. Amsterdam: John Benjamins, pp. 13–31. https://doi.org/10.1075/pbns.125.02jef

Kendrick, T., & Drew, P. (2016). Recruitment: Offers, requests, and the organization of assistance in interaction. *Research on Language and Social Interaction*, 49(1), 1–19. https://doi.org/10.1080/08351813.2016.1126436

Koshik, I. (2002). A conversation analytic study of yes/no questions which convey reversed polarity assertions. *Journal of Pragmatics*, 34(12), 1851–1877. https://doi.org/10.1016/S0378–2166(02)00057-7

La Pradelle, M. de (2006). *A Market Day in Provence. Translated by Amy Jacobs*. Chicago: University of Chicago Press.

Lindström, A. (2005). Language as social action: A study of how senior citizens request assistance with practical tasks in the Swedish home help service. In A. Hakulinen & M. Selting, eds., *Syntax and Lexis in Conversation: Studies on the Use of Linguistic Resources in Talk-in-Interaction*. Amsterdam: John Benjamins, pp. 209–230. https://doi.org/10.1075/sidag.17.11lin

Lindström, A., & Heinemann, T. (2009). Good enough: Low-grade assessments in caregiving situations. *Research on Language and Social Interaction*, 42(4), 309–328. https://doi.org/10.1080/08351810903296465

Moerman, M. (1988). *Talking Culture: Ethnography and Conversation Analysis*. Philadelphia: University of Pennsylvania Press.

Mondada, L. (2014a). *Conventions for multimodal transcription*. Available at: www.lorenzamondada.net/multimodal-transcription

  (2014b). Requesting immediate action in the surgical operating room: Time, embodied resources and praxeological embeddedness. In P. Drew & E. Couper-Kuhlen, eds., *Requesting in Social Interaction*. Amsterdam: John Benjamins, pp. 271–304. https://doi.org/10.1075/slsi.26.11mon

Sacks, H. (1992). *Lectures on Conversation, Vol. 1*. Ed. by G. Jefferson. Oxford: Basil Blackwell.

Sorjonen, M.-L., & Raevaara, L. (2014). On the grammatical form of requests at the convenience store: Requesting as embodied action. In P. Drew & E. Couper-Kuhlen, eds. *Requesting in Social Interaction*. Amsterdam: John Benjamins, pp. 243–268. https://doi.org/10.1075/slsi.26.10sor

Wootton, A. (1997). *Interaction and the Development of Mind*. Cambridge: Cambridge University Press. https://doi.org/10.1017/CBO9780511519895

7 The Request-Return Sequence
What Can Happen at the Interface between Picking up a Repaired Item and Paying for It

Barbara Fox and Trine Heinemann

7.1 Introduction

One of the defining features of commercial service encounters is the exchange of objects that takes place between the participants. Service encounters are routinely organized around such exchanges; customers ask for a product, some information, or a service, are provided with what they ask for, and are in turn expected to pay for what they receive. Each of these sequences is contingent on the successful outcome of the previous sequence: a customer must be able to specify their wants and needs in order for the seller to provide it; in turn, a customer can only be expected to engage in a monetary exchange after having received the goods or services specified. How the participants move between the sequence in which the request is made and granted, on the one hand, and the exchange of money, on the other hand, appears to vary quite significantly across different types of service encounters. For service encounters in convenience stores, for instance, where relatively standard items, such as cigarettes, tickets, and candy are requested and provided, the move from one sequence to the other takes place in a largely seamless fashion and the participants engage in the payment sequence directly after the requested item(s) has been placed on the counter (see, e.g., Halonen & Koivisto, this volume). For service encounters in the beauty salon, by contrast, where a service is typically personalized and involves some alteration of the customer's personal appearance, a specific type of sequence, the *service-assessment sequence*, is routinely employed by the participants between the two sequences (e.g., Oshima & Streeck 2015).

In this chapter, we explore the varied ways in which customers and service providers proceed from requesting to paying in another particular type of service encounter, namely that of a shoe repair shop in North America. The shoe repair shop seems to reside somewhere between the convenience store and the beauty shop: the service that is provided is – as in the beauty shop – typically some type of alteration, but – as in the convenience store – the requesting sequence is typically concluded by the service provider placing the item to which an alteration has been made on the counter in front of the customer. This we find reflected in the variation we find in how customers and service providers in the shoe repair shop proceed from the requesting sequence to the payment sequence: customers in the shoe repair shop only verbally acknowledge the work that has been done to their shoes, boots, purses, etc. in about half of all cases. Moreover, both the service providers and the customers produce a wide range of behaviors in the context of returning an altered item: the service provider may, for instance, merely place the item on the counter, hand it directly to the customer, present it verbally (e.g., *there you go*), demonstrate the alteration manually (e.g., by making visible or directly manipulating the area of the alteration), both show and tell the customer what alteration has been made, or pursue assessments with questions (e.g., *how do they look*). In turn, customers may merely glance at the item or inspect it both visually and manually; if they produce a verbal acknowledgment it can be in the form of acceptance, gratitude, or assessment, and assessments can be positive or negative, high-grade (e.g., *they look beautiful*), or more neutral (e.g., *good*; see Antaki et al. 2000, for this distinction between assessment terms).

Based on this variety, we propose that when customers in the shoe repair shop come to pick up their repaired items, the encounter is organized around a basic sequence that we call the request-return sequence: the customer enters the shop and produces a request for having their repaired item returned. This request serves as an initiating action, or first pair part; the staff then retrieve the now-repaired item and bring it to the counter to return it to the customer. We understand this return of the item as the preferred responsive action, or second pair part. The request-return sequence is potentially complete at this point, and is often treated as complete by the participants, who may move immediately into the next sequence, the payment sequence (which customers may have actually bodily prepared for prior to this, by having a credit card already in hand, for example, see Halonen & Koivisto, this volume). The staff appear to treat the absence of any reaction on the part of the customer at this point as passing on the opportunity to initiate 'repair on the repair' and thus as implicit acceptance of the work that was done. Moreover, though customers often engage in inspection of the item, both before and during the staff's shift in position to ring the sale up at the register, such inspection is not treated as making relevant any next action: unless the customer deploys facial or other bodily-visual practices for indicating trouble, the inspection is also treated as passing on the opportunity to initiate a complaint sequence about the work, and the staff continue to move into the payment sequence.

Though the basic organization of the request-return sequence does not in itself make relevant that customers overtly acknowledge the work that has been done to their item, some type of verbal acknowledgment is nevertheless produced relatively often, in just under half of all cases in which a repaired item is returned to the customer. As we shall show in the following, such acknowledgments can be *volunteered* by the customer; alternatively, the staff can either *mobilize* a customer to acknowledge the work that has been done through a variety of verbal and embodied practices or more explicitly *invite* the customer to assess the work by asking questions such as *how do they look*.

In this study, we examine how the request-return sequence is organized; by paying particular attention to matters such as how the returned item is presented (or not) by the staff and how the returned item is received and oriented to (or not) by the customer, we explore how customers' acknowledgment of the service rendered can become part of a sequence in which this is not otherwise a conditionally relevant action to engage in. In revealing the nuanced organization of the request-return sequence, we thus explore the ways in which a range of different factors, including the spatio-temporal organization of the encounter, the nature of the repaired item, its relationship to both the customer and the staff, the nature of the service provided, and the need to provide payment, shape the multimodal practices engaged in by both customers and service providers when returning and receiving a repaired item.

7.2 Data

Our research site is a shoe repair shop in a small town in North America. The shop is a family-owned business, having been opened over 90 years ago by the grandfather of the current owner. The main staff are the owner, his wife, and their adult daughter, although other employees work there as well. Because 'staff' in English is a collective noun and cannot be used for individuals, we have coined the term *shoetender*, on the model of bartender, for individual staff members.

We recorded for roughly two years in the shop and have approximately 50 hours of data. Customer visits to the shop in general involve two steps, separated in time by minutes, days, or weeks: first the customer drops off an item for repair, with the date the repair will be completed specified at that time, and written for them on a 'pink slip', which also specifies details of the requested repair. On the appointed date, or later, the customer returns to pick up the now-repaired item. The shoetenders refer to these two activities as 'dropping off' and 'picking up'.

In the current study, we are focusing on instances of customers picking up their repaired items, what we here term the request-return sequence. These interactions typically begin with the customer producing their 'pink slip', or a request in a form like *picking up for* [*name*]. The shoetenders then go to the relevant part of the shop to retrieve the item, which in many, but not all, instances, is enclosed in a plastic bag. As we will see below, in many (but not all) cases, the shoetenders bring the bag to the counter, and either on their way to the counter, or immediately after arriving at the counter, they open the bag

The Request-Return Sequence 217

and bring out the repaired item. As we shall explore in the following, there is a range of possible next actions that can be done by the participants once the repaired item has been made available to the customer, each of these possible next actions being contingent on a variety of interactional relevancies.

Our collection consists of 105 request-return sequences. These have been transcribed using the notations and conventions of Conversation Analysis, e.g., Jefferson (2004) for verbal contributions and Mondada (2014) for multimodal aspects of the interaction. All interactions take place in American English.

7.3 The Organization of the Request-Return Sequence

As noted above, the core of the interaction examined in this study is the request-return sequence. In this most basic version of the sequence, the customer produces an initiating 'pick-up' request, and the shoetender returns the item to the customer, typically by placing it on the customer's side of the counter (cf. Mondada & Sorjonen, this volume). The shoetender then moves immediately to ring up the sale. Excerpt 7.1 illustrates:

Excerpt 7.1 (150 06/28/2013; SHO = shoetender, CUS = customer)

```
01 SHO:    ⊃h↑i:,
   sho     ⊃comes to counter-->
02 CUS:    hi dear hh
03         #⊇(0.4)
   sho        ⊇extends hand-->
   fig     #fig.7.1
```

Figure 7.1

```
04 SHO:    [(how are you)
05 CUS:    [>somehow I< thought I'd #∇picked this∧ up,⊃
   sho                                          -->⊃
   cus     >>comes to counter--------------------∧
   cus                            ∇extends hand with slip-->
   fig                            #fig.7.2
```

Figure 7.2

```
06         ⊃>and #∇then when I looked at the shoe,< I ∇⊃
    cus           ∇places sl on c, slaps sl once and retracts hand∇
    sho    ⊃............................takes slip--⊃
    fig           #fig.7.3
```

Figure 7.3

```
07         realized #>wait a #⊃minute< I got one (he)
    sho                       ⊃walks to back of shop-->
    fig           #fig.7.4 #fig.7.5
```

Figure 7.4

The Request-Return Sequence

Figure 7.5

```
08          [shoe(heh) ⊃ m(hhehe)issing [huh heh .heh
09 SHO:     [(oh okay::,)                [(let's get that)=
   sho              -->⊃
10 CUS:     =so I'm s(h)orry it take so long to get it heh
11 SHO:     tha:t's fine.
12          (9.3) ⊃ (0.5)
   sho             ⊃comes to counter with shoe-->
13 SHO:     #there  Δyou⊃ #⊋go:,⊋
   sho              -->⊃  ⊋puts shoe on counter⊋
   cus             Δgazes down towards purse-->
   fig      #fig.7.6       #fig.7.7
```

Figure 7.6

Figure 7.7

```
14 CUS:      ∆#⊃uh hu:h,
   cus       ∆gazes right, to paper on counter-->
   sho         ⊃goes to till-->
   fig       #fig.7.8
```

Figure 7.8

```
15           #(4.8)∆⊃#
   sho          -->⊃
   cus          -->∆ looks up, then to S-->
   fig       #fig.7.9 #fig.7.10
```

Figure 7.9

Figure 7.10

The Request-Return Sequence   221

```
16 SHO:      seven twentyΔ# nine,
   cus                -->Δlooks to purse-->>
   fig                #fig.7.11
```

Figure 7.11

```
17           V(0.8)
   cus       Vtakes money out-->>
```

In this example, the request is done through the customer laying the pink slip on the counter, co-produced with an account for her lateness in coming to pick up the item (lines 5–6, Figures 7.2–7.3). As we can see from Figure 7.1, before this account is produced the shoetender has already gauged from the visibility of the slip that the customer is there to pick up, rather than drop off an item (Heinemann & Fox 2019) and is holding her hand out to receive the slip. The shoetender takes the slip from the counter and goes to retrieve the item (a single sandal) (lines 7–12, Figures 7.4–7.5). As the shoetender, now with a sandal in her hand, approaches the counter again, the customer looks up at her, and gazes briefly at the sandal (Figure 7.6). She then shifts her gaze to her wallet (Figure 7.7) even before the shoetender's presenting utterance (*there you go*) is complete. While the shoetender moves toward the cash register, the customer shifts her gaze to a piece of paper on the counter (Figure 7.8). As Figures 7.9–7.11 illustrate, there is no further inspection and the shoetender does not pursue any acknowledgment from the customer of the repair.

While Excerpt 7.1 illustrates the most basic version of the request-return sequence, we find that most customers inspect their repaired item more closely than does the customer in that example. Typically, this inspection is done following the shoetender's shift away from the customer and toward the cash register, i.e., at a point at which the customer's implicit acceptance of the repair has been taken for granted. Consequently, a customer's inspection does not engender the production of a subsequent acknowledgment. Excerpt 7.2 provides an example of this (here and in the remainder of the chapter we present only the 'return' part of the request-return sequence):

Excerpt 7.2 (132 04/09/14)

```
01         (0.2)≥
   sho     >>comes to counter, shoe in hand≥
02 SHO:    #∪+here you #±↑go:,
   cus       ∪looks at shoe-->
   sho       +extends arm with shoe towards counter-->
   sho                  ±looks towards register-->
   fig     #fig.7.12   #fig.7.13
```

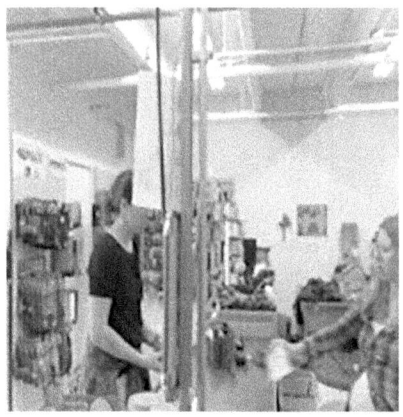

Figure 7.12

Figure 7.13

```
03         +(1.0)+
   sho     +lets go of shoe, it lands on counter+
04         #⊇(.)⊇
   cus       ⊇takes shoe⊇
   fig     #fig.7.14
```

Figure 7.14

```
05         ≥⊇(2.0)≥⊇
   sho     ≥goes to register≥
   cus      ⊇lifts and tilts shoe then puts shoe on counter⊇
06         ⊇(1.0)
   cus     ⊇lifts shoe-->
07 SHO:    n:i#⊇ne thirty ∪eight,⊇
   cus       -->⊇puts shoe down and looks towards S⊇
   cus                   ∪brings hand to pocket of wallet-->
   fig           #fig.7.15
```

Figure 7.15

```
08            ∪(3.0)
   cus     -->∪looks to wallet, opens it and takes out card
```

The shoetender approaches the counter with the repaired item in her hand and the customer brings her gaze to the approaching shoe (lines 1–2, Figure 7.12). At the same time the shoetender verbalizes the return with the presenting utterance *here you go*. Before completing that utterance, and before placing the shoe on the counter, the shoetender has already shifted her gaze to the cash register, which is her next destination (Figure 7.13). At line 3 she places the shoe on the counter; at line 4 the customer picks it up and the shoetender continues walking to the cash register (Figure 7.14). Throughout line 5 the customer visually inspects the shoe, including tilting it to see it from another angle. She briefly places the shoe back on the counter and at line 6 picks it up again to inspect it. Just as the shoetender begins to announce the price in line 7, the customer puts the shoe back on the counter, looks toward the shoetender and begins to take her credit card from her wallet (Figure 7.15).

In Excerpt 7.3, we see a similar pattern, except that here the customer acknowledges the repair overtly with an expression of gratitude, before inspecting the item. Again, neither the customer nor the shoetender orient to the production of an acknowledgment as necessary, or conditionally relevant, after the inspection. This customer has dropped off two pairs of shoes, requesting that one pair be 'tapped' while he waits. SH2, the shoetender who originally dealt with the request, is now serving another customer, while SH1, who has been doing the 'tapping', brings the shoes back to the customer, placing them on the counter with the presenting utterance *there you go* (line 1, Figure 7.16):

Excerpt 7.3 (66 22/03/14)

```
    sh1    Λ>>comes to counter with shoes-->
01 SH1:    >th[ere yΛou #go.<
02 CUS:       [I appreciate that. thanks.
    sh1          -->Λplaces shoes on counter-->
    fig                #fig.7.16
```

Figure 7.16

The Request-Return Sequence 225

```
03         (0.5)Λ#⊃(1.7)⊃
   sh1      -->Λ
   cus              ⊃>>comes to counter, grabs shoes⊃
   fig          #fig.7.17
```

Figure 7.17

```
04 SH1:    t∇hi:s
   sh1     ∇points to CUS-->
05         (0.4)
06 SH2:    (        ∇    ) (         )#∪+u:hm
   sh1              -->∇
   cus                              ∪looks at shoes-->
   sh2                              +...finds CUS' slip in box->
   fig                              #fig.7.18
```

Figure 7.18

```
07         (1.3)+∇∪(0.7)∇∪(0.8)∪#
   sh2     -->+
   sh1           ∇takes slip∇,looks at slip-->
   cus       -->∪turns shoes over∪torques right w shoes in hand∪
   fig                     #fig.7.19
```

Figure 7.19

```
08 SH2:    ⊇ (well +      )⊇+
   cus     ⊇places shoes on bench⊇
   sh2             +points to CUS+
```

Before coming to the counter and reaching for the shoes (Figure 7.17), the customer produces an expression of gratitude (*I appreciate that. thanks*) in line 2. Though he subsequently looks at the shoes and in particular at the area that has been tapped (Figure 7.18), it is quite evident that SH1 does not expect any further acknowledgment of the repaired item; he turns immediately to SH2, indexing the customer both verbally and gesturally (line 4). From SH2's subsequent action we see that he understands this as a request for information about how to proceed: SH2 finds the receipt slip in a box on the counter and hands it to SH1, while saying something that is inaudible to us. SH1 takes the slip, and the customer clearly interprets this as moving into the payment sequence, as he now turns the shoes over (line 7, Figure 7.19) and places them on a bench (line 8), thus freeing his hands to get his wallet (not shown here).

As illustrated by Excerpts 7.2 and 7.3, the return can – and typically does – engender an inspection sequence of some sort, in which customers look at the work that has been done to their item. In fact, we have only a very few cases where customers do not engage in any kind of inspection. With the exception of Excerpt 7.1, this is typically the case if the repair is a stretch (which is not visually accessible) or a shoeshine (where the repair is minor and the result predictable), or when customers pick up a repaired item for someone else. Unlike the hairdressers in the study by Oshima and Streeck (2015), however, the shoetenders in Excerpts 7.2 and 7.3 do not make this inspection conditionally relevant: in both cases the shoetender hands over the item in an almost perfunctory way, while maintaining a trajectory to the cash register, and does not wait for a response from the customer. Notably, then, the inspection is done *after* the repair has been acknowledged, either implicitly, i.e., through the absence of a complaint, as in Excerpt 7.2, or overtly, i.e., through the customer producing, for instance, an expression of gratitude, as in Excerpt 7.3. By subsequently inspecting the item but doing nothing more, the customer passes on the opportunity to initiate some kind of 'repair on the repair', the service rendered has been tacitly accepted, and the interaction proceeds to payment.

7.4 Customer Acknowledgment

While more than half our examples – as illustrated above – do not engender any acknowledgment of the repair by the customer, such acknowledgments may nevertheless come about, either as (a) volunteered acknowledgments, produced at the first point at which the customer has visual access to the repaired item, (b) mobilized acknowledgments, produced in response to the shoetender's demonstration of the work that has been done to the repaired item, or (c) invited acknowledgments, produced after the shoetender has explicitly asked for an evaluation (or some other form of acceptance) from the customer. As we shall see, the different ways in which customers' acknowledgments come about typically also has an impact on what type of acknowledgment is produced by the customer.

7.4.1 Volunteered Acknowledgments

One of the most important factors with respect to the production of acknowledgments, such as for instance assessments, is the degree of access that participants in interaction have to the item that is to be assessed (e.g., Pomerantz 1984; Goodwin & Goodwin 1992; Oshima & Streeck 2015). In the shoe repair shop, access can be visual, tactile, or both; for some repairs it may be sufficient to see the item in order to acknowledge or access the repair, while some repairs (e.g., stretching) are not visible and can only be evaluated through touch (trying the shoe on); for still other repairs it might be necessary to manipulate the shoe in order to establish whether a repair is sufficient (e.g., when the repair involves stitching or gluing). What is evident overall, however, is that the earliest point at which a customer can produce an acknowledgment of the work that has been done is at the point at which they have some degree of visual access to the repaired item.

On very rare occasions, we thus find customers producing acknowledgments as soon as their item is visually accessible to them, and before the return has been completed. This is the case in the following example, in which a customer is picking up her boots. The shop has just gotten a new computer-based cash register. SH2, who is the shoetender serving this particular customer, has gone to the back of the shop to get the boots. When she returns, she is accompanied by SH1 and SH3, both wanting to watch the new cash register in use for the first time, which is what SH2 and SH1 announce in lines 1–3. As soon as the customer's boots are minimally visually available to her, she produces an acknowledgment in the form of a high-grade assessment (line 13):

Excerpt 7.4 (36 31/01/15)

```
01 SH2:     I wanna try'er
02          (0.7)
03 SH1:     oh let's ≥try'er
   sh2            ≥comes to counter with shoes in bag-->
04          (0.2)
05 CUS:     ⊃.pt≥ oh >I get to use< the:,
   cus      ⊃shifts left towards cash register-->
   sh2         -->≥unties the slip from bag-->
06 SH2:     we'll see,
07 SH1?:    hhh
08 CUS:     (c[⊃ool,)
09 SH2:        [(              )≥
10 SH1:        [we're going square,
   cus      -->⊃
   sh2                            -->≥
11 CUS:     ni:ce,
12          #+∪(3.9)+∪
   sh2       +takes boots out of bag+
   cus       ∪looks at boots/bag∪
   fig      #fig.7.20
```

Figure 7.20

```
13 CUS      .pt #+.ahh!+⊃∪ they [look be⊃autiful:::,
14 SH2:                         [(here's your boots,)
   sh2       +puts boots on counter + walks to register-->
   cus              ⊃...lifts boot--⊃
   cus                 ∪leans head right and down, inspects boot->
   fig         #fig.7.21
```

The Request-Return Sequence   229

Figure 7.21

```
15          +(0.2)∪
    cus        -->∪looks at S3-->
    sh2     +moves hand to cash register-->
16 CUS:     tha:n[k you::,
17 SH2:          [s:o:,+ ∪
    sh2                -->+
    cus                    -->∪
18 SH2:     +∪you+ go [to repair,
19 SH3:                [do you still ring it up?
    sh2     +presses screen+
    cus      ∪looks at boot-->
20          #(.)
    fig     #fig.7.22
```

Figure 7.22

```
21 SH1:     re[pair?
22 SH2:       [yup,
23          (0.7)∪
    cus        -->∪
24 SH2:     (s[o then)
25 CUS:     ⊇[>oh my god<⊇ they look⊇ ∪brand new,
    cus     ⊇places boot on counter⊇ grabs the other boot⊇
    cus                                  ∪looks at boot-->
26          (1.4)
```

```
27 CUS:     [thank you so much,⌣
28 SH2:     [what's twenty five.
   cus                    -->⌣looks twrds SHs and cash register
29          #⊃Δ(0.7)Δ
   cus      ⊃puts boot on counter-->
   sh1         Δlooks towards CUSΔ
   fig      #fig.7.23
```

Figure 7.23

```
30 SH3:     Δ[uh
31 SH2:     [o:h, fine [line⌣
32 SH3:                 [fine line,⊃
   cus                     -->⌣looks at boot-->>
   cus                         -->⊃
   sh1      Δlooks to cash register-->>
33 SH2:     so soles, (0.2) twenty five,
```

At the counter and still discussing the use of the new cash register, SH2 begins to take the customer's boots out of the bag, with the customer and SH1 looking on. As is evident from Figure 7.20, the customer monitors the 'unveiling' of her boots closely; and just before SH2 places the boots on the counter, she produces the assessment .pt .ah! they look beautiful (line 13). The request-return sequence in this extract is remarkable in two ways: first, the customer's acknowledgment is early; it is delivered (just) before the boots have been transferred to her interactional space (Mondada & Sorjonen, this volume), i.e., before the boots are on the counter – as evident also by the shoetender's overlapping presenting utterance *here's your boots* in line 14. The acknowledgment is also delivered at a moment where the customer has relatively limited visual access to the boots, as evidenced by her subsequently picking up the boots and inspecting them more closely (Figure 7.21 and 7.22), before producing yet another assessing acknowledgment (*they look brand new*) and an expression of gratitude (*thank you*) in lines 25 and 27, respectively.

From Excerpt 7.4 we can see that visual access to an item is a prerequisite to an acknowledgment of it, and constitutive of an opportunity to assess. Moreover, this excerpt illustrates the work customers do to make acknowledgments produced in this position come across as 'early', volunteered and authentic. The high-grade assessment *they look beautiful* is preceded by an audible ingressive click (.*pt*, see Ogden 2013) and the ingressively produced change-of-state token .*ah* that serves to index a change of affective state (Aston 1986). The assessment as a whole is thus designed as a response cry, i.e., as a displacement of an emotional or affective state to the verbal channel (Goffman 1978), through which the customer implies that by merely seeing the shoes she is overcome with positive emotions that she simply has to 'let out' (Robles 2012).

Early volunteered assessing acknowledgments such as in Excerpt 7.4 are very rare in our data, occurring only seven times in a total of 105 cases in which customers are picking up a repaired item. And as we can see from Excerpt 7.4, such acknowledgments are not treated as conditionally relevant and are in fact frequently ignored by the shoetenders: While the customer's assessment is still underway, SH2 begins to move toward the cash register; from line 17 onward she and the two other shoetenders are exclusively orienting to the cash register and their discussion of how to enter the sale. Notably, though the customer is still visibly inspecting (and admiring) the boots, none of the shoetenders look at her, let alone respond to her assessment or her first expression of gratitude in line 16. Nor do they respond to her second assessment and expression of gratitude in lines 25–27, though SH1 briefly looks up from the cash register and smiles (Figure 7.23).

The following excerpt illustrates a more common use of volunteered acknowledgments: as rational, thoughtful evaluations that are based on carefully gathered evidence. Here then, the acknowledgment is not designed to come across as a response cry; rather, it is produced after the customer has had a chance to inspect the repaired item at his own leisure.

Excerpt 7.5 (5/16/2014)

```
01         ≥(1.5)≥(4.6)≥(2.9)≥(2.1)≥
   sho     ≥walks to counter with shoes in bag≥ places bag on
           counter and attempts to untie the slip≥ looks right,
           then slides bag left on the counter≥ attempts to untie
           the slip, then rips it free of bag≥
02 SHO:    let go,
03         +(0.2)+
   sho     +slaps right hand on counter+
04 CUS:    #⊇heh heh ≥[heh⊇≥
```

232   B. Fox & T. Heinemann

```
05 SHO:                      [hhh
   cus          ⊇...grabs bag-⊇
   sho                  ≥turns to register≥
   fig          #fig.7.24
```

Figure 7.24

```
06           #⊇(0.8)⊇(1.2) #∪(0.6) # ⊇ (0.4)⊇
   cus       ⊇puts LH in bag⊇takes out shoe⊇tilts shoe with sole
                                           up and grabs with RH⊇
   cus                      ∪looks at shoe-->
   fig       #fig.7.25      #fig.7.26#fig.7.27
```

Figure 7.25

Figure 7.26

The Request-Return Sequence   233

Figure 7.27

```
07 CUS:    look like new shoes,
08 SHO:    #⊇well ∪that's what we want.=
   cus     ⊇grabs bag with right hand and puts shoe in bag-->
   cus        -->∪
   fig     #fig.7.28
```

Figure 7.28

```
08 CUS:    #=heh heh heh
   fig     #fig.7.29
```

Figure 7.29

234   B. Fox & T. Heinemann

```
09            (2.0)⊇
    cus       ->⊇
10 SHO:    #⊇they're⊇ good at what they do:,
    cus       ⊇lets go of bag and takes card w RH⊇gathers b in hand-->
    fig    #fig.7.30
```

Figure 7.30

```
11            (2.1)⊇
    cus       ->⊇
12            ⊇∪(0.8)⊇
    cus    ⊇lets go of bag⊇
    cus    ∪looks towards register-->>
20 SHO:    fif⊇ty eight ≥twenty nine, on a card,
    cus       ⊇holds up card--->>
    sho              ≥turns to CUS--->>
```

In this example, the shoetender brings the item to the counter in a bag; after some struggle, she is able to get the tag off of the bag (lines 1–3), and at line 4 the customer grabs the bag (Figure 7.24). A few beats later the shoetender turns toward the register. During line 6 the customer removes a shoe from the bag and for about one second engages in visual inspection, tilting and rotating the shoe (Figures 7.25–7.27). At line 7 he produces the evaluation *look like new shoes*. Like the assessing acknowledgment in Excerpt 7.4, *look like new shoes* is clearly volunteered; the shoetender has moved to the register to begin ringing up the sale during the inspection, thus displaying her understanding that the repair has already been tacitly accepted (cf. Excerpts 7.1–7.3). *Look like new shoes*, however, does not share the same prosodic and temporal characteristics of the assessment in Excerpt 7.4; rather, it is designed to come across as being sincerely offered in the face of gathered evidence: The customer has, after an extended period of inspection, determined that the repaired shoes do in fact look like new shoes. Perhaps because of the way in which the inspection and acknowledgment are done, the shoetender treats the acknowledgment as a compliment by normalizing the work achieved at line 8 (*well that's what we want*), and simultaneously accounting for the work and shifting the praise to someone else at line 10 (*they're good at what they do*) (Figures 7.28–7.30).

The acknowledgments produced in Excerpts 7.4 and 7.5 both illustrate that though such acknowledgments are clearly not required in the request-return sequence, they can be volunteered. Notably, the two acknowledgments are clausal and are both formatted to refer to the visual aspect of the repaired item (*look*). This particular combination of features is recurrently used in volunteered acknowledgments, and much less commonly so when either mobilized or invited by the shoetender (see below). With this type of acknowledgment, customers seem to specifically evaluate the appearance of the repaired item as a whole and do so typically in quite generous terms, i.e., with high-grade assessment terms such as *beautiful* or by likening the result to the original state of the item, *like new shoes*. These acknowledgments can thus be said to be formulated as expressions of appreciation (i.e., compliments or praise), and by producing them customers seem to orient to the repair of their item as being an accomplishment (Bilmes 1988; Golato 2004).

7.4.2 Mobilized Acknowledgments

While we have seen above that customers can volunteer acknowledgments, shoetenders can also do work that appears to mobilize the production of an acknowledgment by the customer. With the term mobilize, we follow Stivers and Rossano (2010: 29) in proposing that participants in interaction have a range of resources available that can be used to increase "the accountability of a recipient to produce a response." In the shoe repair shop, such mobilization is done when the shoetender does not merely return the repaired item to the customer, but also presents the work that has been done. Such presentations can be done either verbally and manually, by the shoetender describing and demonstrating the work that has been done, as in Excerpt 7.6, or by manual demonstrations only, as in Excerpt 7.7. In either case, we find that such presentations are consistently responded to with an acknowledgment (see also Raclaw et al. 2016 on how descriptions can make assessments relevant).

In Excerpt 7.6, the customer is waiting at the counter for the shoetender to return with the repaired item. While the shoetender is still approaching the counter, the two engage in small talk; during this, the customer prepares himself for the monetary exchange by taking his card out of his wallet (line 8). Meanwhile the shoetender reaches the counter and takes the shoes out of the bag (lines 3–13). At the point where the small talk is potentially complete at line 18, the shoetender has the shoes in one hand and has picked up the tag attached to the bag where the details of the repair are listed (Figure 7.31). On the *so* in line 20, he torques (Schegloff 1998) toward the customer while apparently reading what is on the tag (Figure 7.32):

Excerpt 7.6 (116 15/03/14)

```
01 SHO:    how's it going today, hh
02         Λ(0.6)
   sho     Λ>>walks to counter with shoes in bag-->
03 CUS:    it's going wellΛ thank you. and you?
   sho                    -->Λunties the band on bag-->
04         (0.2)
05 SHO:    >very good.<
06         (0.8)Λ
   sho         -->Λ
07 SHO:    it's almost over,
08         +V(0.7)
   cus     +takes card out of wallet-->
   sho      V...puts bag on counter-->
09 CUS:    almost over.+V
   cus               -->+
   sho                -->V
10         (0.3)
11 SHO:    (close early)
12         V(0.8)V
   sho     Vopens bagV
13 CUS:    Vnot the day, just the- (0.3) just
   sho     V...takes shoe out of bag-->
14         the [work day,
15 SHO:        [work part.=yeah.=
16 CUS:    =eh heh .h[eh
17 SHO:              [the day 's just st[arting.
18 CUS:                                 [ye(heh)he hehV
   sho                                              -->V
19         #V(0.9)V
   sho      Vtakes order slipV
   fig     #fig.7.31
```

Figure 7.31

The Request-Return Sequence 237

```
20 SHO:     #Δ(so did we do)  #±Δ(0.6)Δ
   sho      Δtorques left to customer, shoes in right hand,
            slip in left hand Δ turns shoes sole up Δ
   cus                         ±looks at shoes-->
   fig      #fig.7.32           #fig.7.33
```

Figure 7.32

Figure 7.33

```
21          #Δhush plates, #Δ (0.1) Δ
            Δtouches plate with left hand pinky Δturns shoes overΔ
   fig      #fig.7.34        #fig.7.35
```

Figure 7.34

238   B. Fox & T. Heinemann

Figure 7.35

```
22 SHO     #Δ>clean and poΔli+sh::,<
           Δmoves shoes towards customerΔ
    cus                         +moves hand to and above shoes
    fig    #fig.7.36
```

Figure 7.36

```
23 CUS:    good.
24         Δ+(0.8)Δ
    sho    Δputs shoes on counterΔ
    cus    +...grabs shoes-->
25 CUS:    great.+
                -->+
26         #+(0.2)
    cus    +lifts shoes, soles facing up-->
    fig    #fig.7.37
```

Figure 7.37

```
27 SHO:     ↑yep,
28          (0.2)+
   cus            -->+
29 SHO:     Δ>>>do you want the bag?<<<Δ
   sho      Δlifts edge of bagΔ
30 CUS:     yes please.
31          (0.2)
32 SHO:     (>>>s'good/okay<<<)
33          #Δ(2.0)± +(1.7)+ Δ(0.3)
   sho      Δlifts and turns bag so opening faces cΔ
   cus            -->±
   cus                 +puts shoes in bag+
   fig      #fig.7.38
```

Figure 7.38

With the customer looking on, the shoetender informs the customer of the work they have done to his shoes (lines 20–22). As an informing, the shoetender's utterance makes relevant a response from the customer (see Thompson et al. 2015). In addition, he presents the area(s) they have worked on to the customer and manually demonstrates the work (Figures 7.31 and 7.32; cf. Fox & Heinemann 2015): on *hush plates* (a type of sole that can be added to shoes to make them less noisy) he turns the shoes over to present the soles, at the same time touching the relevant place with his little finger (line 21, Figures 7.33 and 7.34); on *clean and polish* he presents the shoes upside first (Figure 7.35). He then places the shoes on the customer's side of the counter, and the customer, who is already holding his hand out (Figure 7.36), takes the shoes and inspects them further (Figures 7.37 and 7.38). Before engaging in this inspection, however, the customer produces two acknowledgments, one after the other, *good* (line 23) and *great* (line 25).

In Excerpt 7.7 we similarly see how the shoetender can apparently mobilize the production of an acknowledgment from the customer by presenting the work that has been done. In this case, the presentation is done purely through making the repaired area accessible to the customer, with no verbal explication accompanying this demonstration:

Excerpt 7.7 (130 04/08/15)

```
01         #Δ(0.6)
    sho    Δ>>walks to counter-->
    fig    #fig.7.39
```

Figure 7.39

```
02 SHO:    alright hhΔ
    sho              -->Δ
03         #Δ+(0.8)#Δ
    sho    Δmoves shoe towards CUS, sole upwardsΔ
    cus    +extends hand towards shoe-->
    fig    #fig.7.40 #fig.7.41
```

Figure 7.40

The Request-Return Sequence 241

Figure 7.41

```
04 CUS:    #Δ+great.Δ+
   sho      Δlets go of shoeΔ
   cus       +takes shoe+
   fig      #fig.7.42
```

Figure 7.42

```
05         #+(3.4)+
   cus      +rotates shoe to inspect top and side+
   fig     #fig.7.43
```

Figure 7.43

```
06 CUS:    and they were stretched too,
```

The shoetender comes to the counter, holding the shoes in front of his body (Figure 7.39). As he reaches the counter, he says *alright*, after which both he and the customer prepare for the return, the shoetender by holding one shoe toward the customer, the customer by beginning to retract his right hand from his pocket and move it toward the shoe (Figure 7.40). Most notably, we can see that the shoetender is holding the shoe with the soles up (Figure 7.41), thus making visible the area on which the repair has been done. The customer produces an acknowledgment (*great*) as soon as he has visual access to the sole of the shoe, at which point the shoetender relinquishes his hold of the shoe (Figures 7.42–7.43).

The mobilized acknowledgments produced in Excerpts 7.6 and 7.7 illustrate that though these are clearly not required in the request-return sequence, the shoetenders can do relatively subtle work to mobilize an acknowledgment from the customer. That the presentation of the repaired item is enough to engender an acknowledgment from the customer has an interesting side effect in that the customer produces an acknowledgment without having had the opportunity to thoroughly inspect and manipulate the item with his own hands. And while inspection may be done, it is always done subsequent to the acknowledgment and is not oriented to by either shoetender or customer as making further evaluative work relevant: in Excerpt 7.6 the shoetender initiates the move to the payment sequence by asking whether the customer *want the bag* for his shoes, once this is confirmed the two cooperate in putting the shoes back in the bag and the shoetender moves to the cash register; in Excerpt 7.7 the inspection that is done concerns an additional repair that has been done to the item, a stretching, which the customer overtly displays by specifically inspecting the sides and top of the shoes before inquiring of the shoetender whether they have also applied the stretch. Mobilized acknowledgments thus seem to constitute one alternative for accepting the repair work that has been done, an alternative to the more tacit acceptance that is implemented by the lack of a complaint (as in Excerpt 7.2) and to expressions of gratification (as in Excerpt 7.3). In this respect, it is perhaps noteworthy that mobilized acknowledgments are – as in both Excerpts 7.6 and 7.7 – typically lexical, i.e., consisting of an evaluative term only. The evaluative terms themselves also seem to come from a restricted set of options; *great* and *good* are relatively prevalent, as are *perfect* and *cool*. In other contexts, it has been noted that some evaluating or assessing terms are routinely used not to evaluate prior talk or action, but to "claim a closure on the previous material as having been, in the circumstances, successfully completed as a section in a segmented whole" (Antaki et al. 2000: 236; see Lindström & Heinemann 2009 and Aggerholm & Asmuß 2016 for similar observations). In the shoe repair shop it seems evident that mobilized acknowledgments such as those produced in Excerpt 7.6 and 7.7 are similarly understood less as assessments proper and more as acceptance of the request-return sequence as being successfully completed.

7.4.3 Invited Acknowledgments

In addition to mobilizing acknowledgments, shoetenders can also do work that makes the production of an acknowledgment conditionally relevant. Such actions are typically done through the shoetender posing a question to which an answer would be noticeably and accountably absent. We find that shoetenders typically produce these questions in two contexts: (a) when the repair has been somewhat complicated and/or the result may not meet the customer's expectations, or (b) when the customer, during the inspection phase, either through verbal or embodied means, indicates potential dissatisfaction with the repair. Excerpts 7.8 and 7.9 illustrate each of these situations, respectively.

In Excerpt 7.8, the customer has come in to pick up a purse. While one shoetender has gone to the back to retrieve the purse, the customer engages another shoetender to advise her on what type of creamer she needs for treating the strap of the purse. When the first shoetender returns with the purse, the customer is busy looking at creamers; Excerpt 7.8 begins with the customer returning to the counter, where the shoetender is waiting to hand over the purse:

Excerpt 7.8 (40 31/01/15)

```
01 SHO:    #∧⊃so, (0.3) this #was ⊃really# ∇weak, ⊃
   sho     ∧leans over counter to purse-->
   cus       ⊃...puts bag on counter⊃shifts to the left⊃
   sho                                ∇points to place
                                             on strap-->
   fig     #fig.7.44           #fig.7.45    #fig.7.46
```

Figure 7.44

Figure 7.45

Figure 7.46

```
02 CUS:     yeah.
03          (0.2)
04 SHO:     and >I backed it< can you tell?
05 CUS:     (oh[ no) that's fine.
06 SHO:        [I put a little piece of leather on
07          the ba:c[k,∇
08 CUS:             [that's great,
   sho              -->∇
09          (0.4)
10 SHO:     so to mail- make it a little stron[ger,
11 CUS:                                       [great.
12          # ∇(0.5)
   sho      ->∇lets go of bag and straigthens up-->
   fig      #fig.7.47
```

Figure 7.47

```
13 CUS:     awesome.∇
   sho          -->∇
```

The shoetender launches the handover of the purse with *so* (Bolden 2008), thus indicating that this business has been pending for a while. She then goes on to provide an account for needing to do a repair (*this was really weak*, line 1) and describes what the repair is (*and I backed it*, line 4). These informings may by themselves make some type of response relevant next (i.e., mobilize an acknowledgment, as in Extracts 7.6 and 7.7, see also Thompson et al. 2015); by attaching an acceptance inquiry (*can you tell?*) to the informing, however, a response becomes conditionally relevant. The customer's response is nicely designed to deal with the relevancies of the shoetender's question: during the production of the shoetender's turn she prepares herself to inspect the purse by placing her bag on the counter and shifting her body so that the purse is in her visual field (Figures 7.44–7.46). She then rejects the inference that the work is potentially complainable with *no* (Raclaw 2013), emphasizing this rejection by prefacing it with *oh* (Heritage 1998). Finally, she produces the positive assessment *that's fine*, thus accepting the repair as adequate (Figure 7.47). This acceptance is further emphasized through subsequent assessments (*that's great* in line 8, *great* in line 11, and *awesome* in line 13).

While the potential trouble with the repair is introduced by the shoetender in Excerpt 7.8, in Excerpt 7.9 the trouble only becomes apparent during the customer's inspection of the repaired item. Again, however, we see the shoetender orienting to such trouble by inviting the customer to acknowledge the repair. Here, the customer is picking up two items, a purse and a strap for a different purse. The excerpt begins when the shoetender comes to the counter with both items and places the strap on the counter (Figures 7.48–7.49):

Excerpt 7.9 (1 01/03/15)

```
01         #∇⊇(0.3)∇ ⊇#
   sho     ∇places the strap on the counter∇
   cus     ⊇takes hands out of pockets⊇
   Fig     #fig.7.48   #fig.7.49
```

Figure 7.48

Figure 7.49

```
02  CUS:      (okay       ▽[     )
03  SHO:                    [and here's the extra
    sho                    ▽...begins to detach slip from strap-->
04  CUS:      m'kay,
05            (5.1) ▽ (0.1)▽ #⊇(2.0)
    sho       -->▽slides strap towards CUS▽
    cus                     ⊇extends left hand-->
    fig                    #fig.7.50
```

Figure 7.50

```
06  ???:      ▽ (       ) ▽
    sho       ▽lets go of strap▽
07            ⊇(0.4)⊇
    cus       ->⊇grabs strap⊇
08  ???:      (     )
09            #▽⊇(2.0)▽#    (6.2)    #
    sho       ▽places purse on counter▽looks at CUS, then at strap-->
    cus       ⊇aligns the ends of the strap, looks-->
    fig       #fig.7.51 #fig.7.52 #fig.53
```

Figure 7.51

The Request-Return Sequence 247

Figure 7.52

Figure 7.53

```
10 SHO:     good?
11          (0.1)
12 CUS:     .tch u:hm (1.8) ye- ye:a(heh)r(hehheh) I g(hhe)uess
13          so=>∇I would have liked them< to match,
   sho        -->∇leans over counter, looking at straps-->
14          (1.0)
15 CUS:     but;
16          (1.0)
17 CUS:     it's probably too late for that
18          now [(huh),
19 SHO:         [.hhh ∇ u:hm: ∇ there'll probably be ho:les that
   sho              -->∇leans back∇
20          you'll see.
21 CUS:     yeah
22          (1.3)
23 SHO:     you[ think (.) [anybody'll ever notice that?>
24 CUS:        [u:hm
25 CUS:     I'll notice. but (0.6) it- it is what
26          it is. okay.=
```

As is evident from Figures 7.48–7.50, lines 3–5, the shoetender has some trouble detaching the tag from the strap. The customer, however, has been preparing to inspect her returned items for a while: as soon as the shoetender's approach toward the counter is evident, the customer takes her hands out of her pockets (Figure 7.48); once the item, a purse strap, is on the counter, the customer leans gradually in over the counter, keeping her gaze fixed on the strap. As soon as the shoetender lets go of the strap, the customer grabs it and starts inspecting it (Figures 7.51–7.53). Noticeable in this example is both the duration of the customer's inspection, as well as the way in which this inspection is done. Initially, the shoetender attends to placing the customer's second item on the counter (a purse), but when this is done, the customer is still inspecting the first item. The shoetender seems to take on a demonstrated 'waiting position' and to monitor the customer's inspection of the purse strap quite closely (see Figure 7.53). Moreover, the customer's inspection is detailed, and she continues her inspection despite the fact that the shoetender is now clearly waiting for her to finish so that she can return the second item. Finally, we can see that the customer's face is set in what can best be described as a somewhat sulky expression throughout her inspection: her lower lip is protruding and she has a distinct eyebrow frown (Kaukomaa et al. 2014). In this case, the shoetender clearly orients to acceptance as lacking, perhaps because the customer's delay and demeanor foreshadow a possible complaint and/or negative assessment of the work that has been done. At line 10 the shoetender produces the questioning *good?*, which makes relevant an agreement or confirmation of the assessment produced by the shoetender (Lindström & Heinemann 2009). As indicated by the perturbations in the customer's response, however, a dispreferred response is pending (Schegloff 1998, 2007; Kendrick & Torreira 2015); the customer next produces a somewhat hedged confirmation (*yeah I guess so*), and then states what she would have wanted the straps to look like (line 13) but that *it's probably too late for that*. This extract thus illustrates that extended inspection without acknowledgment is treated as problematic if the customer's bodily comportment (such as frowning) displays a potential negative evaluation.

Excerpts 7.8 and 7.9 together illustrate how acknowledgments are typically invited in contexts of trouble, i.e., where the shoetender has had to repair an item in a manner that may not be expected by the customer (as in Excerpt 7.8), or where the customer's behavior during the inspection phase indicates a lack of satisfaction. By inviting acknowledgments, shoetenders can be seen to propose the relative scale with which the repair should be evaluated (see Lindström & Heinemann 2009); in both Excerpts 7.8 and 7.9, for instance, the relevance of whether the repair is 'noticeable' is introduced as the primary grounds for acknowledging the repair. Unlike volunteered and mobilized acknowledgments, invited acknowledgments do not as a group show particular structural similarities. Rather, each invited acknowledgment is typically formulated in a way that displays its responsiveness, for instance by being preceded by response particles such as *no* (as in Excerpt 7.8) or *yeah* (as in Excerpt 7.9).

7.5 Conclusion

We have seen that pick-ups at the shoe shop are organized such that customers produce a request to pick up their now-repaired item, either by handing over a receipt slip or with a verbal request in a form such as *picking up for [name]*. Shoetenders grant this request by going to the back of the shop, retrieving the item, and delivering it to the counter, to the space on the counter designated as the customer's space (Mondada & Sorjonen, this volume). The shoetender then moves directly to the payment sequence, either by turning to the cash register or by stating the cost of the repair. In this way, shoetenders treat the absence of any reaction from the customer at the point of the return as tacit acceptance of the repair. During the shoetender's move to the cash register, customers regularly engage in inspection of the item after its return to the counter. The inspection may be entirely visual, or it may involve physical manipulation of the item, either to provide multiple angles of visual access, or to provide tactile information about the results of the repair work.

This organization of the request-return sequence suggests that as in convenience stores the production of an acknowledgment is not made conditionally relevant in the shoe repair shop – in contrast to what seems to be the case in the beauty salons explored by Oshima (2009, 2014) and Oshima and Streeck (2015). The return sequences in the shoe repair shop do, however, set up *conditions* under which an acknowledgment can be produced: upon the return of their item, the customers have visual – and often tactile – access to their item, and such access is a precondition for making an acknowledgment. Indeed, as we have shown, acknowledgments are in fact relatively regularly produced as part of the request-return sequence: they can be volunteered by the customer, but they can also be made relevant with various degrees of strength, i.e., the shoetender can mobilize the production of an acknowledgment by demonstrating the work that has been done to the item, or they can explicitly invite an acknowledgment by making inquiries of the customer.

When making a volunteered acknowledgment, customers seem to orient specifically to the visual availability of the item in so far as these acknowledgments are produced either as soon as the item becomes visible to them, or after some inspection has been done, i.e., never before visual access has been established. In the former case, the acknowledgments are specifically designed as being 'early': they typically consist of high-grade assessment terms (e.g., *beautiful, fantastic, really good, so good*) and are marked with indicators of 'authenticity' such as gasps, response cries, and high pitch. When produced after some inspection, volunteered acknowledgments are stripped of many of these features to instead present them as being grounded in a thorough and rational evaluation of the repaired item. In both cases, however, volunteered acknowledgments typically formulate the evaluation as being grounded in visual access, i.e., *they* look *beautiful/better than new* and treat the repair as an accomplishment.

When shoetenders mobilize an acknowledgment, they do so by describing or demonstrating to the customer the result of the work that was done. While these descriptions or demonstrations seem in and by themselves to make acknowledgment relevant, they only provide the customer with limited access to the repaired item and further inspection often follows the acknowledgment. Mobilized acknowledgments are correspondingly constituted typically through an assessing term only, i.e., *great/cool*, that seem less intended as evaluations of the repair per se, but rather as explicit confirmations that the request-return sequence has been successfully completed.

Like mobilized acknowledgments, invited acknowledgments are contingent on interactional work being done by the shoetender. By producing a question about the customer's satisfaction with the repair, shoetenders make some form of explicit acceptance conditionally relevant. As we have shown, shoetenders can invite acknowledgments in two different contexts: when they are concerned that the work they have done may not be what the customer expected, or when a customer through his or her behavior during inspection may indicate a lack of satisfaction with the work that has been done. Invited acknowledgments can be either positive or negative, but they are typically designed to be explicitly responsive.

7.6   Discussion

The difference between having a service-assessment sequence where the move to the payment sequence is contingent on a (positive) assessment, as in the beauty shop, and a request-return sequence where even an acknowledgment of the repaired item is voluntary and require extra work, as in the shoe repair shop may, we think, say something about the nature of objects and their relation to human beings.

Unlike assessments in hair salons, which – as evidenced by the work of Oshima (2009, 2014) and Oshima and Streeck (2015) – are routinely pursued by hair stylists, acknowledgments at the shoe shop are only occasionally invited by the shoetenders, and many request-return sequences are accomplished without them. A casual examination of one of our other research sites, a bike shop, reveals that when customers pick up a repaired bike, they acknowledge the repair even more rarely than customers in the shoe repair shop, and the bike repair staff never do work to mobilize or pursue acknowledgments. In fact, customers at the bike shop rarely inspect the repair work that has been done; rather, they immediately take hold of their bike and wheel it to the counter for payment.

What motivates this variation in moving from providing a requested service to payment? Here we note some of the factors that might be at work in shaping this sequence across different kinds of shops. The first factor that appears to be at work is whether the repair or alteration that has been done is of an aesthetic character or not. In the bike shop, most repairs are purely functional and may not even be visually accessible. At the hair salon, at the extreme end, our hair is considered to be a vital part of our physical appearance, and thus has mainly aesthetic value. In the shoe shop, repairs may be functional, aesthetic, or both. In both volunteered and invited acknowledgments, we clearly see both customer and shoetender orienting to the relevance of aesthetics; customers may volunteer that an item looks beautiful or looks like new, and shoetenders may invite customers to assess the degree to which a repair is noticeable. For other repairs that are largely functional (new soles, hush plates, and 'taps'), by contrast, acknowledgments are rarely volunteered or invited.

Another factor at work in shaping the service/return/completion sequence is the relative expertise of customers and staff with respect to the object that has been repaired or altered. Many customers in the bike shop are not familiar with the structural details of their bike (if they were, they could have done the work themselves); customers may thus not be able to evaluate the quality of the work done, except perhaps to say that now the bike 'works better'. Shoes and other leather items, on the other hand, are relatively simple in their structure, and most shoe owners are able to inspect and evaluate how their new heels look, or how the shoe shining turned out, or even how the new elastic looks. And of course a haircut requires little expertise to inspect and assess.

In fact, if aesthetics and expertise are explored together, we can see that at the hair salon, the customer is the real 'expert', in that it is the customer and the customer alone who can say if they like the new cut or not, because the aesthetics of a haircut are a purely subjective matter. Thus the customer's inspection and assessment are crucial in the process of hair styling, while at the bike shop, whether the customer likes the appearance of a newly fixed brake line or the new chain may be subordinated to the shop owner's determination of its necessity for functional reasons. The shoe shop is once again somewhere in the middle, with the customer's subjective opinion of the aesthetics of a repair being balanced with the shoetender's expertise of knowing what is possible, how it can be done, what it would cost, and so on. This factor leads to no pursuit of acknowledgments (or inspection) in the bike shop, some pursuit at the shoe shop, and mandatory pursuit at the hair salon.

A third factor involves the nature of the repair or alteration and how its completion can be determined. At the bike shop, repairs are telic; that is, they have a natural ending point: a new seat has been put on, tires have been inflated to the manufacturer-set specifications, new brakes have been installed, etc. At the shoe shop as well, many repairs are telic: new heels have been put on, toes have been glued, etc. Of course at the shoe shop not all repairs have a natural end point (such as stretching), but many do. However, at the hair salon, there is no natural end point to a haircut (except perhaps when all the hair is gone). Even if a customer asks to have a specific amount cut off, they could always ask for more to be cut off. A related factor is that at hair salons there is no possibility of dropping the head off and having the work done while one is away. Thus the customer is immediately present for the work and can inspect the work throughout the process. While customers at the bike and shoe shops do occasionally wait while the work is done, and especially at the bike shop the work is done in visual range of the customer, customers at those shops cannot inspect the work being done with the same intimacy as at a hair salon. And certainly a majority of cases at the shoe shop involve having the work done while the customer is away. A telic granting action thus does not need customer inspection and assessment to determine its completion, while an atelic granting action does. Customers at hair salons are thus pushed to give acknowledgments – in the form of assessments – more often than at the shoe shop, and never at the bike shop.

In addition, when we buy shoes, they are in a pristine state, and customers at the shoe shop are often keen to see if their shoes can be restored to that original state. Hair, by contrast, does not have an original pristine state – it is ever-changing, and presumably no customer wants to have their hair restored to its state at their birth. Bikes also have an original pristine state, but at least in our data, customers often request to have an upgrade done (such as better brakes, or a more comfortable seat, or more durable tires), in addition to requests to have certain things (like broken brake lines) restored to their original state. Customers who request 'restoration' work can thus compare the result of the repair work with the original state of the item to determine if the repair was successful. The state the item was in at drop-off, the state at pick-up and the original state are all relevant at the moment of inspection and acknowledgment, so it is a historical, multidimensional time-grounded activity. Customers at the shoe shop often produce acknowledgments of the sort *they look like new shoes*, which is presumably not the kind of assessment we would find at a hair salon and perhaps only on occasion at a bike shop.

The economic organization of the different types of shops may also play a role in how and when customers inspect and assess. At the shoe shop and bike shop, customers are charged a particular fee, and that is all they pay. At hair salons, in contrast, stylists can expect to be tipped for work that the customer appreciates (at least in North America). A happy customer, whose positive assessment is pursued, may be more likely to tip than an unhappy customer. In addition, a hair stylist is likely to have regular customers who come for a haircut every month or two (except for large chains, which have a first-come, first-served basis for assigning stylists, unless a particular person is requested), which is another motivation to try to make sure customers are pleased with the work. While some customers at the shoe shop may be 'regulars', the frequency of visiting may not be as frequent as at a hair salon, and of course many customers come in only once in a great while. The same appears to be true at the bike shop. Of course, the shoe-tenders and bike repair people work hard to please their customers too, but the economic implications of a displeased customer may not be as noticeable for them as for hair stylists (complaints posted on social media aside).

In all three types of businesses the service sequence could be possibly complete with the initiating request and the completion of the service. However, for all the reasons noted above, at a hair salon the completion of the service is not treated as knowable without assessment from the customer; that is why there is a service-assessment sequence at the hair salon. 'Completion' is thus always an interactional achievement at the hair salon. By contrast, in many of our cases at the shoe shop, the return of the item is treated as completing the sequence unless there are signs of dispreferred uptake from the customer, or if for other reasons the shoetender pursues acknowledgment from the customer (perhaps when the repair work has more to do with aesthetics than functionality). Thus the way these sequences unfold across shop types can be seen to be shaped by a range of contingencies particular to each shop.

References

Aggerholm, H. K., & Asmuß, B. (2016). When "good" is not good enough: Power dynamics and performative aspects of organizational routines. In J. Howard-Grenville, C. Rerup, A. Langley, & H. Tsoukas, eds., *Organizational Routines*. Oxford: Oxford University Press, pp. 140–178. https://doi.org/10.1093/acprof:oso/9780198759485.003.0007

Antaki, C., Houtkoop-Steenstra, H., & Rapley, M. (2000). "Brilliant. Next question...": High-grade assessment sequences in the completion of interactional units. *Research on Language and Social Interaction*, 33(3), 235–262. https://doi.org/10.1207/S15327973RLSI3303_1

Aston, G. (1986). Ah: A corpus-based exercise in conversational analysis. In J. Morley & A. Partington, eds., *Spoken Discourse: Phonetics, Theory and Practice*. Camerino: University of Camerino Press, pp. 123–137.

Bilmes, J. (1988). The concept of preference in conversation analysis. *Language in Society*, 17(2), 161–181. https://doi.org/10.1017/S0047404500012744

Bolden, G. (2008). "So what's up?": Using the discourse marker *so* to launch conversational business. *Research on Language and Social Interaction*, 41(3), 302–337. https://doi.org/10.1080/08351810802237909

Fox, B., & Heinemann, T. (2015). The alignment of manual and verbal displays in requests for the repair of an object. *Research on Language and Social Interaction*, 48(3), 342–362. https://doi.org/10.1080/08351813.2015.1058608

Goffman, E. (1978). Response cries. *Language*, 54(4), 787–815. https://doi.org/10.2307/413235

Golato, A. (2004). *Compliments and Compliment Responses*. Amsterdam: John Benjamins. https://doi.org/10.1075/sidag.15

Goodwin, C., & Goodwin, M. H. (1992). Assessments and the construction of context. In A. Duranti & C. Goodwin, eds., *Rethinking Context: Language as an Interactive Phenomenon*. Cambridge: Cambridge University Press, pp. 147–190.

Heinemann, T., & Fox, B. (2019). Dropping off or picking up? Professionals' use of objects as a resource for determining the purpose of a customer encounter. In D. Day & J. Wagner, eds., *Objects, Bodies, and Work Practice*. Bristol: Multilingual Matters, pp. 143–163. https://doi.org/10.21832/9781788924535-009

Heritage, J. (1998). Oh-prefaced responses to inquiry. *Language in Society*, 27(3), 291–334. https://doi.org/10.1017/S0047404500019990

Jefferson, G. (2004). Glossary of transcript symbols with an introduction. In G. H. Lerner, ed., *Conversation Analysis: Studies from the First Generation*. Amsterdam: John Benjamins, pp. 13–31. https://doi.org/10.1075/pbns.125.02jef

Kaukomaa, T., Peräkylä, A., & Ruusuvuori, J. (2014). Foreshadowing a problem: Turn-opening frowns in conversation. *Journal of Pragmatics*, 71, 132–147. https://doi.org/10.1016/j.pragma.2014.08.002

Kendrick, K. H., & Torreira, F. (2015). The timing and construction of preference: A quantitative study. *Discourse Processes*, 52(4), 255–289. https://doi.org/10.1080/0163853X.2014.955997

Lindström, A., & Heinemann, T. (2009). Good enough: Low-grade assessments in caregiving situations. *Research on Language and Social Interaction*, 42(4), 309–328. https://doi.org/10.1080/08351810903296465

Mondada, L. (2014). *Conventions for multimodal transcription*. Available at http://icar.univ-lyon2.fr/projets/corinte/documents/convention_transcription_multimodale.pdf

Ogden, R. (2013). Clicks and percussives in English conversation. *Journal of the International Phonetic Association*, 43(3), 299–320. https://doi.org/10.1017/S0025100313000224

Oshima, S. (2009). *Beauty and Consensus: Practices for Agreeing on the Quality of Service in Client-Professional Interactions*. PhD dissertation, University of Texas at Austin.

(2014). Balancing multiple roles through consensus: Making revisions in haircutting sessions. *Text & Talk*, 34(6), 713–136. https://doi.org/10.1515/text-2014-0024

Oshima, S., & Streeck, J. (2015). Coordinating talk and practical action: The case of hair salon service assessments. *Pragmatics and Society*, 6(4), 538–564. https://doi.org/10.1075/ps.6.4.04osh

Pomerantz, A. (1984) Agreeing and disagreeing with assessments: Some features of preferred/dispreferred turn shapes. In J. M. Atkinson & J. Heritage, eds., *Structures of Social Action: Studies in Conversation Analysis*. Cambridge: Cambridge University Press, pp. 57–101. https://doi.org/10.1017/CBO9780511665868.008

Raclaw, J. (2013). *Indexing Inferables and Organizational Shifts: 'No'-prefaces in English Conversation*. PhD thesis, University of Colorado.

Raclaw, J., Robles, J. S., & DiDomenico, S. M. (2016). Providing epistemic support for assessments through mobile-supported sharing activities. *Research on Language and Social Interaction*, 49(4), 362–379. https://doi.org/10.1080/08351813.2016.1199089

Robles, J. S. (2012). Troubles with assessments in gifting occasions. *Discourse Studies*, 14(6), 753–777. https://doi.org/10.1177/1461445612457490

Schegloff, E. A. (1998). Body torque. *Social Research*, 65(3), 535–596.

(2007). *Sequence Organization in Interaction: A Primer in Conversation Analysis, Vol. 1*. Cambridge: Cambridge University Press. https://doi.org/10.1017/CBO9780511791208

Stivers, T., & Rossano, F. (2010). Mobilizing response. *Research on Language and Social Interaction*, 43(1), 3–31. https://doi.org/10.1080/08351810903471258

Thompson, S. A., Fox, B., & Couper-Kuhlen, E. (2015). *Grammar in Everyday Talk: Building Responsive Actions*. Cambridge: Cambridge University Press. https://doi.org/10.1017/CBO9781139381154

8 Moving Money
Money as an Interactional Resource in Kiosk Encounters in Finland

Mia Halonen and Aino Koivisto

8.1 Introduction: Money as an Accessible Interactional Resource in Kiosk Encounters

In kiosk encounters, the ultimate institutional goal is simple: the exchange of products and money; the clients get the goods they came to buy and the seller receives the payment. Paying as an activity is an obligatory part of the encounter; as the last part, it is also implicative of closing. That is, when paying is accomplished, the encounter can be brought to a close. However, we will show that although paying constitutes a specific phase in the encounter, money as a physical object is also often present from the very beginning of the encounter, and clients typically orient toward the imminent paying phase from the very start. Displaying, i.e., making the money observable to the co-participant, means that money is used as an interactional resource that affects the temporal and sequential trajectory of the whole encounter.

The Finnish kiosks studied here are small stores offering multiple services from lottery cards and betting to uploading travel cards for public transportation; and goods such as stamps, newspapers and magazines, candies, giftware, cards, cigarettes, soft drinks, and beer. Some of the services and goods, such as uploading travel cards or cigarettes, are located behind the counter or need to be requested from the seller. Some products have an individual barcode that the seller has to read; the codes for other frequently bought items are already on the counter, so that the seller does not even have to handle the item to read the price. The fact that the sales encounter generally progresses smoothly on a routine basis shows what a familiar and frequent type of activity going to a kiosk is in Finland. This also stems from the fact that the kiosks belong to a nationwide uniform chain (called R-kioski), and all function similarly (see also Sorjonen & Raevaara 2014).

A kiosk encounter typically involves certain chronologically organized phases, some of them realized in only some encounters. The core actions include either a verbal or nonverbal request(s) and paying. None of them necessarily requires verbalization. The client can, for example, bring a product to the counter and pay without speaking at all. This is, however, very rare. The following schema illustrates the typical phases of the encounter. We have separated the typical actions especially relevant for paying with dash lines (for similar illustrations, see Raevaara & Sorjonen 2006: 127–128; Koivisto & Halonen 2009: 122–123). Our main focus is the evolvement of the encounter to the point at which the money is transferred from the client to the seller. We do not systematically discuss what happens after this, e.g., if the seller gives the customer change.

1 S: greeting
2 C: greeting
3 C: request(s)
4 S: ((grants the request(s)))

---

5 S: inquiry regarding possible additional purchases (*tuleeko muuta* 'come-Q else-PAR' 'anything/something else?')
6 C: negative answer, i.e., claiming no further purchases ('no')
7 S: announcement of the price
8 C: ((hands the money over to the seller))
9 S: goes to cash register, comes back with change

---

10 Thank yous + Goodbyes

One way to describe the payment phase is that it starts with the announcement of the price by the seller (turn 7) and is completed by the subsequent payment (i.e., when the payment is transferred from the client to the seller). However, we can also argue that the transfer from the request phase to the payment phase actually starts earlier, that is, when the seller makes an 'anything/something else' inquiry (turn 5, beginning indicated with a dashed line).[1] Elsewhere we have shown that while providing the last opportunity for the client to make more requests, the inquiry also indicates the seller's preparedness to receive the payment. The client's negative answer then serves as a 'go-ahead' for moving on to the payment phase (Koivisto & Halonen 2009). In fact, we found in most of the encounters a four-part sequence consisting of (1) 'anything else' inquiry, (2) negative answer, (3) announcement of the price, and (4) paying. This means that the 'anything else' inquiry is not so much a genuine inquiry for possible additional requests as it is a gateway to the paying sequence. That is, after the client's negative answer, the participants have established a mutual agreement on the completion of the request phase and their preparedness to move to the paying phase.

---

[1] In Finnish, the grammatical design of the turn (typically *tuleeko muuta*, come-Q else-PAR), lacking any polar modifier such as *something* or *anything* in English, anticipates neither a positive nor a negative response but is in this respect neutral, which the English paraphrase does not convey (on the polarity of *some* and *any*, see, e.g., Heritage et al. 2007). For the sake of brevity, we will refer to this inquiry as the 'anything else' inquiry in the remainder of the chapter.

Even though paying typically is done in a specific sequential slot within the encounter, the participants can orient to the imminent payment already in the beginning of the encounter. We show this by examining how money as a physical object is handled during the encounter. We focus on (1) the client's ways of handling the money at the beginning of the encounter, (2) the timing of handing over the money in relation to the seller's announcement of the price, and (3) the ways in which the customer hands the money to the seller. We show that the money is often present from the outset of the encounter, and the way in which it is handled is used for managing the temporal and sequential trajectory of the encounter. In the next section, we present the general background of our study, after which we analyze the payment sequences in more detail.

8.2   Background

The present study can be placed within research on interaction in service encounters but with a very specific focus on money as an object. We are interested in cases where money is employed as a resource for *organizing* the interaction by, for example, making the payment phase imminent. The study can thus be seen as part of the emerging field of research on the use of physical objects as resources in interaction. In the introduction to their edited volume, *Interacting with Objects*, Nevile et al. (2014) make a distinction between objects as situated resources and as practical accomplishments. As situated resources objects are used to manage interactional demands and relevancies, while as practical accomplishments objects are formed, constituted, and potentially altered in and through social interaction. In kiosk encounters, one of the goals of the encounter is the exchange of money from the client to the seller (a practical accomplishment), but it is also used as a situated resource to organize the interaction during the encounter. In Nevile et al.'s terms (2014: 15) we focus on money as an object for managing interactional order in kiosk encounters.

As money is the foundation for all trade, including kiosk encounters, it is in a sense self-evidently and nonaccountably present in them. However, it is exactly this status, we argue, that allows money to be used as a resource that, for example, indicates whether all the requests have been made or whether a client is in a hurry. Furthermore, money as a physical object, comes in various forms – coins, bills, and cards – and, consequently, has various semiotic and multimodal dimensions. Money can be shown and seen, but it can also be, for example, heard. For these modalities, the various multifaceted objects connected to handling money, such as wallets, purses, pockets, or cash boxes and tills can also be used as resources (cf. Matthews 2014: 386).

Approaching money as an interactional resource means that actions should be understood as profoundly multimodal and simultaneous while at the same time sequential. Goodwin (2002: 19, also 2013: 21) describes this 'multiplicity of temporalities' as emerging from chains of prior actions providing participants with a dense, rich 'now' which contains diverse resources of language, gestures, and objects in hand. Displaying money, whether this means showing it visually or making it audible, can be used to establish or maintain interactional space in kiosk encounters. For us, 'common interactional space', as studied and theorized by Mondada (see, e.g., 2009, 2014), is a central concept. Common interactional space captures not only the ideal of the spatial arrangements of the context that are needed for encounters but also the time dimension in which this space can and should be created. In this space, "mutual orientation is achieved through the establishment of a common focus of attention, creating an interactional space, shaped by the bodies of both persons, becoming now co-participants to a joint action" (Mondada 2009: 1983, 1994–1995; see also Mortensen 2009; Keisanen & Rauniomaa 2012). The concept of interactional space in kiosk encounters has been applied in research by Raevaara and Sorjonen, who showed (2006: 132) how customers use their body movements to establish their role as customers and create a joint interactional space for launching requests in kiosks (see also, e.g., Mortensen & Hazel 2014). In this chapter, we argue that interactional space does not even need physical proximity; it can be established and preserved through using an object, money, by making it sensorily available – visible or audible. For example, in the phase of the encounter in which the customer and the seller do not share eye contact or are not facing each other, the customer can make their money perceivable by, for example, bouncing coins audibly in their hand. By this action they create a common interactional space in which they indicate through the sound that they are ready with their purchases and thus ready to pay.

Even though studying objects and the use of space is already an established line of research (see, e.g., Goodwin 1981; Streeck 1996), explicit focus on paying and money exchange has only recently evolved, since the late 2000s. In addition to our own previous research (Halonen & Koivisto 2009; Koivisto & Halonen 2009) on the topic, money as a physical object organizing interaction has been studied in streetwise sales by, for example, Llewellyn and Burrow (2008), in a bar by Richardson (2014), in street-market stalls by vom Lehn (2014), and in a gallery by Llewellyn (2015). These studies show how timing and ways of displaying money (or some other payment equipment) are crucial in organizing the interaction. Even though the settings in these studies are different from ours, the careful use of space and time, and the employment of cash money and cards to project upcoming actions seems parallel.

8.3 Data

Our data come from 175 video-taped kiosk encounters in Southern Finland with two different sellers, recorded during the fall of 2002 by the research

Institute for the Languages of Finland. What is particular in the data presented in this chapter, in relation to the present practices in kiosks (or anywhere in trading markets), is that in 2002 most clients still paid in cash, thus operating with notes and coins. Furthermore, Finland changed currencies from the Finnish mark to the euro at the beginning of 2002. Some debit and credit cards were also in use in the data, and 'displaying money' seemed to work similarly with them, independent of the paying medium.

In our previous research (Halonen & Koivisto 2009; Koivisto & Halonen 2009), we focused on the announcement of the price as the marker of a shared understanding of the phase of the encounter. For this chapter, we have divided our data into analytic categories based on the function of the price announcement in relation to actual paying. That is, the announcement of the price can function as either an indication of readiness to receive payment or an actual request for payment. A shared feature for all the encounters in the data is that the seller does not produce the price announcement at the point when they become knowledgeable of the total price of the purchases (e.g., after reading the bar code(s)), but at the point when it is clearly established that the client does not intend to make any further requests and all the action related to fulfilling these are completed. The clients, on the other hand, seem to monitor the seller's readiness to receive the payment and accommodate their actions to it. In Table 8.1, we have divided our data into three categories with respect to the timing of payment in relation to the seller's announcement of the price of the purchase.

In the 'on-time payments' (115/175), the default cases, money has already been made visible by the client before the price announcement, but is kept in the client's own space until the price announcement, after which the client gives the money to the seller. In anticipatory payments (36/175), the money is 'pushed' to the seller, that is, to the common space before the announcement. This practice gives the impression that the client is in a hurry. In delayed payments (16/175), displaying money is delayed in relation to the announcement turn. That is, it is not delayed in any dispreferred or problematic way. In a few other types of cases (8/175), the client and the seller are involved in some other activity, such as chatting, or the clients do not buy anything but have come in to ask something, for example. In this chapter, we analyze and discuss the three types – default, anticipatory and delayed – in that order.

Table 8.1. *Distribution of the timing of payment*

Default cases: 'On-time payments'	115
Anticipatory payments	36
Delayed payments	16
Other	8
All	**175**

8.4 On-time Payments: Money Made Visible before Announcement of Price

We start our analysis with the most frequent cases in our data. In these cases, the client hands over the money to the seller directly after the price is announced or simultaneously with it. This way of handling the money is the 'default' option, employed by the majority of the customers. Besides the timing of handing over the money, i.e., 'on time', we observed another recurrent feature. In these cases, the client makes observable preparations for paying even before the actual paying sequence. That is, the client shows preparedness to either pay by having the money available and observable from the start, or by starting a visible search for it right after their request. This resembles what Richardson (2014: 184–196) calls 'preselected payments' in her analysis of paying in bars. Typically, the client in kiosks comes to the counter holding their wallet but starts to dig out the money only after the request, or in the case of multiple requests, after the last one. At this point, the client has the money ready, but they wait for the 'go-ahead' (i.e., the price announcement) from the seller before actually paying. The client thus shows early orientation toward the ultimate goal of the interaction, the exchange of money and goods, already at the beginning of the interaction. Early preparedness also indicates orientation toward the progressivity of the encounter (see also Richardson 2014: 177).

Figures 8.1–8.3, from three different encounters, are taken from the same place in the sequence, that is, when the clients have just made their requests. In

Figure 8.1

Moving Money 261

Figure 8.2

Figure 8.3

Figures 8.1 and 8.2, the client is in the process of opening his wallet, whereas in Figure 8.3, the client already has a suitable note between her two fingers. The note is also clearly visible to the seller.

Let us look at the progression of one of these default cases in more detail (see Figure 8.1).

Excerpt 8.1 (T516; CUS = customer, SEL = seller)

```
((CUS comes to the picture holding his wallet))
01 CUS:    hyvää huomen[ta.
           good morning.
02 SEL:               [>(no)< hei.
                      PRT hello.
03         (0.2)
04 CUS:    kym↑menen sarjal *#<lip:[pu>; *
           ten-trip ticket.
                            *opens wallet*
                            #fig.8.4
```

Figure 8.4

```
05 SEL:                       [Helsingin sisä[inev °(vai)°;]
                              inside Helsinki (area.)
06 CUS:                                      [joo:         ]
                                              yeah.
07         sisäi+ne.             +
           inside.
   sel                           +reads barcode+
08         *+(1.0)         * (1.6)
   cus     *takes a note fr w*
   sel     +starts to take the ticket out-->1.11
09 SEL:    ja sittem    muu-ta.h=
           and then(PART) else-PAR
           and then anything else.
10 CUS:    =ei *#muuta; (.)  tällä [kertaa°.
           nothing else; (.) this time.
               *starts handing note--->
   fig       #fig.8.5
```

Moving Money 263

Figure 8.5

```
11 SEL:                    [kakstoista ja
                            twelve and
12         kahdeksan↑ky+mmen*#tä kiitos:;
           eighty thank you;
                      -->+
    cus                -->*
    fig                   #fig.8.6
```

Figure 8.6

```
13            (5.4) ((SEL works at the cashier))
14  SEL:     (ja) sei:tsemän kakskymmentä ole hyvä.
              and seven twenty here you are.
15  CUS:     kii↑tos:;
              thank you
```

When the recording starts, the client approaches the counter holding his wallet. Simultaneously with his request, he opens his wallet (line 4, Figure 8.4). While responding to the seller's clarification question, he draws out a note, which suggests that he knows the price of the product in advance, or at least knows that the note is enough to pay for the product (lines 6–7). However, he does not hand over the money nor place it on the counter; he keeps the note in 'home position' (Sacks & Schegloff 2002), close to his body (Figure 8.4). That is, the money is still in his personal physical space. At the same time, it is in their joint interactional space, and thus mutually perceivable. It is only after the seller has produced the closing implicative 'anything else' question that the client starts to move his hand holding the money gradually toward the seller (Figure 8.5). The seller takes the money from the client's hand after putting the ticket on the counter (that is, after having fulfilled the request). Simultaneously, she announces the price (lines 11–12; Figure 8.6). The turn formulation, NP, suggests that the price announcement is indeed an announcement rather than a request (Halonen & Koivisto 2009). The seller's announcement of the price and 'thank you' are produced in the same turn and within the same prosodic unit, which further demonstrates that the seller does not have to wait for the payment. In general, price announcements do not typically function as requests for payment but rather as announcements of readiness to move on, to receive the payment. 'Thank you' then marks receipt of the payment (see also Koivisto 2009).

Excerpt 8.2 shows a case in which the client presents two requests in two different turns. As in the previous excerpt, the client has her wallet visible in her hands, but she opens it only after the last request, which shows orientation toward the imminent paying sequence and may also function as an index for the completion of the list of requests.

Excerpt 8.2 (T514)

```
((C walks to the counter holding the wallet and the research
brochure))
01  SEL:     +huomenta?
              good morning?
              +walks to counter-->
02            (.)
03  CUS:     huomenta;
              good morning;
04            (0.4)+
    sel        -->+
```

```
05 CUS:     hookooällän kymmene matkan kortti.
            HKL's ten trip ticket.
06          +(1.0)          + (0.8)
   sel      +reads barcode+
07 SEL:     ja  sitte      muu-ta    [vielä. ]
            and then(PART) else-PAR   still
            and then anything else.
08 CUS:                              [sit *lot]too; (0.2) kolme
                                      then lottery; (0.2) three
                                          *starts to open wallet--->
09          rivii.hh
            rows.hh
10          (.)
11 SEL:     tuleekos joke>rei[ta<.
            do you want Jokers.
12 CUS:                      [ei #tuu jokerii.*
                              no Jokers.
                                          -->*
   fig                       #fig.8.7
```

Figure 8.7

```
13          *(3.0)                *
   cus      *takes note out of w*
14 SEL:     ja ↑sitte.
            and then.
15 CUS:     kiitos ei muu°ta°.
            that's all thank you.
16 SEL:     n:eljätoist *+kuus#kymmentä+.
            fourteen sixty.
   sel                  +puts purchases on the counter+
   cus                 *starts handing the money-->
   fig                      #fig.8.8
```

Figure 8.8

```
17            (0.2)
18  SEL:      *kitos::;
              thank you
    cus       ->*
19            (6.0)
20  SEL:      ja viisneljäkymmentä näi.
              and five forty there you are.
21  CUS:      joo kiit:os;
              yeah thanks;
```

In this encounter, the client starts to open her wallet when producing the second request (line 8). The wallet is fully open in line 12, which is when she produces an answer to the seller's specifying question (line 12, Figure 8.7). At this point, she shifts her gaze from the seller to her wallet, thereby also shifting her attention from verbal interaction to the solitary activity of taking out a suitable amount of money. She takes out a 20-euro note while the seller works at the lottery machine. As in Excerpt 8.1, however, she does not place the note on the counter nor does she try to hand it over before the seller has completed the 'request phase', i.e., has gathered all the requested items and placed them on the counter. Upon completion of this activity, the seller announces the price (line 16, Figure 8.8) and the client starts to extend her arm toward the seller (i.e., give her the money, Figure 8.8). Again, the price announcement turn is formulated as an NP. 'Thank you' is produced at the same moment as when the seller takes the note from the client's hand.

The analyses in this section showed that the clients indicated their preparedness to pay early on in the encounter but did not initiate the paying sequence itself (i.e., transfer of the money). Typically, they had the wallet in their hand and took out the money simultaneously or directly after the (last) request. However, the clients held the money in their own space until the seller indicated readiness to receive the payment by announcing the price. The detectable signs of the completion of the request sequence (e.g., seller has put all the requested items on the counter) also served as an indication that the seller was ready to receive the payment. The clients were thus prepared to pay, but closely monitored the seller's activities and left the control of the progression of the encounter to the seller. In the next group of cases, we see how the presence of physical money clearly affects the way in which the encounter is organized.

8.5 Anticipatory Payments: Client Pays before Price Announcement

The second most frequent groups of encounters are those in which the client pays early, that is, prior to the announcement of the price. The customer is thus 'proffering payment' (see Richardson 2014: 209). Paying early means that the client begins the paying phase on their own initiative, before the announcement of the price. This typically happens simultaneously with the last request. There are two possible accounts for early payment:

(1) Speeding up the progression of the encounter. Typically, this gives the impression of 'being in a hurry'. In these cases, the request is 'small', commonplace and apparently recurrent (a single bus ticket, a newspaper, etc.). The client places the money on the counter or gives it directly to the seller at the beginning of the encounter, i.e., when making the request. In so doing they may indicate haste, the routine character of the request and the fact that the requested item is the client's only purchase.
(2) The encounter contains talk beyond the actual business itself. For example, in some of the encounters in our data the seller provides information on the ways in which the client can order an electronic travel card. The client may then show their willingness to get back to the ongoing purchase activity by handing over the money on their own initiative and resuming the main line of talk and moving toward the end of the encounter.

In terms of money handling, the money was transferred to the seller in two distinct ways. The client put the money in the seller's hand (1/3 cases) or placed it on the counter (2/3 cases). We provide an example of each type. Both cases represent the routine type of encounter in which the payment is carried out simultaneously with the request and the impression of being in a hurry is conveyed. The money is thus not merely preselected (cf. Richardson 2014) but also handed to the seller even before the verbal request (line 3).

Excerpt 8.3 (T522)

```
01 CUS:    hei;=
           hello
02 SEL:    =hei;
           hello
03         *(0.2)
    cus    *hand with coins towards counter-->
04 CUS:    kerta*#lip°pu°.
           a single ticket
               -->*
    fig           #fig.8.9
```

Figure 8.9

```
05         +(1.4) *(0.6)  * (3.0)            +
    cus           *opens w*
    sel    +reads barcode, takes ticket out+
06 SEL:    se on ↑euroneljä↓kymmentä +kiit↑ti;        +
           that's one euro forty thank you
                                     +takes coins from counter+
07         *(5.2)                     *
    cus    *takes ticket and puts it to w*
08 SEL:    >j[a< nä:]in;
           and like this;
09 CUS:      [k'tti;]
           thanks;
```

In Excerpt 8.3, the client puts the money on the counter simultaneously with the request (line 4, Figure 8.9). Her initiative is also shown in her greeting the seller first, as usually the seller is the first to greet (Raevaara & Sorjonen 2006: 128; Lappalainen 2009). The fact that the payment is carried out early from the seller's perspective is evident in the seller's conduct: after the request and the payment, the seller does not yet take the money from the

Moving Money 269

counter. Instead, she reads the barcode and takes a ticket from the drawer, that is, fulfills the request, which suggests that she is not ready to receive the payment at this point. After completing all the sequences that are required for fulfilling the request, she announces the price and thereby shows her readiness to receive the payment. As in Excerpt 8.1, the seller's 'thank you' is produced in the same turn and in the same prosodic unit with the price announcement. Here, the seller picks the coin(s) from the counter at the moment she says 'thank you'. The client, again, speeds up the encounter not only by giving the money simultaneously with the request but also by opening her wallet immediately after putting the coin on the counter and continuing to keep it open in anticipation of change. Each move and its timing is thus designed to spare time, displaying a strong preference for rapid progressivity (see also Kuroshima 2010; Richardson 2014: 184). What is noteworthy is how the client's behavior affects the seller's behavior. In contrast to Excerpts 8.1 and 8.2, there is no 'anything else' inquiry, which is the seller's way of displaying an understanding of the client's activity orientation. Placing the money on the counter at the beginning of the encounter is thus a sign of having no more than one request. What is also noteworthy is how the client makes the payment detectable to the seller: dropping the coin(s) on the counter makes an audible sound (beginning of line 4). The client's way of handling the money thus results in a condensed encounter and some of the typical sequences are not realized. Furthermore, the detectable presence of money (both visibly and audibly) during the encounter sustains the interactional space and shows orientation toward rapid completion of the institutional task.

Consider another case. Here, the client puts the money in the seller's hand.

Excerpt 8.4 (T566)

```
((encounter starts when previous client is still at counter))
01 CUS:    hei.
           hello
02 SEL:    hei;
           hello
03         (0.2)
04 CUS:    ^*ilta*leh:°ti°.
           ((name of a newspaper))
            *step*
           ^starts handing the money--->
05         +(0.3)
    sel    +starts to extend arm--->
06 SEL:    #↑se_o yh+^de [↓euro°n°.
           that's one euro.
                    -->+
    cus             -->^
    fig    #fig.8.10
```

Figure 8.10

```
07         (.)
08 SEL:    kiit+ti;              +
           thank you;
                  +reads barcode+
09         *(4.4)                        *
   cus     *takes paper from stand*
10 CUS:    ki[itti;   ]
           thanks;
11 SEL:       [>ole hy]vä<_
                you're welcome,
```

This encounter starts when the previous client is still standing in front of the counter. As in Excerpt 8.3, but unlike in most kiosk encounters (Raevaara & Sorjonen 2006: 128), the client establishes contact with the seller by greeting first. After the greetings, the client makes a verbal request (Iltalehti, name of a newspaper), simultaneously stretching his right arm toward the seller (lines 4 and 5; see Figure 8.10).

Interestingly, the requested item is located in a stand in front of the counter, which means that the client would not have to ask the seller to give it to him. The need for a verbal request might be partly because the previous client is still standing in front of the counter and the newspaper stand. In response to the client's initiating action, the seller stretches out her arm and announces the price. That is, the ordering of the obligatory sequences changes in response to the client's behavior: the seller reads the barcode after receiving the money and simultaneously thanks the client (line 8). Thus, as in the other cases, thanking is a way of claiming and marking the receipt of money (see also Koivisto 2009). In addition, as in the previous excerpt, there is no 'anything else' inquiry. The whole encounter then shows considerable adjustment on the part of the seller.

In Excerpts 8.3 and 8.4 we saw that clients actively steered the interaction toward completion by directing the money to the seller 'early', prior to the announcement of price, which gave the impression of being in a hurry. In these cases, in contrast to the 'on-time payments', it was the client who set the pace of the encounter. Interestingly, the seller did not decline the payment (as the bartenders do in similar cases in Richardson's 2014: 209–222 data) even though it was misplaced. Instead, the seller then adjusted her actions to the client's actions by 'speeding up', that is, skipping some sequences (such as the 'anything else' question) or changing the order of the obligatory phases (such as reading the barcode late, only after receiving the money). Early payments thus result in a 'condensed' encounter, and the way in which the clients handle the money affects the trajectory of the encounters, i.e., organizes its course.

8.6 'Delayed' Payments: Preparedness to Pay Not Visible at Outset

In the last group of cases the client is not ready to pay when the price is first announced. These cases could thus be considered deviant cases in comparison to 'on-time' and 'early' payments, where the orientation toward the progressivity of the encounter and its outcome (paying and exchange of goods) is clearly visible. However, we show how also in these cases, the client displays orientation toward the upcoming paying phase. Delays can often be accounted for by the fact that the client is occupied with tasks related to other objects or has difficulties finding their wallet or a suitable amount of money right away. These things typically happen when the client is able to walk to the counter straight away after entering the kiosk instead of having to wait in line. Standing in line gives the client the opportunity to prepare for paying while waiting. In the 'delayed' cases, it is the absence of money that organizes the interaction, i.e., affects its temporal and sequential trajectory.

In Excerpt 8.5 we see that even though the client does not have the money readily available, they start an observable search for it as soon as possible by, for example, going through their pockets. Even though going through one's pockets is an activity carried out in one's personal space, it is still publicly produced in the participants' interactional space, thus displaying orientation toward the pending, obligatory phase of the encounter. This means that these cases also have a visible orientation toward the progressivity of the encounter on the client's part. In fact, our data had no cases in which the client just stood idly and did nothing while the seller fulfilled the request.

We look at one case of delayed payments, focusing on its beginning. Before the actual encounter starts, the client has been talking to the members of the research group (off camera), and the seller has been observing them. After this, the client walks straight to the counter holding up an envelope indicating that what he needs is a stamp (line 1). At this point, it becomes clear to the seller what the client wants, and, consequently, she initiates the encounter by making a candidate understanding of the requested item ('so a stamp', line 2) (Sorjonen 2018).

Excerpt 8.5 (T743)

```
01            *(0.6)
    cus       *walks to counter holding up an envelope--->
02 SEL:       +>eli< kirjemmerk°ki°.*      +
              so a stamp
              +looks at stamps in her hand+
    cus                                --->*
03            (0.2)
04 CUS:       kirjemmerkin os[t#*an ↓joo.
              I'm buying a stamp yeah.
                              *starts to dab pockets-->
    fig                       #fig.8.11
```

Figure 8.11

```
05 SEL:                  [e:likä kuuskyt sent°tiä°.
                          so sixty cents
06            (0.8) +(0.2)      + #*(2.2)                    *
    sel             +reads barcode+
    cus                              *takes w from breastpocket*
    fig                              #fig.8.12
```

Figure 8.12

```
07 SEL:    jos mä liimaan sen siihen viä >(saman tein)<.
           if I stick it on it right away
08         (0.2)
09 CUS:    joo se o hyvä.
           yeah that's good
10         #(1.0) *(2.0)
   cus            *starts to dig into coin pocket--->1.16
   fig     #fig.8.13
```

Figure 8.13

```
11 SEL:      *ton:ne ↓noin.
              right there.
    sel      *puts the stamp on
12           (0.6)
13 CUS:      joo.
              yeah.
14           (1.2)
15 SEL:      se_on nyt siinä valmiina sit°te°.*
              now it is ready there then
    cus                                          -->*
16           *(1.0)          *    ^(0.8)       ^
    cus      *looks at coins*
                                    ^hands coins^
17 SEL:      kit↑ti;
              thanks
18           (4.2)
19 SEL:      ^↑ja nelkyt ↓senttiä;       ^
              and forty cents
              ^hands the exchange coins^
20 CUS:      kitti:;
              thanks
```

The client's first action when he reaches the counter is to put his briefcase in front of the counter. While providing a confirming response to the seller (line 4), the client puts the envelope on the counter and immediately after this, starts patting his pockets, evidently in search of his wallet. This activity begins slightly before the seller's price announcement and thus shows strong orientation toward paying. Even though he did not yet have the money ready when placing the envelope on the counter, putting the search on display shows his orientation toward paying. It takes up to 12 seconds (a fairly long time in the context of a kiosk encounter) after the price announcement before the client is actually able to give the money to the seller (Figures 8.11–8.13).

What is noteworthy is that the seller orients toward the delay not by just standing and waiting but by performing additional tasks that are not part of the routine service: she offers to stick the stamp on the envelope (line 7). Since this is quickly done, she also provides a verbal commentary which comes close to being small talk, which is typically initiated in the 'silent' sequences of the encounter (Raevaara & Sorjonen 2006: 146) (lines 11 and 15). By doing these extra things, she avoids creating the impression of waiting impatiently. In addition, the way in which the price announcement is formulated ('so sixty cents') may reflect the client's initial unpreparedness at the point at which the price was announced. Even though at the local level the turn seems to be formulated as a 'result' of the client's prior confirmation (line 4), longer formulations in price announcements (such as clauses and the employment of turn-initial particles) may also be used to give a client more time to take out their money (Koivisto & Halonen 2009; cf. also Sorjonen & Raevaara 2014 on requests).

Moving Money 275

In the case of delayed payments, the apparent 'problem' is that clients are not ready to pay when the price is announced and/or the paying sequence is prolonged. However, we have seen that although the clients are 'late' in their paying with respect to the timing of the price announcement, they begin the search for money as soon as possible, thereby orienting toward the norm of 'early preparedness' and progressivity. The seller may adjust to the delay by 'slowing down' their activities through, for example, the design of the price announcement (see Halonen & Koivisto 2009; cf. also Sorjonen & Raevaara 2014).

8.7 Conclusions

In this chapter we have analyzed how money, as a physical object, is used for displaying orientation toward the progression of the interaction. More specifically, we have shown how displays of money can be used to manage the temporal and sequential trajectory of the payment phase in kiosk encounters. We focused on the client's ways of handling the money at the beginning of the encounter, the timing of the handing over of the money in relation to the announcement of the price by the seller, and the ways in which the customer handed the money to the seller.

In Section 8.4 we analyzed default cases, in which the clients held the money in a visible way but kept it in their own space until the price announcement turn and the detectable completion of the request sequence. The clients thus indicated their preparedness to pay early on in the encounter but did not initiate the paying sequence itself, leaving the control of the progression of the encounter to the seller. In the anticipatory payments, the clients directed the money to the seller's space early, during their request (Section 8.5). In these cases, in contrast to the 'on-time payments', it is the client who sets the pace of the encounter. The seller then adjusted her actions to those of the client by 'speeding up', or changing the order of the obligatory sequences, resulting in a 'condensed' encounter. This practice treats the encounter as routine-like, easy and quick, and shows that the client is in a hurry. In the cases in which the money was not displayed at the time the seller announced the price, the cases we called 'delayed payments' (Section 8.6), the client still searched for their money in a clearly observable manner. In this way the clients showed their understanding of the default structure of encounters, i.e., even though they were not initially prepared for paying, they were preparing to do so. In general, it can be said that the way in which money is handled and the close monitoring of the timing of the paying showed an orientation to a short and routine-like encounter that requires little time and effort. This also manifested a strong common ground between the participants (cf. Enfield 2006; see also Sorjonen & Raevaara 2014).

This chapter has shown how the elementary ingredient in encounters at shops – the transfer of money from the seller to the client – is in fact both *an accomplishment* and *a situated resource* for organizing the interaction (Nevile et al. 2014). In most of the encounters, the client and the seller align with each other's actions so that client does not pay until the seller is ready to receive the payment. The seller, on the other hand, does not typically announce the price until the client has indicated that they are ready to pay. This – a smooth and coordinated transfer of money from the client to the seller – is clearly an interactional accomplishment. However, we have also seen that money as physical object can be used as a resource, to steer the interaction in a nonaccountable way. For example, the client can place a coin or a note to the counter or give it to the seller early, before the seller has indicated readiness to receive the payment, thus showing willingness to complete the encounter as soon as possible. This shows that money as physical object is a resource that is used to organize, e.g., speed up the encounter. We have thus seen that the handling of money is intertwined with the sequential organization of the encounter but also has its own life that happens simultaneously with the verbal conduct.

References

Enfield, N. J. (2006). Social consequences of common ground. In N. J. Enfield & S. Levinson, eds., *Roots of Human Sociality: Culture, Cognition and Interaction*. Oxford: Berg, pp. 399–430. https://doi.org/10.1075/pbns.314.05yam

Goodwin, C. (1981). *Conversational Organization: Interaction between Speakers and Hearers*. New York: Academic Press.

(2002). Time in action. *Current Anthropology*, 43(S4), 19–35. https://doi.org/10.1086/339566

(2013). The co-operative, transformative organization of human action and knowledge. *Journal of Pragmatics*, 46(1), 8–23.

Halonen, M., & Koivisto, A. (2009). Neljä viiskyt: Miten ilmoittaa asiakkaalle ostosten hinta? [Four fifty: How to announce the price of the purchase to the customer?] In H. Lappalainen & L. Raevaara, eds., *Kieli kioskilla*. Helsinki: Finnish Literature Society, pp. 153–173.

Heritage, J., Robinson, J. D., Elliott, M. N., Beckett, M., & Wilkes, M. (2007). Reducing patients' unmet concerns in primary care: The difference one word can make. *Journal of General Internal Medicine*, 22(10), 1429–1433. https://doi.org/10.1007/s11606-007-0279-0

Keisanen, T., & Rauniomaa, M. (2012). The organization of participation and contingency in prebeginnings of request sequences. *Research on Language and Social Interaction*, 45(4), 323–351. https://doi.org/10.1080/08351813.2012.724985

Koivisto, A. (2009). Kiitoksen paikka. Kiittäminen asiointia jäsentämässä [Time to say thank you: Thanking in organizing the kiosk encounter]. In H. Lappalainen & L. Raevaara, eds., *Kieli kioskilla [Language at the Kiosk: Studies on Routines of Kiosk Encounters]*. Helsinki: Finnish Literature Society, pp. 174–200.

Koivisto, A., & Halonen, M. (2009). *Tuleeko muuta?* Maksaminen osana R-kioskiasiointia [Paying as a part of the kiosk encounter]. In H. Lappalainen & L. Raevaara, eds., *Kieli kioskilla [Language at the Kiosk: Studies on Routines of Kiosk Encounters]*. Helsinki: Finnish Literature Society, pp. 120–152.

Kuroshima, S. (2010). Another look at the service encounter: Progressivity, intersubjectivity, and trust in a Japanese sushi restaurant. *Journal of Pragmatics*, 42(3), 856–869. https://doi.org/10.1016/j.pragma.2009.08.009

Lappalainen, H. (2009). "Tervehtiminen ja tervehtimättä jättäminen. Ollaanko kioskilla epäkohteliaita?" [Greeting and not greeting. Are people impolite at kiosk?]. In H. Lappalainen & L. Raevaara, eds., *Kieli kioskilla. Tutkimuksia kioskiasioinnin rutiineista [Talk at Convenience Store. Studies on the Routines in Convenience Store Encounters]*, pp. 32–55. Helsinki: Finnish Literature Society.

Llewellyn, N. (2015). 'Money talks': Communicative and symbolic functions of cash money. *Sociology*, 50(4), 796–812. https://doi.org/10.1177/0038038515585475

Llewellyn, N., & Burrow, R. (2008). Streetwise sales and the social order of city streets. *The British Journal of Sociology*, 59(3), 561–583. https://doi.org/10.1111/j.1468-4446.2008.00208.x

Matthews, B. (2014). Trajectories of the object in interaction. In M. Nevile, P. Haddington, T. Heinemann, & M. Rauniomaa, eds., *Interacting with Objects: Language, Materiality, and Social Activity*. Amsterdam: John Benjamins, pp. 381–388. https://doi.org/10.1075/z.186.17mat

Mondada, L. (2007). Multimodal resources for turn-taking: Pointing and the emergence of possible next speakers. *Discourse Studies* 9(2), 195–225. https://doi.org/10.1177/1461445607075346

  (2009). Emergent focused interactions in public places: A systematic analysis of the multimodal achievement of a common interactional space. *Journal of Pragmatics* 41(10), 1977–1997. https://doi.org/10.1016/j.pragma.2008.09.019

  (2014). The temporal orders of multiactivity: Operating and demonstrating in the surgical theatre. In P. Haddington, T. Keisanen, L. Mondada, & M. Nevile, eds., *Multiactivity in Social Interaction: Beyond Multitasking*. Amsterdam: John Benjamins, pp. 33–75. https://doi.org/10.1075/z.187.02mon

Mortensen, K. (2009). Establishing recipiency in pre-beginning position in the second language classroom. *Discourse Processes*, 46, 491–515. https://doi.org/10.1080/01638530902959463

Mortensen, K., & Hazel, S. (2014). Moving into interaction: Social practices for initiating encounters at a help desk. *Journal of Pragmatics*, 62, 46–67. https://doi.org/10.1016/j.pragma.2013.11.009

Nevile, M., Haddington, P., Heinemann, T., & Rauniomaa, M. (2014). On the interactional ecology of objects. In M. Nevile, P. Haddington, T. Heinemann, & M. Rauniomaa, eds., *Interacting with Objects: Language, Materiality, and Social Activity*. Amsterdam: John Benjamins, pp. 3–26. https://doi.org/10.1075/z.186

Raevaara, L., & Sorjonen, M.-L. (2006). Vuorovaikutuksen osanottajien toiminta ja genre: Keskustelunanalyysin näkökulmia [Interactants' action and genre: Conversation analytic perspective]. In A. Mäntynen, S. Shore, & A. Solin, eds., *Genre – tekstilaji*. Helsinki: Suomalaisen Kirjallisuuden Seura, pp. 122–150.

Richardson, E. (2014). *The Order of Ordering: Analysing Customer-Bartender Service Encounters in Public Bars*. PhD thesis. Loughborough University. https://dspace.lboro.ac.uk/

Sacks, H., & Schegloff, E. A. (2002). Home position. *Gesture*, 2(2), 133–146. https://doi.org/10.1075/gest.2.2.02sac

Sorjonen, M.-L. (2018). Reformulating prior speaker's turn in Finnish: Turn-initial *siis*, *eli(kkä)*, and *nii(n) et(tä)*. In J. Heritage & M.-L. Sorjonen, eds., *Between Turn and Sequence: Turn-initial Particles across Languages*. Amsterdam: John Benjamins, pp. 251–286.

Sorjonen, M.-L., & Raevaara, L. (2014). On the grammatical form of requests at the convenience store: Requesting as embodied action. In P. Drew & E. Couper-Kuhlen, eds., *Requesting in Social Interaction*. Amsterdam: John Benjamins, pp. 243–268. https://doi.org/10.1075/slsi.26.10sor

Streeck, J. (1996). How to do things with things: Objects trouvés and symbolization. *Human Studies*, 19(4), 365–384. https://doi.org/10.1007/BF00188849

vom Lehn, D. (2014). Timing is money: Managing the floor in sales interaction at street-market stalls. *Journal of Marketing Management*, 30(13–14), 1448–1466. https://doi.org/10.1080/0267257X.2014.941378

Appendix   Transcription Conventions

General Features

Talk is transcribed using Jefferson's (2004) conventions and embodied conducts using Mondada's (2018) conventions.

Overview of basic transcript elements:

SEL:	Speaker identification (pseudonym or category)
cus	Participant doing the embodied action (identified when (s)he is not the speaker; for the speaker, the embodied annotation is placed on the lines(s) immediately following the transcribed turn, without any identification in the margin)
???:	Speaker identification unsure
->	Phenomena in focus are highlighted in various ways, with arrows in the left margin (as here), grey color of the target portion of the line, or boxed portions of the annotation.

Organization of multi-linear transcripts:

- The first line of the transcript is dedicated to the original language and presented in **bold black**.
- The second line, if applicable, contains grammatical glosses and is presented in `normal`.
- The third line is dedicated to translation, and is presented in *italics*.
- The forth and following lines describe embodied conduct. They are in **bold grey**.

Conventions for Transcribing Talk

Talk is transcribed using the conventions developed by Gail Jefferson (2004).

Temporal and sequential relationships, including tempo:

wo[rds] [word]s	Onset and end of overlap (simultaneous talk), at the start of an utterance or later

280   Appendix

word==word	Latching (no intervening beat of silence) between TCUs or between turns by different speakers
(0.6)	Elapsed time (pause or silence); length is timed relative to the delivery of the preceding talk or based on absolute measures.
(.)	Micro-pause (less than 0.2 seconds)
no:, no::	Lengthening/stretching of the sound before the colon (: = 0.1 sec)
>word word<	*Accelerando*/rushed/compressed talk: increase in tempo relative to surrounding talk
<word word>	*Rallentando*/stretched-out talk: slowing down in tempo relative to surrounding talk
wo- word´	Hyphens mark an abrupt ending through oral or glottal cut-off (glottal closure) before a word is complete.

Speech delivery:

word.	Period: Pitch at the end of a prosodically determined unit is falling to low.
word;	Semicolon: pitch at the end of a unit is falling to mid.
word_	Underscore: pitch at the end of a unit is level.
word,	Comma: pitch at end of a unit is rising to mid.
word?	Question mark: pitch at end of a unit is rising to high.
word!	Exclamation point: animated tone (wide pitch range on the preceding syllable), not necessarily an exclamation
be<u>fore</u>, <u>in</u>	Stress or accent prominence on the underlined syllable. For stronger prominence, volume or pitch marking is added.
WORD WOrd	Much higher volume relative to the surrounding talk
°word°	Lower volume
°°word°°	Particularly low volume/quiet voice
↓word	Marked step down in pitch on following syllable
↑word	Marked step up in pitch on following syllable

Transcriptionist's uncertain hearings, comments, and added elements in the translation:

(word)	Transcriber's uncertain hearing
(word)/(weird)	Transcriber's alternative hearings
( )	Unintelligible stretch of talk
((clears throat))	Description, not transcription: Additional transcriber comments and descriptions are provided in double parentheses.

Conventions for Transcribing Embodiment

Embodied actions are transcribed using the conventions developed by Lorenza Mondada (cf. Mondada 2018). For a full version (updated August 2022) and a tutorial see www.lorenzamondada.net/multimodal-transcription.

Transcription Conventions

* *	Descriptions of embodied actions are delimited
+ +	between two identical symbols (one symbol per participant) and are synchronized with corresponding stretches of talk.
*--->	The action described continues across subsequent lines until
--->*	the same symbol is reached.
>>	The action described begins before the excerpt's beginning.
--->>	The action described continues after the excerpt's end.
....	Action's preparation
----	Action's full extension is reached and maintained.
,,,,,	Action's retraction
fig	The exact moment at which a screen shot has been taken is
#	indicated with a specific sign showing its position within turn at talk and with a figure number on a separate line.

Glossing of Talk

Interlinear morpheme-by-morpheme glossing is provided selectively for non-English data. Glossing symbols are based on the Leipzig glossing rules (Bickel et al. 2015). See www.eva.mpg.de/lingua/resources/glossing-rules.php.

1	first person
2	second person
3	third person
ADE	adessive case
ADJ	adjective
ALL	allative case
ART	article
AUX	auxiliary
CLI	clitic
DEM	demonstrative
DEM2	demonstrative *nuo*, a plural form (Finnish)
DEM3	demonstrative *se*
FIG	figure
LOC	locative
NEG	negation, negator, negative
PAR	partitive case
PL	plural
PREP	preposition
PRT	particle
Q	question particle/marker
REL	relative
SG	singular

References

Bickel, B., Comrie, B., & Haspelmath, M. (2015). *The Leipzig Glossing Rules: Conventions for Interlinear Morpheme-by-Morpheme Glosses.* Leipzig. www.eva.mpg.de/lingua/pdf/Glossing-Rules.pdf

Jefferson, G. (2004). Glossary of transcript symbols with an introduction. In G. H. Lerner, ed., *Conversation Analysis: Studies from the First Generation.* Amsterdam: John Benjamins. 13–31. https://doi.org/10.1075/pbns.125.02jef

Mondada, L. (2018). Multiple temporalities of language and body in interaction: Challenges for transcribing multimodality. *Research on Language and Social Interaction*, 51(1), 85–106.

Index

accountability, 181
acknowledgment, 221
　invited, 227, 243–250
　mobilized, 227, 235–242, 250
　pursuit of, 251
　volunteered, 227, 235, 249
action formation, 145, 180
advice, 119–122, 131
aesthetics, 250–251, 253
altruistic actions, 196
'anything else' inquiry, 256, 264, 269
assessment, 25, 115, 118, 120, 125, 127, 131, 189, 207, 215, 227–228, 231, 252
　high-grade, 235, 249
　negative, 248
assistance, 211

bakeries, 4, 23, 79
barcode reader, 147, 152, 154, 157
benefactor, 24, 110–111
beneficiary, 24, 138–139
bike repair shop, 250
branding, 77
bystander, 189, 195

candidate understanding, 272
characterization, 76
cheese shops, 4
claim of not knowing, 118, 127–131
closings, 21–22
collaborative action, 185, 196, 204
collaborative move, 200, 204, 210–211
common ground, 275
common noun, 79, 82, 90, 104
complaint sequence, 215
conditional relevance, 243, 249
consumption, 2
convenience stores, 144, 146, *See also* kiosks
cooperative move, 196
counter, 26–27, 147, 151, 180, 239, 264
couplehood, 23, 38, 41–43, 55, 68

decision to buy, 76, 82, 85, 92, 102, 111, 115–116, 118, 127, 130–131, 139–140
decision-making practices, 41, 68
deictic expression, 78
delicate action, 110, 112, 115
demonstrative, 80, 83, 88, 93, 96, 122, 124, 130, 166–167
description, 80, 83, 85, 89, 103–104, 114, 126, 128, 138
display of not knowing, 118, 123
dispreference, 131
dispreferred response, 248

economic values, 145
economy, 1–2
economy of sale, 24
embodied trajectories, 179–180
embodiment, 145
English, 111, 216
　American, 217
　lingua franca, 79
environmental noticing, 46
epistemic stance, 118, 131

farmer's market, 25, 184
Finland Swedish, 79
Finnish, 79, 111, 146, 255
French, 79, 111, 146

German, 79, 111
gift, 109, 111, 139
　economy of, 109, 140
giving, 159
giving and taking, 151, 154–158, 179
　early visible projection, 164–168
　embodied movement, initiation, 168
　form of the hand, extending, 168
　form of the hand, taking, 168, 179
　hand shape, 164
　initiative, customer, 165
　initiative, seller, 165–166
　taking over the counter, 168

283

284   Index

giving and taking (cont.)
  timed reciprocity, 164
grasping, 189
gratitude
  expression of, 224, 227, 230, 264, 270
  language of, 204
grocery stores, 38

helping gestures, 201, 212
helping hand, 210–211
home position, 264

identification, 76, 103
inspection, 191, 215, 221, 234, 239, 245, 248–249, 252
inspection sequence, 226
institutionality, 76
interactional history, 41, 66, 69
interactional semantics, 73, 79, 104
interactional space, 258, 264, 269, 271
interculturality, 12
Italian, 37, 146

kiosks, 4, 24, 26, 146, 255, *See also* convenience stores

materiality, 1, 4, 7, 18–21, 145, 180
membership categorization, 9
misunderstanding alternative actions, 176
mobility, 9, 15, 37
money, 26–27, 147, 255, 257
monitoring, 196, 198, 200, 230, 275
morality, 146, 150, 164, 168, 176, 181, 185
multimodality, 4
multisensoriality, 4, 15
mutual monitoring, 189

navigation, 38

object category, 48
offer, 109, 113, 200
  format, 128, 133, 135, 137–138
  of assistance, 211
  pre-emptive, 122
  refusal, 109, 131–137
  to taste, 24
openings, 14–16, 39, 119, 132
options between products, 119–120
orientation to visibility of placing the product, 171, 175

packing, 25, 184
participation framework, 68
payment

  anticipatory, 259, 267–271
  delayed, 259, 271–275
  on-time, 259, 271
  preselected, 260
payment phase, 255–257, 271
phone (versus face to face), 5, 14
pitching, 8
placing, 146, 152, 159
  as unilateral action, 159
placing and grasping, 151–154, 179
  asymmetric accessibility of the other, 164
  form of the hand, grasping, 179
pointing, 78, 80–81, 84, 89, 95, 103, 120, 122, 126, 130, 152, 163, 189, 191
politeness, 2, 9–13, 145
potentially purchasable item, 47, 58, 63, 65, 67
precondition for collaboration, 196
preference for a quick transition of reciprocal actions, 168, 171
preference for giving over placing the product, 168, 171
price announcement, 150, 224, 256, 259–260, 267, 269, 271, 274
product, 61, 104
  characterization, 77
  identification, 73, 77
  location, 78
  name, 77
product label
  reading, 125, 127
professional service, 211
progressivity, 131, 139, 145, 164, 168, 176, 180, 260, 269, 271, 275
projectability, 164
proper name, 77, 79–80, 83, 89, 104
purchasability, 55, 61
purchase
  payable to paid, 144
  possessable vs. possession, 144, 147, 150

question, 73–74, 77–79, 101, 119, 122–127, 131
  clarification, 264
  polar, 76, 79, 90–92, 96–103, 119
  specification, 74
  wh-, 76, 79–89, 93–96, 101–103, 124

recognition, 104
recognizability, 77, 95, 168
recommendation, 119–120, 122
recruitment, 185
reference, 76, 78–79, 92, 102–103

Index

request, 1, 4, 16–18, 22, 24, 74, 78, 81, 86, 103, 110–112, 133, 145, 150, 152, 163–164, 185, 193, 215, 249, 255
   for advice, 120
request phase, 266
request-return sequence, 25, 215, 249

sensorial access, 111, 114, 122–123, 126, 138, 227
sensorial features, 126, 128
sensoriality, 76, 139
service-assessment sequence, 214, 250
shoe repair shop, 4
shopping, 2
small talk, 7, 11
sociability, 1, 7–8, 151
social categories, 204, 211–212
sociality, 4, 212

Spanish, 111
spatiality. *See* interactional space
spatio-temporal organization, 216
supermarkets, 37, 41
Swedish, 186
Swiss German, 79, 111, 146

tasting, 111, 120, 128, 138
trajectory
   sequential, 271, 275
   temporal, 271, 275
transfer of objects, 144

value, 1–2, 150
verbal acknowledgment, 215
verbal offer, 201, 204
visual access, 227, 230, 242, 249
visual appearance, 126, 128

For EU product safety concerns, contact us at Calle de José Abascal, 56–1°, 28003 Madrid, Spain or eugpsr@cambridge.org.

www.ingramcontent.com/pod-product-compliance
Ingram Content Group UK Ltd.
Pitfield, Milton Keynes, MK11 3LW, UK
UKHW040058310825
462435UK00019B/433